Zeppelin and the United States of America
(Pages 3 – 148)

Zeppelin und die Vereinigten Staaten von Amerika
(Seiten 151 – 255)

"Towards the sky
with my friend
Pierre "der Zeppeliner"!

from the
"Friedrichshafen Zeppelin
Reederei"

yours Uwe

HANS G. KNÄUSEL

ZEPPELIN
AND THE UNITED STATES
OF AMERICA

An Important Episode
in German-American Relations

20.10.85 1981
Friedrichshafen, Germany

Knäusel, H. G.: Zeppelin and the United States of America –
An Important Episode in German-American Relations
1st edition 1976
2nd revised and enlarged edition 1981
Translated from the German by M. O. McClellan
Published by Luftschiffbau Zeppelin GmbH
and Zeppelin-Metallwerke GmbH, Friedrichshafen, Germany
Printed in Germany
by Zeppelin-Druckerei, Friedrichshafen, Germany

ISBN 3-9800552-0-5 (Geb/iU)
ISBN 3-9800552-1-3 (Pb/iU)

The relationship between the United States of America and Germany is a long one, rich in tradition. Perhaps no other two countries enjoy the warm bonds of friendship which join the United States and the Federal Republic of Germany. It cannot be denied that the two world wars of our century seriously damaged these ties. But the freedom-loving American people, with their pronounced sense of fair play, were always the first to push for a swift return to normal relations. They did not see fit to place the burden of responsibility for events on the entire German people when smaller groups must bar the blame. A man such as Dr. Hugo Eckener, for instance, denied the respect of the regime in his own country, was even more highly esteemed by the American people as the representative of the majority of Germans, who could not be held responsible for the machinations of the National Socialists. For Americans, Dr. Eckener and his airships were a symbol of the peace-loving soul of Germany and thus a symbol of peace and friendship throughout the world. Zeppelin aerial navigation had its origins in the little town of Friedrichshafen on Lake Constance. May this book help keep alive the spirit of that era and contribute to deepening the mutual understanding between the United States and Germany and strengthening the bonds of friendship which unite them.

Friedrichshafen, Germany, spring 1981

Martin Herzog

Lord Mayor of the
City of Friedrichshafen

Chairman of the Board
Luftschiffbau Zeppelin GmbH and
Zeppelin-Metallwerke GmbH

Willy Kaldenbach and *Heinrich Kollmann*

General Managers
Luftschiffbau Zeppelin GmbH and
Zeppelin-Metallwerke GmbH

FOREWORD

In 1976, as the subject of "Zeppelin and the U.S.A." was first dealt with during an exhibit in Friedrichshafen to honor the American Bicentennial, it was clear to all that the complexity of the task at hand had not yet been fully recognized. But numerous tips and suggestions, above all from the United States, were the inducement to revise the book which had appeared as a supplement at the time of the exhibit. The author owes his gratitude above all to F. W. von Meister, who has since passed away, for his generous inspirations. Special thanks also go to Captain Franklin D. Buckley, U.S. Navy (Ret.), whose patient, long-distance correspondence helped keep the subject alive, and to Henry Cord Meyer, University of California, whose own works still await publication, works which will further serve to keep the topic vivid. But there were conscientious experts and critical apologists of the Zeppelin Story in Germany as well who recognized that the sole purpose of recording Zeppelin history today could not be the verbal and optical presentation of the complete works in outline form. Alfred Weber, the clever and farsighted private scholar, was one of them; Hans von Schiller another. Both were instrumental in the initial preparations for this edition, but can no longer experience the finished work.

The diversity of U.S.-German cooperation in airship development cannot be represented in its entirety here. For – aside from Count Zeppelin's early experiences in the United States – the contacts, the exchange of ideas and experiences, the personal encounters which occurred during the years between 1919 and 1939 cannot be condensed into a few pages. The aim of this book is to inspire the reader to an examination of history and to incorporate the fruits and experiences of one of its chapters into the analytical observation of his own behavior. May the bilingual nature of the book help provide an insight into the other country.

Munich/Erdweg, Germany, March 1981   *H. G. Knäusel*

CONTENTS

INTRODUCTION

The articles, papers and books published about Zeppelin surely number in the hundreds. To further add to this abundance would mean a repetition of considerable details. There remain, however, aspects which have been ignored, mentioned only in passing or even, in some cases, entirely forgotten. There are perhaps two reasons for this: the subject was either not discernible due to its historical dimensions, or it was disclaimed and repressed, because it was, at least at times, unpleasant. An example of the latter case is the topic dealt with here, laden with resentment from the beginning of the era of national socialism; at the latest from 1938 on, sooner expunged not only from the archives but from memory as well, had that been possible: the successful passage of the LZ 126 (ZR 3) to the U.S., considered by the entire world after World War I a tremendous achievement, but for the national socialists in Germany following Hitler's rise to power in 1933 a blot on history. A German airship as war reparation! The Treaty of Versailles was rejected point-blank by Hitler. The efforts of the American President Wilson, over the objections of the other victor nations, to create a just peace, to include the Germans in a supranational League of Nations, encompassing all the peoples of the world did not fit into Hitler's idea of the way the world should be. Of all the countries of the world, only the United States was aware in 1918, as again in 1945, of the danger involved in condemning the German people as one and leaving them to the mercy of an uncertain future. We know today that developments in Europe and thus in the world would almost certainly have taken a different course, if all the victor nations had been willing to even approximate Wilson's conceptions.

The Zeppelin Story is more than the tremendous achievement of an ingenious inventor, more than the proud, jubilant era of the Empire, when the first airships caused bewildered amazement as they crossed the sky, more than ticker-tape parades for the airship crews on Broadway. The Zeppelin Story is also World War I, the period of world-wide economic depression, Nazi-Germany's preparations for World War II – a dramatic span of world history. The subject at hand may assume subordinate importance when viewed in the light of global history. But the achievements of the German airship builders, the spirit of international understanding radiated by their work and the warm friendship which bound airship builders and crews in America and Germany made history in their own right and surely helped here and there to moderate one or another negative political development. In any case, Dr. Eckener and his people were symbols of that part of Germany which stood opposed to National Socialism, despite the fact that, on orders from above, swastikas were painted on the airships from 1934 on.

The historical efforts of single achievements are hardly noticeable to participants, but are not future generations bound to examine these events in depth in order to learn from them? Woodrow Wilson presented his famous "Fourteen Points" in 1919. It was thwarted by conflicts of interests among the European states, and the resistance of isolationists in his own country. Thus the newly-signed Treaty of Versailles became the basis for renewed world conflict. Even the chapter of airship development, a mere excerpt in the entirety of world history, gains significance when viewed in this light. For seldom, neither before nor since, have technical development, political and economic decision and simple human encounter been so intensively intertwined as during the era of airship development at the peak of international political tensions in the 20s and 30s. Although the small group of active airship crews and builders on both sides of the Atlantic could not change the course of history, Karl Arnstein and Hugo Eckener, Charles E. Rosendahl and Hans von Schiller, Paul Litchfield and Willy von Meister, and many others like them resisted with the only means at their disposal: they tried to hold the world together with bonds of friendship.

Everything that happens in our world affects our personal lives in some way; to recognize the significance of even what are assumed to be side issues and thus the historical position of all concerned, perhaps even the individual himself, is the task at hand. Count Ferdinand von Zeppelin as an observer of the Civil War – a coincidence? At first, perhaps, but of grave consequence for his own later life and possibly for an entire era in the history of technology. The determination of a man like Dr. Eckener to build an airship after World War I, at first to save jobs, and the chance to do this for the United States of America was surely no coincidence, but rather the perception of a need made reality and born of historical facts. And so one thing leads to another. Max Grünbeck, for many years mayor of Friedrichshafen, becomes friends with Richard E. Carver, mayor of Peoria, Illinois and a generation younger. The friendship of the "Zeppelin City" and the "City of Earthmoving" is sealed. A coincidence? Again, the answer is no. For twenty years before, Julius Oesterle, veteran of years of airship navigation, experienced employee of the Luftschiffbau Zeppelin in Friedrichshafen and successor to Hugo Eckener, had taken advantage of the "American connection" and established contact with the Caterpillar Company. The company that once built world-famous airships now represents in Germany the world-famous giant of earthmoving. The historical significance of the Friedrichshafen firm was one of the deciding factors for the American partner. And this decision was the beginning of a new, unmatched development which lent a new and vital aspect to the historical element of the former airship builder. And when as a consequence of its historical tradition, the relatively small town of Friedrichshafen maintains a truly active partnership with the relatively small town of Peoria, the entire world no longer takes part in this intercommunication of peoples, at least a few thousand souls have the opportunity to understand each other better.

"Zeppelin and the United States of America" is a topic that essentially coincides with the absolutely lowest point in German history. But if the study of history has any meaning at all, it is that, due to the intricacy of their relationship, the senseless and tragic confrontation between the United States and Germany that we have seen twice in this century can never occur again. As with Hugo Eckener and his colleagues, from now on it will be these positive contacts that set the tone.

1.
EXPERIENCES
IN AMERICA

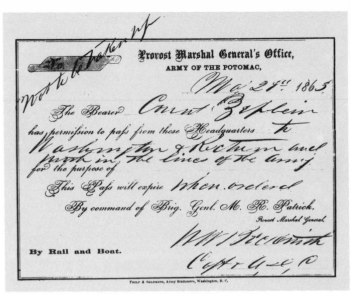

Provost Marshal General's Office,
ARMY OF THE POTOMAC,

Ma 27th 1865

The Bearer Count Zeplein
has permission to pass from these Headquarters to
Washington & Return and
forth in the lines of the Army
for the purpose of
This Pass will expire when ordered
By command of Brig. Genl. M. R. Patrick.
Provost Marshal General

By Rail and Boat.

PHILP & SOLOMONS, Army Stationers, Washington, D. C.

Pass issued to Count Zeppelin, permitting him freedom of movement within the Army of the Potomac. Due to the incorrect spelling of his name ("Zeplein"), it may be assumed that he was issued the pass personally at the pass office, instead of receiving it formally by application.

Paß des Grafen Zeppelin, der ihm Bewegungsfreiheit innerhalb der Potomac-Armee gestattete. Die unkorrekte Schreibweise seines Namens („Zeplein") läßt vermuten, daß er den Paß nicht formell mit einem Antrag, sondern durch direkte Vorsprache bei der Dienststelle erhielt.

Count Zeppelin (1838–1917, 2nd from right) in an Army of the Potomac camp.

Graf Zeppelin (1838–1917, 2. von rechts) in einem Lager der Potomac-Armee.

14

1.1 Count Zeppelin meets President Lincoln

When Count Ferdinand von Zeppelin arrived in the United States in the year 1863, at the age of 25 years, he was yet unknown in that country. A couple of decades later the name Zeppelin had become a household word in America. Since 1861, the country had been rocked by the convulsions of the Civil War. Count Zeppelin wanted to observe, to gain experience. As a professional soldier, he was interested in the methods of warfare, newly developed at the time.

Permission to travel within the lines of the Union troops was granted to Zeppelin as one of only four foreign observers by President Lincoln, who even received the young German visitor at the White House. Count Zeppelin wrote later in his memoirs of this encounter with the American president: "The president expressed his sincere pleasure at my coming and wished me success in my studies. Prior to granting me an audience, the president had ordered inquiries made concerning me. Through the kindness of Herr von Schleiden, the Hanseatic Envoy, I have in my possession, as valuable autograph, a short note written by Lincoln to the Secretary of State and War Secretary Stanton, in which he asks whether the inquiries made about me would permit the granting of my request for a Military pass. I then, indeed, received such a pass, which permitted me complete freedom of movement among the Union armies. Except for myself, only the Duke of Joinville, the Duke of Chartres and the Count of Paris have received such a pass in the entire course of the war."

Soon after his meeting with Lincoln, Count Zeppelin joined a brigade of the Army of the Potomac, under the command of Major General Butterfield. In 1863 the Army of the Potomac was commanded by General Hooker.

The weeks spent in the rear area were not all restful ones. Count Zeppelin took advantage of the opportunities offered him by the military pass for the Army of the Potomac to participate actively in the events unfolding before him. More than once did Zeppelin become involved in dangerous predicaments and only luck and daredevil skill saved his life. Just in case, Count Zeppelin himself relates that he secretly carried with him a "warm letter of recommendation to General Lee from the general's charming niece, whose acquaintance I'd made

Left: Major General Daniel Butterfield (1831–1901)

Links: Generalmajor Daniel Butterfield (1831–1901)

Right: Carl Schurz (1829–1906) as Brigadier General of the Northern Army.

Rechts: Carl Schurz (1829–1906) als Brigadegeneral der Nordarmee.

The French war observers, the Duke of Chartres (second from left), the Count of Paris (centre) and the Duke of Joinville (2nd from right) in General McClellan's headquarters in 1862.

Die französischen Kriegsbeobachter Herzog von Chartres (2. von links), Graf von Paris (Mitte) und Herzog von Joinville (2. von rechts) 1862 im Hauptquartier von General McClellan.

Right: One of the few photographs of Count Zeppelin (2nd from right) during his stay with the Army of the Potomac. The photos (pp. 14, 16, 17 and 19) were taken by Mathew Brady, the famous photographer of the Civil War.

Rechts: Eines der wenigen Fotos mit Graf Zeppelin (2. von rechts) von seinem Aufenthalt bei der Potomac-Armee. Die Fotos (S. 14, 16, 17 und 19) stammen von Mathew Brady, dem berühmten Fotografen des Sezessionskrieges.

in Philadelphia". For, had he been captured by Confederate troops during one of his scouting trips, they would certainly have "shot me in short order or strung me up from the nearest tree", as he himself writes.

Zeppelin also met Carl Schurz. It is interesting to note that the impression this famous General of the Nothern Armies made on him seems to conflict with the way Schurz is often portrayed in German and American literature today. In any event, Zeppelin seemed little impressed at the time with the military abilities demonstrated by Schurz, who had come to the States from Germany following the Revolution of 1848 and, by 1877, would rise to Secretary of the Interior in President Hayes' cabinet. It should be noted there that Carl Schurz, who died in 1906, first gained historical significance later on as a journalist. Thus Zeppelin, himself still a young man, met Schurz when the latter was also relatively young.

1.2 Balloon ascent in America

In August 1863, Zeppelin took part in the launching of a tethered balloon near St. Paul, Minnesota, outside the battle zone. He was surely familiar with the use of balloons for reconnaissance on both sides of the front, as both the North and South used them. It was perhaps here in St. Paul that the cornerstone for his later work was laid. As a soldier, his first concern was the expanded use of barrage balloons for military purposes. Their use as observation stations seemed to him almost ideal. Perhaps the idea of making the balloon navigable and dirigible, possibly even newly designing it, occured to him then – we have no record of this. Only his thoughts on stabilizing

"The last reconnaissance of the war balloon on the James River" was the caption under this picture, which appeared in Harper's Weekly on September 6, 1862.

„The last reconnaissance of the war balloon on the James River" war dieses Bild unterschrieben, das am 6. September 1862 in Harper's Weekly erschien.

Gas generators from Professor Lowe, who made several ascents with tethered balloons for the Union Armies during the initial years of the war.

Gasgeneratoren von Professor Lowe, der in den ersten Kriegsjahren etliche Aufstiege mit Fesselballons bei den Armeen der Nordstaaten durchführte.

the balloon by equipping it with a fixed rudder are mentioned in a letter[1].

As early as June 1863, Solomon Andrews, a doctor from Perth Amboy, New Jersey, had successfully steered his airship Aereon I, an event that Count Zeppelin was presumably aware of.

Following his sojourn with the army, Count Zeppelin accepted an invitation to join an expedition into the headwater region of the Mississippi. According to reports of the day, his adventures during this undertaking equaled those he experienced during his stay with the Army of the Potomac in every respect.

One unique and daring feat deserves mention here, as it was apparently typical of the young Count: While visiting Niagara Falls, he observed that a piece of wood he had thrown into the water was again and again carried towards an adjacent cliff by an eddy. Zeppelin himself then jumped into the water, was carried in the same way to the cliff and rewarded by a magnificent view of the interior of the Falls.

Count Zeppelin returned to Germany on November 1863, after a six-month stay in the United States.

---

[1] Letter of August 19, 1863 from St. Paul, Minn. (cf. Italiaander: F. Graf von Zeppelin, Verlag Stadler, Konstanz 1980, p. 29). A systematic analysis of the some 25 letters written by Count Zeppelin while in America, could perhaps provide final clarification here.

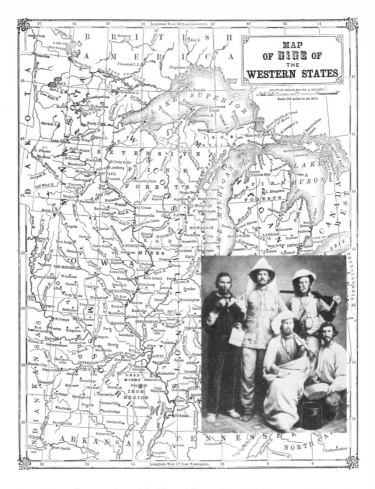

Count Zeppelin (standing with rifle) while participating in an expedition to the headwaters of the Mississippi. Old map of 1863.

Graf Zeppelin (stehend mit Gewehr) als Teilnehmer einer Expedition im Quellgebiet des Mississippi. Alte Landkarte von 1863.

1.3 Analysis of an encounter

Lincoln's positive attitude towards the young Zeppelin is interesting when viewed from the historical perspective of those years. Not much remained of the almost adoring admiration for Germany shown by Americans at the turn of the 19th century. This would disappear altogether after 1870, not to be felt again for decades. The times were gone when a John Quincy Adams, later sixth president of the United States, would translate Wieland's Oberon, when the reading of Goethe and Schiller was a must in intellectual circles.

Germany had undergone a change. The cultural flourish of the Goethe era had given way to a period of cultural boredom. Political conditions had taken on a dimension of despair and feebleness at odds with America's progressive, still fresh and dynamic urge for personal freedom, but also for political strength. Indeed, for the Northern States, the Civil War had been above all else the desperate documentation of this will to preserve freedom and strength by preserving the unity of the nation.

The transformation which had taken place in Germany did not go unnoticed in the U.S.

In his autobiography, "The Education of Henry Adams", Adams – like Zeppelin born in 1838 – describes his deep disappointment at the intellectual and social decay he witnessed in Germany while touring Europe from 1858–1860.[2] The specter of imperial Germany with its nationalistic mien and claims to world power had already been heralded and was strongly rejected above all by American intellectuals.[3]

And it was from this Germany that Count Zeppelin came to America. How he wondered at the casual attitude and unconventional demeanor of the American president. A closer analysis of Zeppelin's recollections of this meeting with Lincoln leads to the notion that the

---

[2] Henry Adams (1838–1918), grandson of John Quincy Adams (see above).

[3] By the outbreak of war with France in 1870, alienation was complete. Paris had replaced Berlin as the intellectual and cultural metropolis of Europe, even for Americans. It is interesting to note, and surely no accident, that the remaining three foreign war observers sanctioned by President Lincoln were Frenchmen. (cf. p. 15/16)

Left: Abraham Lincoln
(1809–1865) as he was when
Count Zeppelin met him in
1863.

*Links: Abraham Lincoln
(1809–1865), so wie ihn Graf
Zeppelin 1863 kennenlernte.*

president must have found Zeppelin's somewhat stiffly formal appearance rather amusing. He had come to petition Lincoln for permission to act as observer – certainly a rather insignificant matter for the president – attired in top hat and tails. But clever insight helped Zeppelin adapt immediately to the new way of life. He certainly had no problems in getting along with his crusty comrades – in – arms in the Army of the Potomac. Nevertheless, he did not forget his ties to his European intellectual mentality, an expression of which was his critical evaluation of Carl Schurz, mentioned previously. His criticism was directed at the attempt by a German officer lacking in military ability to conceal this through vanity, a tactic which, in liberal America, would probably evoke amusement, rather than astonishment or disapproval, even today.

A study of the further course of Count Zeppelin's life readily shows that his experiences in America had a strong impact on him and influenced his later thought and behavior.

1.4 Flights to New York
planned as early as 1895

Whether ist was, as is often assumed, an experience gained during the 1870 – 71 war against France – he watched as prominent personalities escaped Paris by balloon during the siege of that city – or a publication by the Prussian Postmaster-General Heinrich von Stephan on the subject of transporting mail by air[4], the idea of building dirigible balloons had occupied Zeppelin even during his military service. His diary contains an entry dated April 25, 1874 concerning the concept of a balloon – vehicle.

In November 1890, immediately upon being released from military service, he began to seriously pursue his idea of building a dirigible airship. From 1892 on, after commissioning Theodor Kober, design work preceeded at such a fast pace that a patent was granted for an "airtrain" as early as 1895. Even though later "Zeppelins" deviated in some details from the concept established in the first patent document, the basic principle – a rigid hull with an exterior skin and several interior gas cells for buoyancy – were applied down to the last Zeppelin airships and its practicality was proven in a long series of successfully executed airship systems. Count Zeppelin's rigid system alone made possible then the construction of larger, more powerful airships.

A diary entry from the year 1895, in which he sketched plans for the transport of passengers and cargo by airship to New York, among other destinations, clearly disproves the frequent charge that Zeppelin thought only of the military applications of later dirigibles. This concept, however, was not a new one at the time. Several designers, including the Americans John Wise (1843) and T. S. C. Lowe (ca. 1850) had expressed the idea of crossing the Atlantic by balloon. Some even attempted to put their theories to a practical test; none, however, succeeded.

---

[4] Heinrich von Stephan was the founder of the World Postal Union (1874) and authored in 1873 a paper titled "World Postal Delivery and Airship Navigation" [transl.].

Two postcards sent to Count Zeppelin by American fans. The card at the top bears no address ("Whereever he may be"). The cards probably never reached the Count and perhaps were valued even then as collector's items.

Zwei Postkarten von amerikanischen Verehrern an Graf Zeppelin. Die obere Karte ohne Anschrift („Wo er sein mag"). Da die Karten keinerlei Vermerk enthalten, ist anzunehmen, daß sie den Grafen nie erreichten und vielleicht schon damals als Sammlerobjekte dienten.

1.5 The popular Count

On July 2, 1900, the first Zeppelin airship rose from the surface of Lake Constance. The initial years of airship navigation gave little basis for strengthening of ties with the United States. But Count Zeppelin's endeavors did not go unnoticed in America. He achieved considerable popularity in the U. S. through the disaster near Echterdingen in 1908, in which airship LZ4 was destroyed on the ground by a storm, after a much-acclaimed endurance flight. Above all, the many German clubs

HOO'S HOO TODAY

(BY JOHN W. CAREY.)

Who runs a railless railroad— and is welcome to the same—and ranks with Kaiser Wilhelm in the German Hall of Fame? Who blows his choo-choos full of gas and hollers "All aboard!" and waves so-long, as fades away the terra firma horde? Who does not know for certain that he ever will come back—and yet, at least, need have no fear of bovines on the track? Who'll fix it yet so we'll but need to hail a big balloon when we would make a call upon the Man That's in the Moon? Who'll stop at Mars or Neptune when he wants a coupling pin—the Milky Way for gasoline? Boy, page Count Zeppelin.

If you want to get the news— BUY THE TIMES.

Excerpt from the "Denver Times" of June 27, 1913. The poem and drawing appeared in numerous newspapers, among them, the "Washington Star", "Chicago News", "New York Globe" and "San Francisco Post".

Ausschnitt aus der „Denver Times" vom 27. Juni 1913. Gedicht und Zeichnung sind in zahlreichen Zeitungen, u. a. in „Washington Star", „Chicago News", „New York Globe" und „San Francisco Post" erschienen.

Dear Sir:

I hasten to express to you the sympathy of the Aero Club of America in the loss of your wonderful airship. Each step of your progress has been carefully watched by us all and we were preparing to send you our congratulations on your remarkable achievement when the news of the accident reached us and we cannot express how keenly your loss was felt by our Club.

It has given the members of the Aero Club of America much pleasure however to learn that you have already begun the construction of another ship and that your great work is so highly appreciated by all the world and we heartily wish you every success.

Your Highness:

We, the undersigned, representing the Woman's Guild of Christ Church, Boonville, State of Missouri, United States of America, wish to make a small request of the man who steered the Zeppelin II 456 miles through lofty and limitless space so successfully.

All we ask of Your Highness is the small gift of a souvenir pocket h handkerchief. This is the oldest Episcopal Church in the Diocese of Kansas City and the second oldest in the State of Missouri.

The Church fabric and rectory both show the wearing hand of time and we are anxious to make some needed improvements. To this end we propose to hold a Handkerchief Fair and are soliciting this small gift from our friends and welwishers both at home and abroad.

If you will remember us while sailing the Zeppelin II and send us a handkerchief it will be most gratefully appreciated,

Very Respectfully,
Mrs. C. A. Lombart.
Mrs. C. A. Lombart
President.

Your Excellency:

I have the honor to inform you that the Aero Club of Washington, by the unanimous vote of its Board of Management, has elected you to honorary membership in the Club in recognition of your distinguished services in the advancement of Aerial Navigation.

It is the hope of the members of this Club that when you come to America we may have the pleasure of seeing your Excellency in Washington.

A. LESCHEN & SONS ROPE CO.
WIRE ROPE

HENRY LESCHEN
PRESIDENT

JOHN A.LESCHEN
VICE PREST.

W.C.HENNING
SECRETARY

LESCHEN
WIRE ROPE

AERIAL WIRE ROPE TRAMWAYS

918-932 NORTH FIRST STREET

HOME OFFICE
ST.LOUIS,M.O.

BRANCHES
NEW YORK
CHICAGO
DENVER
SAN FRANCISCO

ST. LOUIS,   June 25, 1913.

Count Ferdinand Zeppelin,
    Stuttgart, Herdwegg 66, Germany.
Dear Sir:-

        I address you with the hope that you will grant my request in
asking your autograph to be placed with the list of other great names
that I have been collecting for some years for the purpose of placing
same ultimately with the Historical Society.

        This list was started some fifty years ago by a former Senator
of the United States from Illinois and has come to me through his death.
I was importuned by my friends to add to it the great names of the present
generation, in which undertaking I have met with splendid success.

        Among the list of names when I received the album are the
following, inscribed and signed with original autograph:

Queen Victoria	Charles Dickens	Henry W. Longfellow
Alfred Tennyson	John Ruskin	Ralph Waldo Emerson
Abraham Lincoln	George Bancroft	Washington Irving
John W. Motley	Victor Hugo	Oliver Wendell Holmes
John Howard Payne	Edgar Allen Poe	Nathaniel Hawthorne

and others of world-wide reputation.
        I have since then increased this list to almost three hundred
names, keeping it up to the highest standard possible and the
following are a few of the names received by myself:

Prof. Ernst Haeckel	Thomas A. Edison	James Whitcomb Riley
Admiral Dewey	Rudyard Kipling	Admiral Count Togo
Theodore Roosevelt	G. Marconi	Israel Zangwell
Wm. H. Taft	Clara Barton	S. Weir Mitchell
Lord Roberts	Arthur Conan Doyle	J.Pierpont Morgan
Grover Cleveland	A. J. Balfour	General Count Nogi
Woodrow Wilson	Melville W. Fuller	Winston S. Churchill

        I trust that you will give this your consideration and
favor me with your autograph, for which I enclose a sheet fitting
the album, and if there is any doubt of good faith I should be glad
to refer you to the Honorable Chauncey I. Filley of this City, or
shall be glad to show the autographs to any one whom you might desire
to refer to in this City.
        As to myself I have been Cashier for above Company for the last
twentytwo years and have taken up this matter simply as a matter of
historical collection.
        Thanking you in advance for such courtesy as you may extend to
me, I beg to remain, with greatest respect,

ADDRESS ALL COMMUNICATIONS
TO A.LESCHEN & SONS ROPE CO.   Yours truly H. Amerland

From 1908 until the first World War, Count Zeppelin received letters of
recognition and numerous tributes from the United States, as these examples
show (see also pp. 28 and 170).

*Von 1908 bis zum Ersten Weltkrieg erhielt Graf Zeppelin ständig anerkennende
Briefe und viele Ehrungen aus den Vereinigten Staaten, wie diese Beispiele
zeigen (s. a. S. 28 und S. 170).*

and societies in the larger cities, especially New York and Chicago, contributed to this popularity. For them, Count Zeppelin was a symbol of the "Fatherland" that had been left behind but not forgotten. All important events occurring there were, of course, followed with rapt attention. Thus, as all over Europe, the airship was the talk of America as well.

Zeppelin was deluged with tribute in the form of honorary memberships, invitations and letters of thanks from the U. S. for the world-wide recognition he had gained for the German people and thus for the Germans in America. The German-Veterans societies, in particular, idolized the Count almost to the point of worship. This lavish affection was in no way always welcomed by Zeppelin, and it was certainly not only for lack of time that he rarely expressed his thanks personally for the honors shown him, but had his staff attend to this.

```
                                                              L.-Z.
                    Absohrift.

                                           „The Norfolk".

                         Washington, D.C. June 23 1910.

     Count Ferdinand Zeppelin,
                              Friedrichshafen,
                                        Germany.

     Dear Comrade !
                    I think my help with your first balloon in the Army of the
     Potomac in Virginia should entitle me to a letter from you in reply to my re-
     quest for an opportunity to explait your inventions in America.

          Give me a chance to help you and J will show you that J have the power
     to do you much good.

                         Yours sincerely

                              E.W Whitaker,

     J wrote you July 24.1908.
```

Letter to Count Zeppelin (see p. 27)   *Brief an Graf Zeppelin (s. Seite 27)*

2.
THE ERA
AFTER WORLD WAR I

2.1 The "Shenandoah" ist built in the United States

As a result of World-War I, international communications including the exchange of ideas among airship designers of other countries, were severely limited. One encounter with U. S. sources, however indirect and unintended, did occur on October 20, 1917, when the naval airship L49 (LZ96)[5] ran out of fuel and was forced to make an emergency landing near Bourbonne, France. Virtually undamaged, it literally fell into the hands of the Allied Powers. The ship was dismantled and examined in every detail. The "Shenandoah", built in the U. S. following the war, was based in large part on the plans of the LZ 96. Count Zeppelin died, however, on March 8, 1917, and was unable to witness this first concrete realization of his idea in the United States.

The "Shenandoah" dubbed ZR1, was put into service in the United States in September 1923 and was used primarily for experimentation aimed at improving landing and mooring techniques (especially mooring mast design). The "Shenandoah" was the first airship to use non-combustible helium gas for buoyancy.

In September 1923, the Shenandoah was caught in a storm and

Charles E. Rosendahl, navigator aboard the "Shenandoah" and later captain of the "Los Angeles".

Charles E. Rosendahl, Steuermann der „Shenandoah" und später Kapitän der „Los Angeles".

Top right: The "Shenandoah" at the high mast. In the middle Admiral Moffet.

Rechts oben: Die „Shenandoah" am Hochmast. In der Mitte Admiral Moffet.

Bottom right: The wreckage of the "Shenandoah".

Rechts unten: Teile der abgestürzten „Shenandoah".

---

[5] LZ followed by a consecutive number was the designation for all projects carried out by the Luftschiffbau Zeppelin. Out of a total of 131 projects started between 1900 and 1938, 119 were completed. The navy used other numbers, preceded by an L.

ripped in two while aloft. Charles E. Rosendahl, the "Shenandoah's" navigator, who later made a name for himself as commander of the "Los Angeles", was able to land one half of the ship with part of the crew. In spite of this accident, it was none other than Rosendahl who championed the building of airships in the United States. Rosendahl maintained close and cordial contacts to airship advocates in Germany.

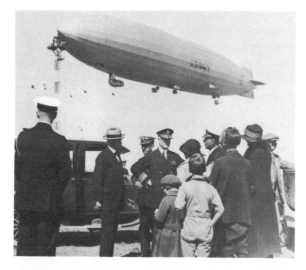

2.2 Production stop for the LZ 124

Following the end of hostilities in 1918, all airships still existing in Germany had to be turned over to the Allies. Interest in the ships was so great that a part, albeit a small part, of the war reparations imposed on Germany could be settled in this manner. Although the United States was among those who showed keen interest, plans to build a giant airship seemed at first to be thwarted by lack of conviction that a crossing of the Atlantic was indeed possible. At this point, however, began a chapter in German – American relations that has influenced the friendly ties between the two nations until the present, in spite of World War II, in spite of the Third Reich and all the grave events which burdened those ties.

With the war over, the most important task for Dr. Hugo Eckener, director of the Luftschiffbau Zeppelin in Friedrichshafen, was to save the jobs of the employees at the plant. This was possible only if an order from abroad for the construction of a giant airship could be obtained. But the building of large-capacity aircraft was forbidden in Germany and the necessary funds were unavailable in any case. Plans for a 100,000 cu. meter airship, which Colonel William S. Hensley on behalf of an American shipping company sought to realize in cooperation with the airship builders in Friedrichshafen, were frustrated by the provisions of the Treaty of Versailles.[6]

In 1919, Hensley had participated as an observer in the return flight of the R34 from the U. S. to Europe (see p. 34). Although his plans called for an airship to be used strictly for the commercial transport of mail, cargo and passengers over the Atlantic and the contract had already been drawn up, the Allies refused to grant their permission. "Project Hensley", along with drawings bearing the serial no. LZ 124, was shelved. An order from the government of one of the victor nations was now the only hope for saving the Luftschiffbau Zeppelin.

---

[6] Law governing the conclusion of a Treaty of Peace between Germany and the Allied and Associated Powers of July 16, 1919; Article 198, Para. 4: "No dirigible airship shall be maintained." Although this ban was later modified and applied only to airships exceeding 30.000 cu. meters in volume, these dimensions alone prevented use in intercontinental passenger service.

2.3 LZ 126, the "America Airship"

A Chicago industrialist by the name of Harry Vissering played a key roll in the development of German – American airship construction. A close friend of President Harding, he was able to make people in Washington understand that the only way for the U. S. to profit from the airship business was to cooperate with the German airship builders. Vissering also aroused the interest of Goodyear's Paul Litchfield in the subject and served as go-between for Eckener and Litchfield.

Paul W. Litchfield, president of the Goodyear Tire & Rubber Company and the Goodyear-Zeppelin Corporation.

Paul W. Litchfield, Präsident der Goodyear Tire & Rubber Company und der Goodyear-Zeppelin Corporation.

And finally, there were numerous other advocates, above all, commander Rosendahl and Rear Admiral Moffet of the Navy. Thanks to their efforts, the U. S. government finally relented and contracted for the construction of an airship worth three million marks, allowing this amount as settlement towards the reparation costs imposed by the Versailles treaty (see appendix 7.1 for excerpts of contract). The project was threatened with failure at the start, however; the ship could be delivered only by air and the German government refused to grant its permission. Furthermore no insurance company willing to underwrite the venture could be found.

Eckener went all out. He put up the entire assets of the airship company as collateral and received approval after all. One risk was wholly disregarded. The United States reserved the right to refuse acceptance of the ship upon its arrival in Lakehurst unless all requirements had been fulfilled. In Friedrichshafen, complete trust had been placed in the know-how that had been acquired in over 20 years of experience.

For the people in Friedrichshafen, LZ 126, designated ZR 3 by the Americans, was the first airship to be built for long-haul, transoceanic passenger service. Eckener was aware of the tremendous responsibility he had assumed when he took on the contract. Among the few precedents for long – distance flights was the African voyage of LZ 104 (L 59), which covered 6750 km nonstop in 1917 and the flight of the British airship R 34 in 1919. R 34 had crossed the Atlantic in both directions in a voyage considered a sensation at the time. The principle of R 34's design was identical to the Zeppelin concept; only a few technical and structural details varied. The ship landed at Roosevelt Field in Mineola, Long Island, before returning to Europe.

The new ship from the Friedrichshafen hangars not only had to meet unprecedented technical requirements, it was also to fullfill a momentous challenge: a succesful crossing of the Atlantic would prove the ship's all weather capabilities and suitability for long distance service, thus demonstrating to Eckener and the Luftschiffbau in Friedrichshafen the potential for Zeppelin airships in large – scale international air service. ZR 3 had to be a standard of dependability and safety for all future airships. The Zeppelin engineers, under the experienced leadership of Dr. Ludwig Dürr, met this challenge with complete success.

Incidentally, the designation "ZR" showed that, even in the U. S., Count Zeppelin's airship concept received the credit due it. Unofficially, the "Z" stood for Zeppelin and the "R" for "rigid". And following ZR 1, the "Shenandoah", which was in essence a reproduction of a Zeppelin airship, and a British rigid airship[7] never put into service in the U. S., ZR 3 was to be the third "Zeppelin" for the Americans.

---

[7] R 38 was to be acquired by the U.S. and renamed ZR 2, but crashed in August 1921 during a test flight. Sixteen of the seventeen Americans on board perished. This disaster at first dampened American enthusiasm for airship construction. At the time, ZR 1, was under construction at the Naval Aircraft Factory in Philadelphia.

2.4 An Atlantic crossing with political consequences

Construction on LZ 126 ws begun in 1922. The U. S. Navy maintained an office at the Friedrichshafen Plant, the "Office of Inspector of Naval Aircraft", to supervise the work. Special engines were developed by Maybach and tested in endless trial runs for the new and unusual task. The future crew underwent intensive training. After nearly 18 months of construction the first test flight was made on August 27, 1924. The tests indicated that the required specifications could be met. Nevertheless, there was great anxiety as to whether the

(Continued on page 39)

During the construction of LZ 126 (ZR 3), the U.S. Navy maintained an office in Friedrichshafen under the direction of Garland Fulton (right).

Während des Baus von LZ 126 (ZR 3) unterhielt die US-Navy in Friedrichshafen ein Büro unter der Leitung von Garland Fulton (rechts).

35

General Description of ZR-3

Construction —

    a) Pertinent parts of general specifications i.e

      1. Capacity and dimensions

      2. General arrangement of Hull, keel, cars, and
Gas bags, form, wiring; ~~~~~~~~; fins, rudders, elevators
and controls; water ballast arrangements; gasoline tank and piping;
oil tanks and piping; ventilation; access hatches; crew space;
freight spaces; passenger accommodations; minor controls;
mooring arrangements (including bow mooring); typical power car
arrangement; control cabin; method of docking (slinging in shed);
communication system; radio and radio compass; lighting system

    Engines — 1. Description of engines; water circulation; gasoline
supply system and storage; lubrication; method of starting and
reversing; ignition

                  (Complete description with sketches and photos of
    Instruments and fittings — Compasses and compass positions (in-
cluding gyro compass); inclinometre; staroscopes; electric thermom-
eters; altimetres; (optical) drift and ground speed instrument;
gas bag pressure indicators; revolution indicators; helm angle indicators
etc.

    Plans — Such plans as will thoroughly illustrate the
above three subjects ie Construction — Engines — Instruments
    Photographs — Where clarity is increased thereby.
    Performance — Graphs showing endurance at different speeds
        1. Performance of fuel, oil consumption @ speeds.
        2. Loss of lift with altitude
        3. Change of lift due to temperature
        4.   "   "   "   "   pressure
        5. Dynamic lift with different ships speed and
    inclination.

        Safety Precautions
    1. speed limits
    2. rudder angle limits at various ships speeds
    3. load distribution under various conditions
    4. Table of tensions for ships wiring.

Notes and sketches for the construction of ZR 3 made by Garland Fulton, head
of the "Office of the Inspector of Naval Aircraft" in Friedrichshafen (see also
p. 38).

*Notizen und Skizzen zum Bau von ZR 3 von Garland Fulton, dem Leiter des
„Office of the Inspector of Naval Aircraft" in Friedrichshafen (s. a. Seite 38).*

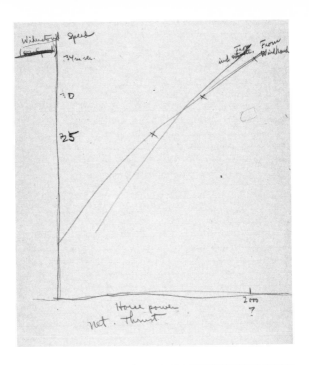

OFFICE OF
INSPECTOR OF NAVAL AIRCRAFT
FRIEDRICHSHAFEN a/B. (GERMANY)

500-936
L-160
126

19 August 1924

Memorandum for Luftschiffbau Zeppelin:-

　　1.　　It is understood

　　(a)　Some proof loading or test of the bow-mooring force
indicator was made after the instrument was installed.

　　(b)　Some proof loading of rudder control leads was made
after being installed in the ship.

　　2.　　It would be appreciated if we could have the opportunity
of seeing copies of any records made of those tests.

　　　　　　　　　　　　　　G. FULTON

500-907
LZ-151

4/8 4 August 1924

Memorandum for Herr Pochhammer.

Reference to Pennoyer Memo. L.Z. 93 of 10 December 1923, and Pochhammer memo of 2 August 1924, the following comments are made:-

Part II, Descriptive Data

1) There may be confusion here between (a) the detailed weight statement requested by I.N.A. Memo.L.Z. 142 of 5 June 1924 and (b) the distribution of weights fixed and usable (trim plan) requested by Pennoyer memo. above.

2a.3 & 4. Opportunity to settle this matter is requested as soon as practicable.

5) The only speed and power curves we have are estimated curves (Sheet PB 601) which gives no data as to the radius of action of ship based on various combinations of engines. This naturally must be based on fuel capacity (American and/or Trans-Atlantic conditions) It is hoped the final descriptive data will include more speed-consumption data than given on Sheet PB 601 and in more convenient form for use by the ship's Commander. Also it is hoped the estimated data will finally be checked and corrected on the basis of information gained during trials.

6) What was wanted here on dynamic lift curves was non-secret data put up in such form as to be useful to the ship commander. As an indication of the form which the information might take see the enclosure (A). (Please return sheets) Any other convenient form will be just as satisfactory.
An example of what was meant in Pennoyer memo on "Lift Curves for varying degrees of bag fullness" is also enclosed.(B & C).

7) Fuel consumption curves. We have not received fuel consumption curves giving consumption curves for fractional powers. Actual fuel consumption curves for engines (and ship) under standard conditions were what was intended in Pennoyer memo. mentioned above (See 5 above.)

10) What was intended by Pennoyer memo. was such a plan as

"Lade plan bei Rückkehr von der Hohenfahrt"#L1024.

If any points in the above are not clear, it is requested we be permitted to explain further.

G. FULTON

LZ 126 reaches New York. *LZ 126 erreicht New York.*

flight over the Atlantic set for October would go off as planned, a flight which would decide the fate of the Friedrichshafen operations and the further development of the trend – setting airship concept.

On October 12, 1924, LZ 126 became airborne on its crucial voyage across the Atlantic. The following 85 hours until the ship touched down in Lakehurst have been described in numerous accounts. Four officers of the U. S. Navy and Army took part in the flight and were among those who were to take charge of the ship once in the United States.[8]

---

[8] As guests on board were: Captain G. W. Steele, Cdr. J. H. Klein, Ltd. Cdr. S. J. Kraus (Navy) and Major G. Kennedy (Army).

On board the LZ 126: Dr. Eckener with American guests (see footnote, p. 39) during the crossing.

Dr. Eckener mit amerikanischen Gästen (s. Fußnote S. 176) während der Überfahrt an Bord von LZ 126.

Right: President Coolidge greets Dr. Eckener, with captain Hans Flemming in the middle.

Rechts: Präsident Coolidge begrüßt Dr. Eckener. In der Mitte Kapitän Hans Flemming.

Bottom: LZ 126, now ZR 3, in front of the hangar in Lakehurst, New Jersey.
Unten: LZ 126, jetzt ZR 3, vor der Halle in Lakehurst, New Jersey.

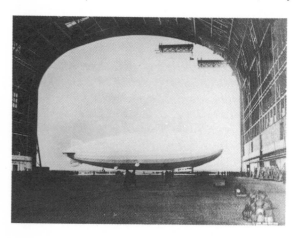

The crossing was completed without serious incident. As the airship circled New York harbor, it was greeted by the din of the city's fire sirens accompanied by those of every sea-going ship in the harbor.

So many had gathered to witness the landing at nearby Lakehurst that it was nearly impossible to maneuver the ship into the giant hangar.

Dr. Eckener and the officers were summoned to Washington by President Coolidge for an official reception at the White House. The president of the United States recognized the significance of the event. For him, the passage was more than a brilliant technical achievement. He described the airship as a messenger of peace, with which Germany would once again gain acceptance in the community of nations after years of war. Thus ZR 3 "Los Angeles", as LZ 126 was henceforth known, had not only fulfilled a mere technical and, for the airship industry in Germany, significant economic function, but had assumed an unexpected political role, as well, a role that would influence relations between Germany and the United States of America for many years to come. The war of only a few years before seemed forgotten when, during a film showing of the transatlantic voyage of ZR 3, the American audience broke into a spontaneous rendition of the German national anthem.

After the endless festivities, Dr. Eckener, accompanied by Captain Ernst Lehmann and Navigation Officer Hans von Schiller, set out on a trip across the United States aimed at making contacts and laying the groundwork for the planned international airship service.

It is interesting to note that more recent accounts of Germany during the 1920s fail to mention this phenomenal enthusiasm of the American public and the subsequent cooperation in airship development. Even special studies such as M. Knapp (a. others) "The U. S. A. and Germany 1918–1975"[9] no more mention the tremendous achievements of Dr. Eckener and his colleagues than they do the almost euphoric enthusiasm on the part of the American public for the German airship or the intricate political and economic processes linked to it. If one considers only the countless prominent honors bestowed on Dr. Eckener, which cannot have remained hidden from today's authors, this ignorance of the airship and its deserving role in the complex relationship between the United States and Germany during those years is all the more incomprehensible.

Part of the LZ 126's crew remained in the U. S. to train the crew of the "Los Angeles" or to promote the climate for a joint effort, as in the case of Captain Lehmann, who stayed with Goodyear in Akron, Ohio. The Germans profited a great deal from the Americans at that time, as the latter had invested generously in the improvement of mooring techniques in trials with the "Shenandoah". Ships had repeatedly been lost in Germany, due to inadequate docking facilities. With the "Shenandoah", the Americans had already highly refined the art of mast docking, an important technique for the giant airships of the 20s and 30s.

---

[9] Knapp, Link, Schröder, Schwabe: The U.S.A. and Germany 1918–1975, Munich 1978, C. H. Beck'sche Verlagsbuchhandlung, Beck'sche Schwarze Reihe No. 177. Subtitle: German-American Relations between Rivalry and Partnership. (In German; original title s. biography p. 142)

ZR-3–A TRIBUTE

IN COMMEMORATION of the Trans-Atlantic flight of the Zeppelin airship, ZR-3, which on October twelve to fifteen, nineteen hundred twenty-four, flew one-fifth the distance around the world in eighty hours, this tribute is presented to Dr. Hugo Eckener and his Zeppelin associates of Friedrichshafen, Germany.

It is appropriate to recall that the father of this new mode of transportation, Count Ferdinand von Zeppelin, served as a volunteer officer in the Union Army of the United States during the Civil War.

After completing a successful career as a Major-General of Cavalry, Count von Zeppelin began his real life's work in eighteen hundred ninety-four at the age of fifty-six years.

Rising again and again above disappointments which would have crushed ordinary men, his indomitable spirit of progress brought him success at the late age of seventy.

In creating this wonderful airship, the ZR-3, which accomplished the remarkable achievement of uniting for the first time the continents of the old world and the new world with a span of only sixty-six hours between coastal ports, the successors to Count von Zeppelin have aided in perpetuating his ideal, which is best expressed in his own words:

"May the rigid airship do its part in bringing men and nations more closely together and facilitate mutual understanding and good will throughout the World."

To this ideal America pledges its faith.

Presented by

DETROIT AVIATION SOCIETY.

Harold S. Emmon
President.

Carl B. Fetsche
Secretary.

Detroit, Michigan, U. S. A.
October thirty, nineteen hundred twenty-four.

One of many tributes to Dr. Eckener and his crew following their successful Atlantic crossing.

Eine der vielen Ehrungen für Dr. Eckener und seine Mannschaft nach der erfolgreichen Atlantiküberquerung.

2.5 Zeppelin and Goodyear

On September 19, 1923, an agreement was signed establishing the Goodyear – Zeppelin Corporation, which was later to have employed a number of prominent engineers from Friedrichshafen, led by Dr. Karl Arnstein. Two-thirds of the new company's shares were held by the Goodyear Rubber an Tire Co., one-third belonged to the Luftschiffbau Zeppelin. All patents owned by Zeppelin and its subsidiary companies were transfered to Goodyear. By the same token, the people in Friedrichshafen were given access to all of Goodyear's airship patents[10]. Only engines were excluded from these agreements. Goodyear made available to the corporation all of its plant facilities and personnel in Wingfoot Lake, Ohio. For the Zeppelin people who

---

[10] Latest publication on the subject: H. G. Dick, "The Golden Age of the Great Rigid Airships." In "Inside the Control Car", Feb. 1979, Issue 27, p. 1. The distribution of shares fluctuates from source to source, due to subsequent modifications of the contract or parts thereof.

Paul W. Litchfield (right) shows Captain Ernst Lehmann, of the Luftschiffbau Zeppelin, a Goodyear blimp.

Paul W. Litchfield (rechts) zeigt Kapitän Ernst Lehmann vom Luftschiffbau Zeppelin einen Goodyear Blimp.

went to Goodyear after the war, this was a unique oppurtunity to continue working on airship development under the most favorable conditions.

Various rigid airships were planned by Goodyear, but not until 1928 was a contract won to build two large airships for the U.S. Navy, only a few days before the LZ 127 "Graf Zeppelin" set out upon its first voyage to the United States. Both the "Akron" and the "Macon" (model designation ZRS-4 and ZRS-5), however, suffered an unfortunate fate; by 1934 they had both been lost at a total cost of 75 lives. It was perhaps fate that the wreck of the "Akron" in the Atlantic was discovered by a German ship, the "Phoebus", and radioed round the

Left: The German engineers from the Luftschiffbau in Friedrichshafen who went to the newly founded Goodyear-Zeppelin Corporation (1923).
1st row (left to right): Eugen Schöttel, Benjamin Schnitzer, Dr. Karl Arnstein, Eugen Brunner, Dr. Wolfgang Klemperer; 2nd row: Walter Mosebach, Lorenz Rieger, Hermann Liebert; 3rd row: Kurt Bauch, Hans Keck, Erich Hilligardt, Paul Helma, Wilhelm Fischer.

Links: Die deutschen Ingenieure vom Luftschiffbau in Friedrichshafen, die 1923 zur neuen Goodyear-Zeppelin Corporation nach Amerika gingen.
1. Reihe (von links): Eugen Schöttel, Benjamin Schnitzer, Dr. Karl Arnstein, Eugen Brunner, Dr. Wolfgang Klemperer; 2. Reihe: Walter Mosebach, Lorenz Rieger, Hermann Liebert; 3. Reihe: Kurt Bauch, Hans Keck, Erich Hilligardt, Paul Helma, Wilhelm Fischer.

RAIL ZEPPELIN
GOODYEAR ZEPPELIN CORP.
AKRON, OHIO

Airships were not the only business of the Goodyear-Zeppelin Corp. Shown here is a design for a high-speed rail car, which was later put into service in a somewhat modified form.

Die Goodyear-Zeppelin Corporation beschäftigte sich nicht nur mit Luftschiffen. Hier der Entwurf für einen später in etwas modifizierter Form zum Einsatz gekommenen Schnelltriebwagen.

Bottom: Model of a Goodyear-Zeppelin rigid airship during a parade in 1925.
Unten: Modell eines Starrluftschiffs von Goodyear-Zeppelin (1925).

Dr. Karl Arnstein, chief designer of the "Akron" and the "Macon".

Dr. Karl Arnstein, Chefkonstrukteur der „Akron" und der „Macon".

world. Of the crew of 76, only four could be rescued by the "Phoebus"; one of them died aboard the ship.

Dr. Eckener always used his visits to the United States to further develop contacts. Work had to go on, of course, at the hangars in Friedrichshafen. The success of the ZR 3 "Los Angeles" was by itself no guarantee for the continued existence of the company.

Eckener, who was convinced of the future success of world-wide airship service, attempted at the time to gain support for a joint German-American airline company. The existence of such a company seemed to him a prerequisite for building large numbers of passenger airships. But Dr. Eckener soon realized that his efforts would not rapidly bear friut. He decided to try another approach.

Note:

Surprisingly, after initial reservation, even Hermann Göring and the German Ministry of Aviation later urged the establishment of an American company for commercial airship service. In an express letter to Dr. Eckener dated September 28, 1936, the Minister of Aviation wrote: "I am in agreement with your plans to travel at the end of this month to the United States of North America aboard the airship "Hindenburg", in order to establish contact with concerned American parties in the matter of cooperation between the Deutsche Zeppelin-Reederei GmbH and an American commercial airship service company yet to be formed. I have noted your assurances that the talks are to be non-binding and will deal with the items mentioned in detail in your letter. I request, however, that negotiations on the matter of the transport of mail be left to the competent postal authorities. I further request a written report on the outcome of your discussions upon your return".

2.6 The Zeppelin-Eckener Fund

Although the success of ZR 3 had a lasting effect on the German public as well, the government of the German Reich remained sceptical and, at first, unwilling to provide funds to build another large airship; even then, the future of aviation was believed to lie with the airplane. Years before, Count Zeppelin himself had provided arguments for this position, for he had also foreseen a great potential for the airplane and had urged the building of planes even before World War I.

Thus, Dr. Eckener took a different approach. For months, he and the crew of the ZR 3 went on tour, showing slides of the Atlantic crossing and collecting some 2.5 million marks in a campaign which became known as the "Zeppelin-Eckener Fund". Nearly 30 per cent of the cost of constructing LZ 127 was financed in this way. This ship was to be of great significance in German-American relations, was to become world-famous and the most successful airship of all time. It was essentialy the LZ 127 "Graf Zeppelin" that inspired our fascination with the "zeppelins", a fascination that has lasted until the present day.

„Zeppelin-Eckener Fund"
call up.

Aufruf zur Zeppelin-Eckener-Spende (s.a.S. 180).

3.
NO AIRSHIPS WITHOUT HELIUM?

Dr. Eckener shows American friends plans for the airship LZ 127. Standing (l. to r.): Lt. Cdr. H. V. Wiley, Lt. R. G. Mayer, Cdr. G. Fulton; Seated: Capt. E. S. Jackson, Eckener, Lt. Cdr. C. E. Rosendahl (Photo 1927).

Dr. Eckener zeigt amerikanischen Freunden Pläne des Luftschiffs LZ 127. Stehend von links: Ltd. Cdr. H. V. Wiley, Ltd. R. G. Mayer, Cdr. G. Fulton; sitzend: Cpt. E. S. Jackson, Eckener, Ltd. Cdr. C. E. Rosendahl (Photo 1927).

3.1 First American voyage of the "Graf Zeppelin"

Four years after the ZR 3's unforgettable Atlantic passage, the LZ 127 took off on its first voyage to the United States. On board was a long-time promoter of airship construction, Charles E. Rosendahl, who hoped to gain further experience on this trip. The press and radio were also represented. Lady Drummond Hay, the daughter of the American newspaper publisher Hearst, produced articles and head-lines. As the only woman on board, she was herself the center of constant attention.

Some problems were encountered during the voyage, which had been prepared with great enthusiasm. Gusty winds over the Atlantic damaged the covering of the left horizontal stabilizer. The remaining covering was secured provisionally during the trip continued with severely reduced speed. This incident, however, did not impair the overall success of the undertaking. On the contrary, the voyage took

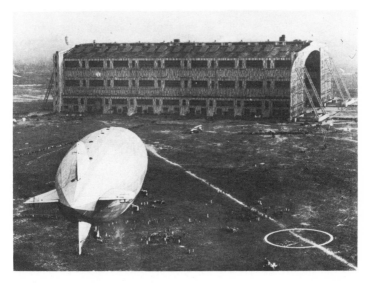

LZ 127 "Graf Zeppelin" over Manhattan and while landing at Lakehurst.
LZ 127 „Graf Zeppelin" über Manhattan und bei der Landung in Lakehurst.

City Roars Approval as Flyers Ride Down Broadway to City Hall

OFFICIALLY WELCOMED TO CITY!—Still dazed by the magnitude of their welcome, the feted flyers were officially received yesterday at City Hall by Acting Mayor McKee. Photo above shows general view of reception.

AT HEIGHT OF GLORY!—Never in his career has Dr. Eckener been accorded a more hearty reception than that accorded him in New York. He is shown on journey down Broadway with Rear-Admiral Moffett beside him.

CONGRATULATIONS!—Acting Mayor McKee is shown above welcoming the flyers in the name of the city and congratulating them on their achievement. Grover Whalen is at Eckener's right and Commander C. E. Rosendahl at McKee's left.

ACKNOWLEDGING PLAUDITS OF ENTHUSIASTIC MOB!—A thundering roar rose from thousands of throats as the procession rolled up Broadway yesterday. Eckener, seated on the top of rear seat, waved his hat in acknowledgement.

NOTHING LIKE THAT IN GERMANY!—Yessir, it's the huge Woolworth Building that is making Dr. Eckener crane his neck so much. He is shown above on City Hall steps at official reception.

Newspapers brimmed with reports of the first American voyage of the LZ 127 (see also pp. 56–59 and p. 202).

Die Zeitungen waren voll von Berichten über die erste Amerikafahrt von LZ 127 (s. a. Seiten 56–59 und 202).

Dr. Eckener meets Charles
Lindbergh. In the middle is
Envoy Otto C. Kiep from the
German Embassy in
Washington.

*Dr. Eckener trifft Charles
Lindbergh. In der Mitte
Gesandter Otto C. Kiep von
der Deutschen Botschaft in
Washington.*

Dr. Eckener in conversation
with Henry Ford. On the left
is Captain Ernst Lehmann, in
the background, navigation
officer Hans von Schiller
(Photo 1924).

*Dr. Eckener im Gespräch mit
Henry Ford. Links Kapitän
Ernst Lehmann, im
Hintergrund
Navigationsoffizier Hans von
Schiller (Photo 1924).*

on a dramatic aspect which, of course, was seized upon and exploited
by the news correspondents on board.

The reception in the U.S. far surpassed the one given the ZR 3. The
crew was led in triumph through the streets of New York. The city did
not let the opportunity go by to arrange a ticker-tape parade, an honor
shown only a few prominent personalities. A reception given by
Mayor Walker and a visit with President Coolidge in Washington
followed. Although the "Graf Zeppelin's" planned tour of Cleveland,
St. Louis and Chicago was cancelled due to inclement weather, Dr.
Eckener did make a formal visit to Chicago, where he received an
extraordinarily warm welcome. In Detroit, he discussed the problems
of air travel with Henry Ford, Walter Chrysler and managers of
General Motors. Eckener was accompanied for the first time on this

Dr. Eckener and his officers paid visits to numerous firms in the U.S. in 1928.
Dr. Eckener besuchte 1928 mit seinen Offizieren zahlreiche Firmen in den USA.

Bottom: The stowaway was mobbed by autograph-seekers upon his arrival.
Unten: Der blinde Passagier muß bei seiner Ankunft Autogramme geben!

trip by F. W. von Meister, his companion on nearly all Eckener's later American tours. Shortly afterwards, von Meister set up an office in New York and represented the interests of the Luftschiffbau Zeppelin until the cooperation came to an end.[11]

(1930)

In those days, every child in America knew not only the name Zeppelin, but Dr. Eckener as well. Wherever he and the crew of the LZ 127 showed up, the public's enthusiasm knew no limits. No other airship voyage – with the singular exception of the global voyage a year later – hardly any other single event of the day received so much attention in the American press. Whereas it was above all the technical and competitive achievement that had evoked such admiration for the ZR 3's Atlantic crossing, the aspect of friendship was now the primary factor in the American public's sentiments towards the German airship people.

One occurrence on the return trip deserves mention. During a check of the ship, Hans von Schiller discovered a stowaway, an American scarely 19 years old, who was probably the only stowaway of all time to achieve word fame. It is claimed that, upon arrival in Germany, he even signed autographs. At any rate, contemporary photos prove that he at least received a tumultuous welcome.

---

[11] F. W. (Willy) von Meister was also vice president of the American Zeppelin Transport Inc., founded by Goodyear-Zeppelin and the German Zeppelin Transport Co. The latter maintained of necessity close ties to the Ministry of Aviation in Berlin. Following the attack on Pearl Harbor, all shares of the company, which had been kept by von Meister since 1938, were confiscated. Most of the material was destroyed in the early 1960s. Thus nearly all important documents which could shed light on the relations between the U.S. and Germany concerning airship navigation no longer exist and a wealth of interesting details are lost.

Pages upon pages of reports on the American voyage and arrival of the LZ 127 "Graf Zeppelin" filled single editions of American newspapers. Shown here is the "New York American" of October 17, 1928 (p. 1).

Seitenweise wird in einer einzigen Ausgabe über die Amerikafahrt und die Ankunft von LZ 127 „Graf Zeppelin" in amerikanischen Zeitungen berichtet. Hier in „New York American" vom 17. Oktober 1928 (Seite 1).

Editorial Telephone, DRY Dock 8000 • NEW YORK AMERICAN "A Paper for People Who Think", WEDNESDAY, OCTOBER 17, 1928

'Hochs' Mingle with 'Hurrahs' in Welcome for Eckener

ROBUST COMMODORE RIDES LIKE 'LINDY' UP BROADWAY

All Clear Ahead

AT CITY HALL

M'KEE'S WELCOME; ECKENER'S REPLY

ON THE BRIDGE.—Lady Drummond Hay and Commander Eckener were chatting together in the control room of the *Graf Zeppelin* when the Hearst camera man snapped this picture. They turned to face the camera just as the shutter clicked.

UP THE BAY ON THE MACOM

Up Lower Broadway

Today's Programme For Flight Heroes

2,000 Reservations For New Dirigible

By Airpost from Germany to New York

'Das Ist Mein Schatz,' Eckener Beams at Los Angeles

BUT IT'S GRAF THAT PROVED VALUE OF AIRCRAFT, HE SAYS

"Three Musketeers" of the Air

HINDENBURG GRATEFUL FOR AID TO LINER

And I Haven't a Thing to Wear,' Sighs Lady Hay

DIRIGIBLE IS FUTURE LINER OF SEA, SAYS VON WIEGAND

Gen. Mitchell Calls Airship 'Best Ever Made'

ZEP MECHANIC MEETS SISTER

B. ALTMAN & CO.
FIFTH AVENUE AT THIRTY-FOURTH STREET
TELEPHONE: MURRAY HILL 7000

Balloon Pioneer Renders Tribute To Dr. Eckener

Golf Sweaters
By Altman
With Matching Hose

Decidedly small patterns or none at all are still most favoured on the links. Altman is showing a large collection in cashmere and fine wool, $6.50 to $15.00

Coat Sweaters in European novelties and fancy designs . $13.50 to $45.00

Imported cashmere mufflers, light and warm, will be much in demand this season for sports and daytime

MEN'S SWEATERS—FIRST FLOOR

"New York American", October 17, 1928 (p. 4)
„New York American" vom 17. Oktober 1928, Seite 4

The advertising value of the Zeppelin airship was soon discovered by commercial interests as well. Shown here is a publicity photo from 1929: "Firestone – first again. First shipment of tires via air New York to Basle, Switzerland … via Graf Zeppelin…"

Schon bald wurde das Zeppelin-Luftschiff auch von der werbenden Wirtschaft als zugkräftiger Werbeträger entdeckt. Hier ein Photo für PR-Zwecke aus dem Jahre 1929. Text auf dem Reifen: „Firestone – wieder Nummer Eins. Erster Reifenversand per Luft von New York nach Basel … mit Graf Zeppelin…"

3.2 "Graf Zeppelin's" world voyage

The successful American voyage inspired not only Friedrichshafen Zeppelin people to new feats. The newspaper publisher Hearst secured exclusive world rights to news coverage of the planned global voyage, thereby guaranteeing the financing of the undertaking. And, after numerous trips, adequate experience had been gained to enable an attempt at a project of such magnitude.

Only three landings were planned for the round- the-world journey. The publisher Hearst had made the launching from the Statue of Liberty in New York a condition for his portion of the financing. And so, the LZ 127 flew first to New York, and it was from there that – at least from the American point of view – the voyage around the world began officially on August 7, 1929. On August 10, the airship was once again in Friedrichshafen and five days later, on August 15, 1929, the "Graf Zeppelin" took off a second time, its course due east. The Americans on board appreciated the fact that, for the Germans, this was the official start of the world voyage.

The stop in Tokyo proved to be an unforgettable experience, not only for the Japanese, but for passengers and crew as well. From there the "Graf Zeppelin" set out on the most hazardous part of its journey – destination Los Angeles over the Pacific Ocean, the world's largest expanse of water – which no man had ever crossed in this way.
Sixty-eight hours later, the ship reached the West Coast of the United States, a few hours after the planned arrival time. As a worried F. W. von Meister, who had awaited Dr. Eckener in San Francisco, questioned him about the delay, Eckener replied: "But Herr von Meister, when, for the first time in human history, an airship crosses the Pacific Ocean, isn't it fitting that it appear over the Golden Gate at sunset?"[12]. It was a psychological trick that worked, for "... his calculations proved completely accurate. The Zeppelin was given a tumultuous welcome"[13].

---

[12] From the record of an interview with F. W. von Meister by Henry Cord Meyer, professor of History at the University of California, Irvine, Ca., and dated Sept. 15, 1979, shortly after von Meister's death.

[13] ibid.

Ticker tape parade in New York
for the crew of the LZ 127 "Graf
Zeppelin" after the global voyage.
*Konfettiparade für die
Mannschaft von LZ 127 „Graf
Zeppelin" in New York nach der
Weltfahrt 1929.*

Right: Dr. Eckener and Mayor
Jimmy Walker.
*Dr. Eckener und Bürgermeister
Jimmy Walker.*

Dr. Eckener describes the course of the world voyage on the globe in front of the New York city hall. In the center is Lady Drummond Hay, on the right, Mayor Walker with Captain Lehmann behind him. On the far left (with cap) is Captain Flemming.

Dr. Eckener trägt die Weltfahrt auf dem Globus vor dem New Yorker Rathaus ein. In der Mitte Lady Drummond Hay, rechts Bürgermeister Walker, dahinter Kapitän Lehmann, ganz links (mit Mütze) Kapitän Flemming.

As the ship continued down the coast, it passed over the festively illuminated estate of the publisher Hearst, who had provided major financing for the voyage.

Los Angeles was merely a stopover; the mood was high to go on and, for the first time, disaster seemed near. But again, Dr. Eckener was in control of the situation. Hans von Schiller, watch officer on board, describes what happened:[14]

"As we prepared to take off that evening, the temperature was considerably higher than expected. We had to remove all excess provisions and water ballast. Finally, it seemed to work, the mooring

---

[14] Hans von Schiller: "Zeppelin – Wegbereiter des Luftverkehrs". Kirschbaum-Verlag, Bad Godesberg 1966. Ist ed., p. 97. (Note: 2nd revised and enlarged ed. in prep.)

crew prodded the ship into the air. But after only twenty meters, we stopped rising and were forced to run all engines at top speed to try to lift the ship dynamically. We began to move foreward – and spotted, about one kilometer away, a high-tension line some 40 meters above the ground and directly in our path. The pressure of the elevator caused the aft section to drop and touch the ground, whirling up grass and weeds and snaring the lower edge of the stabilizer. But we kept on going. Dr. Eckener was tranquility itself. Calmly, he directed his son at the elevator: 'Knut, hold her steady'. And shortly before the obstacle: 'Pull her up now' Though the nose of the dirigible had cleared the cable, we were still worried about the tail. But then, as the mid-section passed over the cable, came Dr. Eckener's calm command: 'And now straighten her out again'. And by a hairsbreadth, we made it."

Incidentally, the Navy was disconsolate about the fact that six crew members were forced to take the train to Lakehurst, because, inadvertently, not enough hydrogen gas had been made available in Los Angeles.

Although the dirigble's crew had by now become accustomed to enthusiastic welcomes, the reception in New York at the end of the world voyage surpassed everything experienced thus far. The "Zeppelin" had conquered the air for all time – or so it seemed. Technology celebrated a triumph without equal. Just how highly the crew was held in esteem was documented in the awarding of the "Freedom of the City" by Mayor Walker.

3.3 Codeword: Helium

While Dr. Eckener remained in the U.S. for negotiations, LZ 127, with Captain Lehmann in command, began the flight back to Friedrichshafen.

The most important object of negotiations during those years of LZ 127's greatest success – including the famous expedition to the Arctic

Left: President Hoover and Dr. Eckener in Washington in 1929.
Links: Präsident Hoover und Dr. Eckener 1929 in Washington.

in 1931 in which two Americans also took part[15] – was the supply of non-combustible helium, larger quantities of which were only abailable in the United States. To enable the development of a world-wide airship transport network, top priority had to be given to safety. What no aviation authority would permit today was still possible in the 1930's: passengers were carried over long distances using highly explosive hydrogen gas. However, it was clear to all concerned that this solution could only be a temporary one, unacceptable in the long run. Thus, LZ 129 "Hindenburg" had already been designed to use helium. When construction began in 1934, it was assumed that helium deliveries from the United States were assured – in part due to the cordial relations in the airship sector. But the efforts of Dr. Eckener, the German and the American employees of the Goodyear-Zeppelin Corporation as well as their colleagues at the U.S. branch of the Deutsche Zeppelin-Reederei, most notably its agent, F. W. von Meister, were all in vain. In the end, political developments in Germany prompted the decision of the Americans not to supply the non-combustible gas. This decision, however understandable politically, was to have grave consequences shortly thereafter.

And so LZ 129 was built for use with hydrogen after all. Trust was placed in the experience won with LZ 127. Furthermore, LZ 129 was far superior technically in many respects to the already aging LZ 127. Thus, after extensive trials, scheduled flights were begun in 1936.

3.4 "Zeppelins" in scheduled service between Europe and America

Since the end of August 1932, the LZ 127 "Graf Zeppelin" had been making regular flights to South America. In October 1933, during a return trip, another visit was paid to the United States. Stops were made in Miami, Florida, Akron, Ohio and Chicago, Illinois. After that, "The Graf", as the LZ 127 was often called, never again flew to

---

[15] Lt. Commander E. H. Smith of the U.S. Navy and Lincoln Elsworth, polar explorer from New York.

October 26, 1933: LZ 127 "Graf Zeppelin" lands at Curtiss-Wright Airport in Chicago.
26. Oktober 1933: LZ 127 „Graf Zeppelin" landet in Chicago auf dem Curtiss-Wright airport.

the United States, the country where it had celebrated its greatest triumphs.

The smooth, even cordial relations between the airship builders in Friedrichshafen and the U.S. Navy were recorded in a variety of written documents. On October 11, 1935, an agreement was signed which secured the use of technical facilities at the Lakehurst Airfield and the Naval Base in Opa-Locka, Florida by the Deutsche Zeppelin-Reederei GmbH, Berlin for the LZ 129, still under construction. For a slight fee, the LZ 129 was guaranteed the use in Lakehurst of the hangar and mooring mast, storage space for approximately 30,000 cubic meters of hydrogen gas for refilling as well as the necessary filling equipment, tank cars etc. In addition, a docking crew of 90 men was provided for each launch and landing for a fee of only $ 250, a truly amicable price. Should the LZ 129 land anywhere else in the United States, it was agreed that up to seven tank cars be provided to

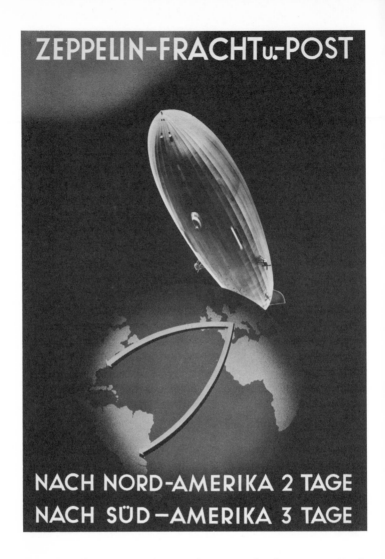

Poster from the year 1936, advertising fast cargo and mail transport to North and South America with the LZ 129 "Hindenburg".

Plakat aus dem Jahre 1936, das mit dem Luftschiff LZ 129 „Hindenburg" für die rasche Fracht- und Postbeförderung nach Nord- und Südamerika wirbt.

secure gas and fuel supplies. Radio facilities at airports could be used as well.

Most surprising of all was the permission to store large quantities of hydrogen. From the beginning, American airships had been filled exclusively with safe helium. Even ZR 3 had been immediately converted to helium operation upon delivery to the U.S. Navy. The support shown the Zeppelin people by the Navy in this respect as well is an expression of the excellent connections maintained by American and German airship advocates.

The first American flight of the LZ 129 "Hindenburg" took place in May 1936 and led, as did later trips, directly to Lakehurst. The airship, the largest ever put into passenger service, flew this route a total of eleven times. And yet each arrival, indeed each time a dirigible was spotted anywhere, caused an excitement which always drew a multitude of spectators as well as reporters and cameramen. A vast quantity of photographic material, some of it not entirely brought to light even today, is evidence of that enduring and unparalleled fascination with airships. In July 1936, the German minister of Aviation, Göring, wrote to the Zeppelin-Reederei in Berlin:

"Having received the suggestion from sources in New York, please advise if it is possible to have the airship "Hindenburg" cruise over New York in daylight hours during one of its next voyages to America. Up till now, the "Hindenburg" has presumably passed over New York only in darkness and the public has not been given any opportunity whatsover to see the much admired airship. According to my information, a cruise over the city lasting hours would be advantageous for propaganda purposes.

I find the American Navy's accommodating offer of the use of the airship terminal at Lakehurst reason enough to deem the proposal justified."

Even the terrible disaster on May 6, 1937 in Lakehurst, in which the LZ 129 was consumed by fire, did not alter the general interest in airships that persists to the present day. The tragic end of this ship was captured on film in every detail. The taped eyewitness account of the American radio reporter Herbert Morrison is one of the most dramatic testimonies of modern journalism ever made.

The wreck of the LZ 129 "Hindenburg" brought an end to the era of passenger airships. Although contruction of the LZ 130 was completed

in Friedrichshafen, the ship was never put into passenger service; only test flights were conducted. Following the tragedy in Lakehurst, the LZ 127 „Graf Zeppelin" was retired after nearly nine years of uninterrupted service.

Goering Stops All Zeppelin Flights

Daily Express Special Reporter
BERLIN, Sunday.

NAZI Air Minister General Goering, who only yesterday proclaimed that the wreck of the Hindenburg would have no effect on Germany's Zeppelin plans, today ordered the Zeppelin Company to discontinue all flights until after airship pioneer Dr Hugo Eckener had investigated the cause of the Lakehurst disaster.

This unexpected action is hailed as confirmation of the sabotage theory by the German man-in-the-street, who refuses obstinately to believe that Germany's pride, the Hindenburg, was not the victim of a time-bomb or incendiary bullet.

It also brought disappointment to Captain von Schiller, commander of the Graf Zeppelin, and his crew, who, undaunted by the Hindenburg's fate, had hoped to fly the Graf to Lakehurst to bring back the bodies of their dead comrades.

This flight would have been the 579th of the nine-year-old Graf Zeppelin, which has flown millions of miles without mishap.

Immediately on returning with 25 passengers to Friedrichshafen yesterday from its second trip to South America this season, Captain von Schiller called together his crew, asked if they were willing to continue the flight. They answered with one shout, "Yes."

Captain von Schiller communicated with the Zeppelin Company, which replied, "Hold yourself in readiness to fly to North America."

Twelve hours later Captain von Schiller received orders from General Goering that the Graf Zeppelin was to remain in its hangar in Friedrichshafen until further notice.

Meanwhile, Hitler is waiting impatiently for the findings of the commission now investigating the shattered wreck lying on the Lakehurst airfield, in the hope of finding a clue to the cause of the disaster.

Top left: Crash of LZ 129 "Hindenburg" at Lakehurst May 7, 1937. American landing crew escaping; one man of the crew was killed.

Links oben: Absturz von LZ 129 „Hindenburg" am 7. Mai 1937 in Lakehurst. Die amerikanische Bodenmannschaft versucht zu fliehen; ein Mann der Gruppe wurde getötet.

Bottom left: An American military honor guard stands watch over the wreckage of the LZ 129.

Links unten: Amerikanische Soldaten halten Ehrenwache an den Trümmern von LZ 129.

Top: Excerpt from the "Daily Express" of May 10, 1937, three days after the "Hindenburg" disaster.

Oben: Ausschnitt aus „Daily Express" vom 10. Mai 1937, drei Tage nach dem „Hindenburg"-Unglück.

TO
THE HONORABLE
 THE SECRETARY OF COMMERCE
  WASHINGTON, D. C.   July 21, 1937

   In an order, dated May 7, 1937, made by the Secretary of Commerce
pursuant to the Air Commerce Act of 1926, as amended, relating to the
investigation of accidents in civil air navigation in the United States,
South Trimble, Jr., Solicitor, Major R. W. Schroeder, Assistant Director of the Bureau of Air Commerce, and Denis Mulligan, Chief, Regulation
and Enforcement Division of the Bureau of Air Commerce, all of the
Department of Commerce, were designated to investigate the facts, conditions and circumstances of the accident involving the airship HINDENBURG,
which occurred on May 6, 1937, at the Naval Air Station, Lakehurst,
New Jersey, and to make a report thereon.

   Commander C. E. Rosendahl, U. S. Navy, Colonel C. de F. Chandler,
U. S. Army, Colonel Rush B. Lincoln, U. S. Army, Colonel Harold E.
Hartney, Technical Adviser to the U. S. Senate Committee on Commerce,
Hon. Gill Robb Wilson, Director of Aeronautics for the State of New
Jersey, and Hon. Grover Loening, Aeronautical Adviser to the U. S.
Maritime Commission, were designated as technical advisers. General-
leutnant Friedrich von Boetticher, German Military Attache, was selected
by the German Ambassador at the invitation of the Secretary of Commerce,
as an observer at the investigation.

Pages 72–75: Extracts from one of the first reports of the investigation into the crash of the LZ 129. Shown is page one with the names of the members of the board of inquiry.

Seiten 72–75: Auszüge aus einem der ersten Untersuchungsberichte über den Absturz von LZ 129. Hier Seite 1 mit den Namen der Mitglieder des Untersuchungsausschusses.

On the fourth day of the hearings, the members of the German Commission appointed to investigate the accident, including Dr. Hugo Eckener,
Lieutenant Colonel Joachim Breithaupt, Professor Guenther Bock, Professor
Dr. Max Dieckmann, Director Dr. Ludwig Duerr, and Staff Engineer
Friedrich Hoffman, appeared and thereafter acted as observers and testified
as witnesses. The U. S. Navy Board of Inquiry was represented throughout
the hearing by an observer.

When the accident occurred, an aeronautical inspector of the Department of Commerce was present. Before midnight of the same day, other representatives of the Department reached the scene of the accident. After
a preliminary inspection had been made, public hearings were held, from
May 10th to May 28th, in the main hangar at the Naval Air Station,
Lakehurst, New Jersey, in Asbury Park, N. J. and in New York City.

In addition to that provided by the Department's representatives,
assistance was received from the U. S. Navy Department, Bureau of Investigation, Department of Justice, Weather Bureau, Department of Agriculture,
Bureau of Standards, Department of Commerce, New York City Police Department, and the Bureau of Explosives. Aviation companies, newspapermen,
newsreel representatives, and photographers, many of whom were eye
witnesses to the event, and others, furnished valuable information.

Page two of the investigators' report with the names of representatives of the
German commission who took part in the investigation.

*Seite 2 des Untersuchungsberichts mit den Namen der Vertreter der deutschen
Kommission, die an den Untersuchungen beteiligt waren.*

<u>CONCLUSION</u>

The cause of the accident w as the ignition of a mixture of free hydrogen and air. Based upon the evidence, a leak at or in the vicinity of cell 4 and 5 caused a combustible mixture of hydrogen and air to form in the upper stern part of the ship in considerable quantity; the first appearance of an open flame was on the top of the ship and a relatively short distance forward of the upper vertical fin. The theory that a brush discharge ignited such mixture appears most probable.

Respectfully submitted,

South Trimble, Jr., Solicitor

R. W. Schroeder, Asst. Director,
Bureau of Air Commerce.

Denis Mulligan, Chief, Regulation and
Enforcement Division, Bureau
of Air Commerce.

Approved

Daniel C. Roper,
Secretary of Commerce.

Summary of the investigators' report (page 56) of July 21, 1937, into the crash of the LZ 129.
Zusammenfassung des Untersuchungsberichts (Seite 56) vom 21. Juli 1937 über den Absturz von LZ 129.

Passengers on board the Airship HINDENBURG on its departure from Frankfurt-am-Main, Germany, on May 3, 1937,
were as follows:

Adelt, Gertrude	Berlin, Germany
Adelt, Leonhard	" "
* Anders, Ernst Rudolf	Dresden, Germany
Belin, Peter	Washington, D. C.
* Brink, Birger	
Clemens, Carl Otto	Bonn, Germany
* Doehner, Hermann	Mexico City, Mexico
* Doehner, Irene	" " "
Doehner, Matilda	" " "
Doehner, Walter	" " "
Doehner, Werner	" " "
* Dolan, Curtis	France
* Douglas, Edward	New York
* Erdmann, Fritz	
Ernst, Elsa	Hamburg, Germany
* Ernst, Otto C.	" "
* Feibusch, Moritz	Lincoln, Nebraska
Grant, George	London, England
Heidenstamm, Rudolf von	
Herschfeld, George	Bremen, Germany
Hinkelbein, Claus	
Kleeman, Marie	
* Knoecher, Erich	Zeulenroda, Germany
Leuchtenberg, Wm.	New York
Mangone, Philip	
Mather, Margaret	
Morris, Nelson	
O'Laughlin, Herbert	
Osbun, Clifford	Chicago, U.S.A.
* Pannes, Emma	New York
* Pannes, John	" "
* Reichold, Otto	Vienna, Austria
Spaeh, Joseph	
Stoeckle, Emil	
Vinholt, Hans	Copenhagen, Denmark
Witt, Hans	

* Indicates those who died in accident.

Passenger list for the last flight of the LZ 129 (attached to the investigators'
report of July 21, 1937).

*Passagierliste der letzten Fahrt von LZ 129 (Anlage zum Untersuchungsbericht
vom 21. Juli 1937).*

3.5 Helium becomes a political issue

Helium had been the subject of lengthy debate in the U.S. Congress since 1925. A bill passed on March 3 of that year severely restricted exports. Following years saw repeated debates on the subject. The debacle at Lakehurst prompted the majority of Americans to favor supplying helium to Dr. Eckener so that he might continue his work. Yet developments took another direction.

Only a week after the catastrophe in Lakehurst, Secretary of the Interior Harold L. Ickes passed on to the cabinet in Washington an inquiry from Germany. The Germans wished to purchase some 300,000 cubic meters of helium for the LZ 130, which was still under construction. The cabinet feared, however, that the gas and the airships might be used for military purposes. President Roosevelt, always well disposed to Eckener and his idea, had the Interior Secretary form a five-man special commission to deliberate the helium issue. Besides Ickes, who later became one of the fiercest opponents of helium sales to Germany, the other members of the commission, which included Secretary of State Cordell Hull, Secretary of Commerce Daniel C. Roper, Secretary of War Harry H. Woodring and Secretary of the Navy Claude A. Swanson, had decided within a few days to recommend to the President that, under certain circumstances, helium be sold "for applications in commercial airship service between the United States and other countries[16].

On May 25, 1937, while the world still felt the shock of the disaster at Lakehurst, the recommendation was passed on to Roosevelt. Of course, steps were to be taken to prevent the military application of the helium – humanitarian considerations were given priority, "…in order to promote science and commerce, relieve human suffering, protect the lives of airship passengers and thereby strengthen international bonds of friendship"[17]. Roosevelt immediately forwarded the commission's findings to the proper congressional committees. Eck-

---

[16] Other uses, including scientific applications, were also stipulated.

[17] From Moltmann, G.: Die Luftschiff-"Hindenburg"-Katastrophe und das Heliumproblem. In "Wehrwissenschaftliche Rundschau", 11/1961.

ener, in America at the time to look into the causes of the wreck, even testified before Senate and House military committees and tried to assure them that military use of the helium was out of the question. This was presumably the first time these committees had ever conducted hearings with a foreigner.

Things seemed to be going well. On December 7, 1937, the German Embassy in Washington sent the following telegram to the Foreign Ministry in Berlin:

1) Just received note from American Government granting extension of 1937 issued air route privileges to year 1938 for Deutsche Zeppelin-Reederei GmbH and approving eighteen flights for airship LZ 130.

2) According to State Department memorandum of yesterday, on the joint recommendation of all members of National Munitions Control Board and Secretary of Interior, 17,900,000 cubic feet of helium have been allotted to American Zeppelin Transport Inc., New York as agent for Deutsche Zeppelin-Reederei GmbH, Frankfurt a/M. This quantity may be exported until October 31, 1938 on the basis of special export licenses. According to Mellon, the export transactions, yet to be applied for, are a mere formality.

signed *Dieckhoff*

Why this telegram was not forwarded to the Deutsche Zeppelin-Reederei in Frankfurt until December 24, 1937, however, is not clear. These delaying tactics were continued by the Berlin ministries, for the complete original of this important memorandum, which surely was received in Berlin at a considerably earlier date, was not received by the Zeppelin-Reederei until January 15, 1938. The letter accompanying the memo read as follows:

"Enclosed please find copy of a memorandum in which the State Department advises the German Embassy in Washington that the air route permit granted to the Deutsche Zeppelin-Reederei for 1937 has been extended to the year 1938 and that 18 flights by the airship LZ 130 will be permitted during 1938. Please take note of conditions of memorandum.

In a publication of the State Department of December 6, 1937,

Daily Washington

MERRY GO ROUND

By DREW PEARSON and ROBERT S. ALLEN.

(The authors of the column which appears daily in this space are given widest latitude. Their viewpoints do not necessarily reflect those of the Daily Mirror.)

WASHINGTON.—With war threatening in Europe there has been a serious inner Cabinet discussion over the sending of 19,800,000 cubic feet of helium to Germany.

This is enough helium to aid materially in blowing up the city of London, or Paris, or to provide gas for the operation of military balloons during an entire war. In fact, it is a priceless military gift to any belligerent nation, and so anxious has Germany been to get it that a Nazi ship has been anchored at Houston, Tex., waiting to load it aboard and race for Hamburg.

THE GAS WAS PRODUCED at Amarillo, Tex., and has been held awaiting final word from Washington before being sent to Houston and loaded aboard the German vessel. It was actually about to be dispatched when watchful Secretary of the Interior Ickes got skeptical regarding Germany's use of the gas and intervened.

The helium was to be sold to Germany under the law passed by Congress last year after the Hindenburg disaster. However, there are some neat jokers in the present sale which went unnoticed until caught by Ickes. One of these is the fact that a Zeppelin only requires 6,000,000 cubic feet of helium, whereas Germany is getting 19,800,000 cubic feet this year.

She has specified that she wants a little extra for experimentation and in order to send the new Zeppelin around Europe—but this does not explain her getting three times as much as required. In addition to this, Germany is to receive 40,000,000 cubic feet of helium within the next two years.

THE HELIUM DEAL was approved by Joe Green, State Department munitions controller, and by Army and Navy experts, on the ground that it was in line with an act of Congress. Since Congress passed the act, however, Europe has been seething, and Hitler has given every indication that he will provoke war if anyone thwarts him.

The inter-departmental committee has asked for pledges that the helium will be used only for scientific and commercial transportation purposes, and apparently Cabinet members have been naive enough to believe that Germany will keep her word.

Meanwhile, a German lobbyist, residing in the Mayflower Hotel, has been urging immediate action; while Herman Goering, Nazi War Marshal, also an official of the Zeppelin company, has been clamoring for the helium.

Note—The United States has virtually complete monopoly on helium—and it is almost indispensable to balloon or Zeppelin operation in war. Helium gas bags cannot be readily shot down, because helium does not explode when hit by a bullet. And the Army has perfected a system of patching balloons in mid-air so that they continue buoyant even when punctured by bullets.

Early 1938: American newspaper maintain constant coverage of helium debates in Congress. Left: the "Daily Mirror" of March 22, 1938; right: the "New York Times" of March 26, 1938 (see also p. 80).

Anfang 1938: Die amerikanischen Zeitungen berichten ständig über die Heliumdiskussionen des Kongresses. Links: „Daily Mirror", 22. März 1938; rechts: „New York Times", 26. März 1938 (s. a. Seite 80).

ASKS HELIUM SALES BAN

Vandenberg Offers Amendment to Act Covering Foreign Airships

WASHINGTON, March 25 (AP).— Senator Vandenberg proposed today that Congress withdraw the nation's supply of helium from commercial airship lines operating between this and foreign countries. He introduced an amendment to the Helium Act which would repeal a section allowing such sales.

The American Zeppelin Transport Company of New York is now awaiting final government approval of a contract to buy a quantity of the gas for the German Zeppelin Corporation.

Secretary Ickes, however, has delayed approval of the sale until President Roosevelt returns from Warm Springs, Ga. Mr. Ickes said he was concerned about conditions in Europe and possible use of the helium for foreign military purposes, which is forbidden by the Helium Act.

concerning export licenses for weapons, munitions and other implements of war, helium is also mentioned:

„On the joint recommendation of all of the members of the National Munitions Control Board and the Secretary of the Interior, an allotment of 17,900,000 cubic feet of helium gas, the exportation of which may be authorized by license during a period of one year after November 1, 1937, was granted on November 23, 1937, to American Zeppelin Transport, Incorporated, New York, as Agent for Deutsche Zeppelin-Reederei G.m.b.H., Frankfurt on the Main, Germany, in accordance with paragraphs (6) and (7) of the Regulations Governing the Exportation of Helium Gas. No licenses have as yet been applied for or issued under this allotment."

Due to time limitations placed on the export licenses, it must be assumed that such licenses will only be issued in future in individual cases".

U. S. Withholds Helium From Warlike Reich

Halts Shipment, Pending Iron-Clad Pledge From Zeppelin Firm That Gas Will Be Used Peaceably

From the Herald Tribune Bureau

WASHINGTON, March 22.—With the express approval of President Roosevelt, the Department of the Interior is holding up the signing of a contract for the sale of 19,800,-000 cubic feet of helium gas to German Zeppelin interests, because of growing skepticism in high official quarters as to the use to which the gas would be put.

The law governing the sale of helium (of which the American government has a world monopoly) to a foreign country requires that positive guaranties be given that none of the gas will be used for military purposes. The German Zeppelin Corporation has represented that the sole use of the gas would be to maintain a commercial airship service to this country. But there is a distinct hesitancy in official quarters here to accept such representations as sufficient guaranty, in view of the recent annexation of Austria and Germany's reported territorial ambitions in other central European areas.

With war threatening Europe, the United States government is said to feel that it must have, in order to comply wih the helium export act, an iron-clad guaranty that the gas will not be used for military purposes. The difficulty in dealing with Germany in her present aggressive mood, as one official explains it, is to draft a form of contract that will provide the required assurances.

The impression here is that the United States government is not disposed to hasten the completion of the deal with the Zeppelin company. It is reported that the matter of guaranties has been referred back to the Munitions Control Board, which approved export licenses several weeks ago. The export approval was conditional on Germany's complying with the requirements of the helium export law, but the matter of drafting the contract of sale was left to the Department of the Interior. Secretary Harold L. Ickes, who has been in constant touch with the President, has rejected as inadequate all of the formulas for exacting guaranties thus far proposed.

The extreme caution in proceeding with the Zeppelin deal is construed here in diplomatic circles as a rather oblique expression by this government of its displeasure over the annexation of Austria and Germany's territorial ambitions.

In full expectation that the sale contract would go through promptly, the Zeppelin company sent a ship loaded with tanks to Houston, Tex., two months ago. The tanks were unloaded and shipped to Amarillo (where the gas is mined) and there they are gathering rust today. The Zeppelin company, moreover, announced a schedule of crossings to start in May.

When the export licenses were approved, it was explained that the entire amount of helium desired by the German company would not be made available at once. Sufficient quantities would be released, it was said, to make up the loss through leakage on each westward crossing. There would also be sent to Germany from time to time a sufficient quantity to make up for the leakage loss on the eastward crossings. To inflate the bag of the ship built to replace the Hindenburg. lost by fire at Lakehurst last summer, 6,000,000 cubic feet are needed.

"New York Herald Tribune" of March 23, 1938.

„New York Herald Tribune", 23. März 1938.

The memorandum delivered by the State Department to the German Embassy in Washington on December 7, concerning air route privileges for the LZ 130, reads as follows:[18]

„The Secretary of State presents his compliments to His Excellency the German Ambassador and refers to previous correspondence concerning the application of the Deutsche Zeppelin Reederei G.m.b.H. to conduct experimental transatlantic flights with the airship. L.Z. 130 during 1938.

The Secretary of State takes pleasure in informing the Ambassador that the Secretary of Commerce has extended for the year 1938 the provisional authority heretofore granted to the Deutsche Zeppelin Reederei G.m.b.H., premised upon the facts and representations appearing in the said application, and under the following terms and conditions:

(1) The round trip flights to be made in the airship L.Z. 130 between Frankfurt, Germany and Lakehurst, New Jersey U.S.A., shall not exceed eighteen in number and, before any flight shall be made in United States territory, a schedule or timetable shall be transmitted to the Department of Commerce, showing the approximate dates when the proposed flights are to be made between foreign territory and the United States.

(2) The flights contemplated in this authorization shall be subject to the terms of the Air Navigation Arrangement between the United States and Germany effective June 1, 1932.

(3) It is understood that the privilege granted herein is for the navigation of the airship L.Z. 130 in direct flight from a place in Germany to Lakehurst, New Jersey and return. The route to be traversed into and out of Lakehurst, New Jersey in such flight shall be over the shortest route in United States territory to and from Lakehurst, New Jersey, unless weather or other emergent conditions make it necessary to vary the said route.

(4) This authorization is granted upon the understanding that the Government of Germany will grant to United States aviation inter-

---

[18] Department of State, Washington, D. C., File 811.79662 LZ-130/8.

ests, upon application duly submitted by this Government, air route and service privileges in German territory equivalent to those already granted or hereby granted by the Government of the United States to German aviation interests.

(5) It is understood that a sufficient number of proving flights will be made with the L.Z. 130 before passengers are carried for hire on flights between the United States and Germany."

The first deliveries of helium were sent to Germany in late 1937. But the annexation of Austria by Hitler on March 13, 1938 brought an abrupt end to the cordial relations with the United States which Eckener had so painstakingly and patiently developed. On March 14, 1938, the House of Representatives passed a law prohibiting the sale of helium to the German Reich, thus reversing its earlier 1937 decision[19]. Although Eckener tried to get approval for the helium deliveries directly from President Roosevelt, the president was bound by the rulings of the helium commission and Congress. The dramatic events of these weeks and months were vividly described by Eckener himself in his book "Im Luftschiff über Länder und Meere"[20]. A German freighter, waiting in the Port of Galveston, Texas since Spring of 1938 to take on an load of helium, was forced to return home empty.

To be sure, the vast majority of American regretted the decision, for now Dr. Eckener and his colleagues were no longer able to continue their work, so popular and admired by the American public in particular. But due to the aggressive policies of Hitler's Germany, most of the American people supported the ruling after all. The newspapers reported daily on the conflict and, in large part due to the helium issue, the highly-charged political situation in Europe was followed attentively by all America.

---

[19] "...the sale of helium gas to the German Reich shall be prohibited." H. R. 9855 on March 14, 1938 (see page 85).

[20] Heyne Paperback Book 5582, Munich 1979, p. 271 ff. (slightly abridged reprint of original 1949 edition, Verlag Chr. Wolff, Flensburg) with foreword by R. Italiaander and additional commentaries.

LZ 130, for which the helium was destined, shortly before its completion in Friedrichshafen in Spring of 1938. On November 14, 1936, Dr. Eckener had reportet (cf. "Werkzeitschrift der Zeppelin-Betriebe" Nr. 4, 1936) that negotiations were being conducted over a possible chartering of the LZ 130 by the United States, flying under American registry with a German crew (!). Meanwhile, however, this dream was doomed to failure.

LZ 130, für das das Helium bestimmt war, kurz vor der Fertigstellung in Friedrichshafen im Frühjahr 1938. Am 14. November 1936 hatte Dr. Eckener noch über dieses Schiff geschrieben (s. „Werkzeitschrift der Zeppelin-Betriebe" Nr. 4, 1936), daß Verhandlungen mit Amerika im Gange seien, wonach LZ 130 eventuell von Amerika gechartert und unter amerikanischer Flagge mit deutscher Besatzung fahren würde (!). Doch dieser Traum war inzwischen längst ausgeträumt.

Galveston, Texas, January 1938: The German freighter "Dessau" unloads empty pressure tanks to be filled with helium, great quantities of which were produced in Amarillo, Texas (photo top). The "Dessau" was finally forced to return home without helium.

Galveston, Texas, Januar 1938: Der deutsche Frachter „Dessau" entlädt leere Druckbehälter, um diese mit Helium, das in Amarillo, Texas, in großen Mengen gefördert wird, füllen zu lassen (Bild oben). Die „Dessau" muß aber schließlich ohne Helium zurückfahren.

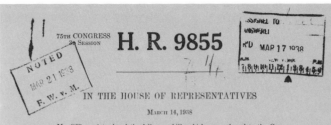

Austria was annexed by Hitler on March 13, 1938. The following day, a law was passed by Congress finally barring the sale of helium to the German Reich.

Am 13. März 1938 annektierte Hitler Österreich, und schon einen Tag später verabschiedet der amerikanische Kongreß das Gesetz, mit dem endgültig Heliumlieferungen an das Deutsche Reich unterbunden werden.

3.6 Dr. Eckener – Mediator between Germany and America

One fact, far better known abroad and especially in the United States than in Germany at the time, was the strained relationship between Dr. Hugo Eckener and the National Socialists. During the initial years of the Nazi regime, Eckener stubbornly refused to allow the airships to be used for propaganda purposes or, for example, to make the airship hangar in Friedrichshafen available for a mammoth Nazi rally. In 1933, the Gestapo demanded from Eckener a public endorsement of Hitler (after Eckener's 1932 radio speech in support of

Charles E. Rosendahl (right) and Hans von Schiller in July 1938 in Berlin. The last meetings of American and German airship advocates before the outbreak of World War II were solemn and nostalgic.

Charles E. Rosendahl (rechts) und Hans von Schiller im Juli 1938 in Berlin. Diese letzten Begegnungen amerikanischer und deutscher Luftschiffer vor dem 2. Weltkrieg waren von Ernst und Wehmut erfüllt.

then Chancellor of the German Reich Heinrich Brüning). Eckener, however, refused, just as he later refused to issue a "declaration of consent" to the invasion of the Rheinland by German troops in March of 1936. Neither did he attempt to conceal his disapproval of the propaganda flights of LZ 127 and LZ 129 to the 1936 Olympic Games in Berlin. He was powerless, however, as from 1934 on, "Graf

Zeppelin" was forced to display the swastika on its stabilizer, which – as later in the case of the "Hindenburg" – occasionally led to manifestations of disapproval in the United States. The fact that Eckener was indeed sometimes forced to give ground, according to his own testimony so as not to jeopardize the airship cause, was wholly the result of Nazi coercion.

His disapproving attitude towards the Nazi regime finally resulted in Hitler's demand that Eckener be removed. The attempt failed, not least of all due to his popularity in the United States. Nevertheless, the German press and radio were barred from further mentioning his name. The American ambassador in Berlin, William E. Dodd, kept his government regularly and accurately informed about the state of affairs in Germany, as can be seen from State Department files in Washington[21] and documents of the Roosevelt Library in New York[22]. In any case, it may be assumed that Roosevelt had accurate information about Eckener's role within Nazi Germany, which explains FDR's decidely congenial relations with Eckener. The Roosevelt Library documents include an inofficial recommendation to bring Eckener to the U.S. and to win his participation in the American airship program[23].

Upon the recommendation of the U.S. Embassy in Berlin, Eckener was given an especially warm welcome when he and the "Hindenburg" landed for the first time at Lakehurst in 1936. After his blacklisting in the mass media this amounted to a rebuff of the Hitler regime. All the honors bestowed on Eckener in the U.S. after Hitler came to power in 1933 must be viewed in this highly political perspective. By no means were Eckener's achievements exploited solely for political purposes in the U.S. But they provided a welcome opportunity to numerous harsh critics of Hitler's policies to compromise Hitler himself. The tremendous public interest in the Lakehurst disaster and the subsequent debate over helium must also be seen in this light.

---

[21] e.g. Embassy report from Berlin of April 14, 1936 ref.: 862.00/3594

[22] e.g. Letter to R. W. Moore of April 18, 1936, Official File 523.

[23] Off. File 2275: Letter from J. Mesmer to President Roosevelt, May 18, 1936.

One episode which demonstrates President Roosevelt's esteem for Eckener was related by F. W. von Meister[24]. During his stay in the United States in October 1933, Eckener received an invitation to the White House for tea with the president's wife. Eckener was somewhat

President
F. D. Roosevelt
and Dr. Eckener.

*Präsident
F. D. Roosevelt
und Dr. Eckener.*

surprised. Upon his arrival at the White House, he was welcomed cordially by the president himself. Roosevelt asked Eckener to excuse the unusual arrangement and explained that it was the only possibility to speak to him alone "without having to invite that Nazi ambassador".

---

[24] See footnote 12, page 61.

4.
THE FUTURE OF AIRSHIPS
IN THE BALANCE

4.1 The War Stops Everything

The outbreak of world War II finally put an end to the always cordial relations between airship advocates in Europe and America. Further development of the airship program was out of the question. LZ 127 and LZ 130 were scrapped in the spring of 1940; the airship hangars in Frankfurt, once proud departure point for a variety of contacts and harmonious cooperation with America, were blown up.[25]

The American journalist, Karl von Wiegand, an old friend of the airship people in Friedrichshafen, met with Hitler in the autumn of 1940, one of the last Americans to do so. Von Wiegand had taken part in the 1929 world voyage of the LZ 127 "Graf Zeppelin" on behalf of William Randolph Hearst. Since then, he had maintained close personal contact with Dr. Eckener and numerous other airship advocates. Hardly any other foreign journalist was more familiar with conditions in Germany at that time. During his visit, he sought to warn Hitler that, following his military campaign in France, a continuation of his policies of conquest could not help but force the United States to intervene. Hitler chose to ignore the warning.[26]

Although the war stopped cooperation between the Goodyear Company and the former "Luftschiffbau" in Friedrichshafen, the ties of friendship endured. Only two examples of these lasting contacts:

Dr. Eckener travelled to America as early as May 1947 as an advisor to the Goodyear Aircraft Corporation. He met with many friends from before the war, including T.G.W. Settle. In 1955, Dr. Max Grünbeck, Lord Mayor of Friedrichshafen was on hand in the chapel of the U.S. Naval Air Station at Lakehurst, as Paul W. Litchfield, president of the Goodyear Aircraft Corporation, presented three stained glass windows depicting the history of aviation. One of them showed the LZ 127 "Graf Zeppelin".

---

[25] At the time (1939/1940), the ZR3 was also scrapped ("Los Angeles" conducted flight operations until June 30, 1932, when she was decommissioned only to save operation expense during the depression. From 1934 till 1936 she was the subject of mooring experiments [Buckley, F. D.]).

[26] Samhaber, E.: Weltgeschichtliche Zusammenhänge, Gütersloh 1976, p. 9.

4.2 The Airship Dream Lives On

With the war over, it was now the airplane that stood in the way of a revival of the airship concept. The airplanes were reliable, fast, suitable for long range service and, above all, larger than before. Nevertheless, the call for new airships can still be heard today.

Countless societies and other groups are still devoted to the further development of the airship. The realists among them know that, despite the potential offered by modern technology, the case against building new airships is strong, especially against commercial uses. They are at least aware that it is unrealistic to try to pick up where they left off more than 40 years ago. However, the efforts of a number of groups show that, independent of this consideration, a concern for airship matters can be a meaningful endeavor. The activities of the American Institute of Aernautics and Astronautics (AIAA), for example, include a "Conference on Lighter-than-Air Technology". The Lighter-than-Air Society, with headquarters in Akron, Ohio, is also occupied with airship development. The society publishes a bulletin which, in addition to featuring articles by its own members, deals with historical events and keeps its membership up-to-date on a wealth of airship-related literature from around the world. The group cooperates closely with German societies, including the Deutsche Gesellschaft für Luft- und Raumfahrt (DGLR).

One aspect is important to all these endeavors: the structural concept of the Zeppelin airship, i.e., a rigid hull with an exterior skin and flexible gas cells inside, had proved its worth in the twenties and thirties and was accepted as the best and most practical design. As a result, all projects resumed later tended to cling to this basic concept; thus, despite the various efforts, hardly any of them got past the drawing board. Of the broad-based programs begun in the early sixties dealing with so-called hybrid airships, a combination of the conventional dirigible and the helicopter principle, only a few were able to rid themselves of the fixation with the former "zeppelin" and even then, the break was seldom complete. Happily, some innovative new projects have begun to take shape in the past few years with an eye, above all, towards marketability. It is not far-fetched to predict a resumption of German-American cooperation in the event large-scale projects are under consideration.

July 3 to August 29, 1976: Exhibition (partial view) "Zeppelin and the U.S.A."
in the Zeppelin Museum in Friedrichshafen. In the middle is a model of ZR 3.

*3. Juli bis 29. August 1976: Ausstellung (Teilansicht) „Zeppelin und die USA" im
Zeppelin-Museum, Friedrichshafen. In der Mitte ein Modell von ZR 3.*

January 20 – February 26, 1978: Exhibition (partial view) "The Zeppelin
History" at the Lakeview Center for the Arts and Sciences in Peoria, Illinois.

*20. Januar bis 26. Februar 1978: Ausstellung (Teilansicht) „The Zeppelin
History" im Lakeview Center for the Arts and Sciences, Peoria, Illinois.*

4.3 Friedrichshafen – still "Zeppelin City" today

Probably no other foreign city of its size is (or least was during the era of the Zeppelin airships) as familiar to Americans as Friedrichshafen with its population of 50,000. Many visitors come from America each year to visit the Zeppelin museum. Many find their way to the grounds of the former Luftschiffbau Zeppelin, today the home of Zeppelin-Metallwerke and the world-famous Zahnradfabrik Friedrichshafen (ZF), both important successors to the former Luftschiffbau. Many a recollection is swapped in conversations with old employees of the companies. Historians from other continents gather for on-the-scene studies of this interesting chapter in the Zeppelin Story and to apply new findings to a better understanding of the common German-American Zeppelin Era.

The close prewar ties between the Luftschiffbau Zeppelin and the United States were renewed in 1954. During that year Zeppelin-

August 26, 1976:
Richard E. Carver and Dr. Max Grünbeck, mayors of Peoria, Illinois and Friedrichshafen, Germany, sign partnership certificate.

Am 26. August 1976 unterzeichnen Richard E. Carver und Dr. Max Grünbeck, die Bürgermeister von Peoria, Ill., und Friedrichshafen eine Partnerschaftsurkunde.

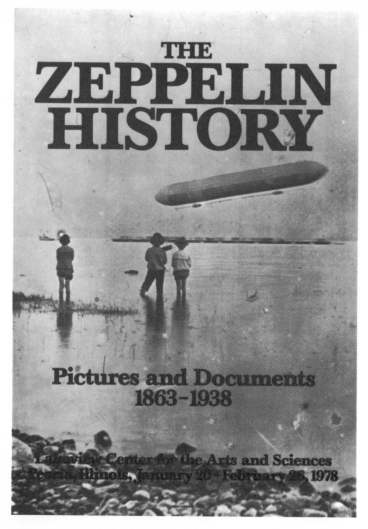

Poster for the exhibition in Peoria, which was one of the largest Zeppelin presentations shown outside Germany (photo: first ascent of LZ 1, July 2, 1900).

Plakat der Ausstellung in Peoria, die eine der größten Zeppelin-Präsentationen außerhalb Deutschlands war (Foto: LZ 1, erster Aufstieg am 2. Juli 1900).

Metallwerke became agents for the Caterpillar Tractor Company in the Federal Republic of Germany. As an expression of the close relations between the two companies, Friedrichshafen and Peoria, Illinois, home of Caterpillar, became sister cities in 1976. A large scale exhibition depicting the history of the Zeppelin airships was sponsored by the Zeppelin-Metallwerke on behalf of the Friedrichshafen Sister City Commission.[27] The exhibition not only acquainted the citizens of Peoria with the airship theme, but was widely acclaimed throughout the United States. The partnership between Friedrichshafen and Peoria has resulted in two honorary citizenship awards,[28] whose accomplishment can be eventually traced back to Friedrichshafen's Zeppelin past and which carry on the topic "Zeppelin and the USA".

Mayor Carver of Peoria, Illinois visiting the Zeppelin-Metallwerke. On the left is Willy Kaldenbach, General Manager of the Zeppelin-Metallwerke GmbH and Luftschiffbau Zeppelin GmbH. (1977)

Bürgermeister Carver, Peoria, Ill., besucht die Zeppelin-Metallwerke. Links Willy Kaldenbach, Geschäftsführer der Zeppelin-Metallwerke GmbH und der Luftschiffbau Zeppelin GmbH. (1977)

---

[27] "The Zeppelin History", exhibition of photos and documents from 1863 to 1938 at the Lakeview Center for the Arts and Sciences, Peoria, Illinois, January 20–26, 1978. Exhibition brochure by author.

[28] 1977: Dr. Max Grünbeck, Lord Mayor of the City of Friedrichshafen from 1948 until 1977 and initiator of the partnership.
1980: Willy Kaldenbach, General Manager of the Luftschiffbau Zeppelin and the Zeppelin-Metallwerke GmbH.

This exhibition (poster) was shown in Friedrichshafen in honor of the American Bicentennial Celebration.

Aus Anlaß des 200. Jahrestages der Vereinigten Staaten von Amerika fand diese Ausstellung in Friedrichshafen statt (Plakat).

5.

RECENT LITERATURE ON THE SUBJECT "ZEPPELIN AND THE USA"

It is well known that technical progress and social development are intimately related. The story of how Zeppelin airships helped to bring the peoples of the world together during the twenties and thirties has yet to be written. This topic will occupy an important niche in both German and American histories of the 20th Century. Although a few recent publications approach the subject, no comprehensive scientific study has yet appeared. At the present time, Henry Cord Meyer, Professor of Modern History at the University of California at Irvine, is working on the subject[29]. Meyer's "comparative study of the four dirigible-building cities of Friedrichshafen, Cardington, Howden and Akron and the technological and social impact of airship construction on modern industrial society" is available in lecture manuscript form[30].

The biographies of Count Zeppelin[31] and Hugo Eckener[32] describe in detail the most significant known experiences of these two most important airship pioneers in America. In his comprehensive book, K. Clausberg[33] devotes the very first chapter to that decisive encounter with the U.S., the delivery of the ZR 3. Recently published American works in the field of aeronautics contain many admiring references to the German airship pioneers and their influence on the development of

[29] South Atlantic Quarterly, Winter 1979, p. 107. Footnote: "Henry Cord Meyer ... is studying the political manipulation of airship technology and operation in Germany, England and the United States from 1919 to 1939."

[30] Henry Cord Meyer: The social impact of emerging technology: The rigid airship in western society, 1900–1936. The manuscript was discussed during the "First Annual Irvine [Cal.] Seminar on Social History and Theory". Comments of Professor Todd Laporte, Berkeley-University, recorded on tape by Meyer (1978).

[31] Rolf Italiaander: Ferdinand Graf von Zeppelin, Reitergeneral, Diplomat, Luftschiffpionier. Konstanz 1980, Verlag Friedrich Stadler.

[32] Rolf Italiaander: Hugo Eckener, ein moderner Columbus. Konstanz, 1979, Verlag Friedrich Stadler.

[33] Karl Clausberg: Zeppelin, die Geschichte eines unwahrscheinlichen Erfolges. München 1979, Schirmer/Mosel Verlag.

the airship in the United States. Among these are R. K. Smith[34] and his outstanding volume on the American airships "Akron" and "Macon" and Z. Hanson[35], whose history of the Goodyear airships contains an elaborate acknowledgement of Zeppelin airship development. And finally, D. Bottling's Time-Life book[36] will certainly portray the airship era to a wide audience, whereby the common German-American efforts of the 1920s and 1930s again form a central theme.

American landing crew at Lakehurst handling LZ 127 "Graf Zeppelin".

Amerikanische Bodenmannschaft in Lakehurst am LZ 127 „Graf Zeppelin".

---

[34] Richard K. Smith: The Airships Akron and Macon. Annapolis, Maryland (USA) 1965, United States Naval Institute.

[35] Zenon Hansen: The Goodyear Airships. Bloomington, Illinois (USA) 1977, Airship International Press.

[36] Douglas Botting (ed.): The Giant Airships. Alexandria, Virginia (USA) 1980, Time-Life Books Inc. (German language edition in preparation).

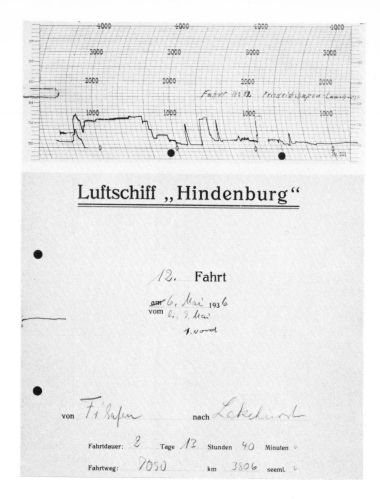

Luftschiff „Hindenburg"

12. Fahrt

~~am~~ *6. Mai* 193*6*
vom *bis 9. Mai*

1. Nord

von *Fr'hafen*   nach *Lakehurst*

Fahrtdauer: *2* Tage *12* Stunden *40* Minuten

Fahrtweg: *7050* km *3806* seeml.

Cover page of the log book and sketch of the altimeter from the first voyage of the LZ 129 "Hindenburg" to Lakehurst, New Jersey.

Deckblatt des Fahrtenbuches und Aufzeichnung des Höhenmessers der ersten Fahrt von LZ 129 „Hindenburg" nach Lakehurst, New Jersey.

100

6.
CHRONOLOGY

1863 Count Zeppelin travels to the U.S. as an observer during the Civil War.

Meeting with President Lincoln.

Encounter with Carl Schurz.

Participant in balloon launch near St. Paul, Minnesota.

Joins expedition to Mississippi headwaters.

1873 Heinrich von Stephan (founder of World Postal Union, 1874) publishes paper on "World Postal Delivery and Airship Transportation" ("Weltpost und Luftschiffahrt")

1874 First entry concerning balloon vehicles in Count Zeppelin's diary.

1895 Diary entry by Zeppelin concerning plans to carry passengers, mail and freight to New York.

1900 First launch of a Zeppelin airship.

1908 LZ 4 lost following endurance flight; donation by German public; Zeppelin concern begins growth. Count Zeppelin receives numerous honors in U.S.

1917 German naval airship L 49 (LZ 96) captured virtually intact by Allied forces. All components are measured; serves later in U.S. as basis for construction of the ZR 1 "Shenandoah".

1919 British airship R 34 crosses Atlantic in both directions. William S. Hensley attempts to build LZ 124 in Friedrichshafen; project is thwarted by Treaty of Versailles.

1920 Dr. Eckener negotiates with the United States for the building of Zeppelin airship as war reparation.

1921 R 38 (ZR 2) crashes during test flight; 16 Americans die.

1922 U.S. Navy contracts Luftschiffbau Zeppelin to build civilian airship (LZ 126 = ZR 3).

1923 ZR 1 "Shenandoah" put into service.

Goodyear-Zeppelin Corp. founded; joint use of all patents agreed.

1924 LZ 126 delivered to the U.S. Operates until 1932 (1936) as ZR 3 "Los Angeles".

1925 Shenandoah disaster; C. E. Rosendahl lands with half of ship, rescues part of the crew.

Congress begins helium debates.

1928 First flight of LZ 127 "Graf Zeppelin" to Lakehurst, New Jersey.

1929 World voyage of LZ 127, financed essentially by American newspaper publisher Hearst;
official launch in Lakehurst; route leads via Friedrichshafen, Tokyo, Los Angeles to Lakehurst and back to Friedrichshafen.

Dr. Eckener negotiates the purchase of helium from the United States; attempts made to form an American-German airship line company.

1931 ZRS-4 "Akron" put into service.

LZ 127 makes expedition to the Arctic; two American scientists, as well as three Russians and a Swede, take part.

1933 ZRS-4 "Akron" crashes; three survivors rescued by German ship.

ZRS-5 "Macon" put into service.

LZ 127 visits Miami, Akron and Chicago.

1935 ZRS-5 "Macon" is lost.

Extensive agreement between U.S. Navy and Deutsche Zeppelin-Reederei for use by LZ 129 of facilities in Lakehurst, New Jersey and Opa-Locka, Florida.

1936 LZ 129 "Hindenburg" begins scheduled passenger service to Lakehurst, New Jersey.

1937 LZ 129 burns while landing at Lakehurst; end of airship passenger service.

"Helium Commission" under Secretary of the Interior, H. L. Ickes, recommends that Roosevelt approve sale of helium to Germany.

First helium deliveries at year's end.

1938   Helium sales to German Reich banned by law on March 14.

1940   ZR 3 "Los Angeles", LZ 127 and LZ 130 scrapped in the United States and in Germany.

1954   The Zeppelin-Metallwerke, successor to the Luftschiffbau Zeppelin, become agents for products of the Caterpillar Tractor Company in the Federal Republic of Germany.

1976   Friedrichshafen becomes sister city to Peoria, Illinois.

"Zeppelin and the USA" exhibit in Friedrichshafen in honor of U.S. Bicentennial.

1978   Exhibit in Peoria, Illinois, "The Zeppelin History".

Willy von Meister, Charles E. Rosendahl and Bob Farley, president of American Zeppelin Transport Inc., await LZ 129 in Lakehurst (1936).

Willy von Meister, Charles E. Rosendahl und Bob Farley, Präsident der American Zeppelin Transport Inc., erwarten LZ 129 in Lakehurst (Foto 1936).

7.
APPENDIX

7.1   Excerpts from contracts
to build ZR 3 (LZ 126) from June 26, 1922,
between the Luftschiffbau Zeppelin, Friedrichshafen
and the United States Department of the Navy*

Contract B:

. . . the Luftschiffbau Zeppelin agrees to build a rigid airship on the basis of the specifications and conditions as set forth hereinafter and shall deliver said airship, fully equipped in every respect and in satisfactory condition, to the Naval Air Station at Lakehurst, New Jersey, USA.

The term "fully-equipped airship" used in this contract shall mean an airship fully equipped in accordance with the technical specifications as approved by the Navy Department and operational in every respect, including engine cars, control car and passenger cabins with galley and dining room equipment, all necessary navigational equipment and instruments, radiotelegraph equipment, machinery and equipment, including such tools and spare parts as are customarily carried during flights. Said vessel shall be a civilian airship and shall contain facilities for carrying approximately twenty (20) passengers in addition to crew. The dimensions and capacities of the vessel shall be approximately as follows:

Length		200 metres
Extreme diameter		28 meters
Height		32 meters
Design gas capacity		70,000 cubic meters
Total lift	with hydrogen at 760 mm air pressure	81,850 kg
Weight empty	0°C Temp; 0.1 relative gas density, 60% relative humidity	41,850 kg

---

*Retranslation from German language.

Actual Load   40,000 kg

Minimum speed in any case 70 statute miles = 112.6 km per hour in calm air at an altitude of 1,000 meters.

Engine Output   2000–2250 rated HP

to be developed by airship engines of the best type available. The airship shall be of the most modern type, with respect to design, construction and materials, comparable to the L-70 and NORDST-ERN classes, modified to the extent that improvements made since the introduction of these classes shall have been made necessary or desireable. Thus, said airship shall embody the most recent concepts and know-how in airship construction. It shall be designed in such a way as to be of adequate strength for its purpose; however, any unnecessay weight shall, at the same time, be avoided. It shall possess good maneuverability while airborne under various load conditions. The equipment and facilities throughout the airship shall be designed and executed in such a way as to achieve a maximum of safety with respect to the use of hydrogen gas and fuels commonly used in airship engines. Special precautions shall be taken to eliminate the hazard from fire in every respect. Special reinforcement shall be built into the nose of the vessel and connectors shall be provided which allow the vessel to be made fast on a mooring mast.

. . . All parties to this contract agree to apply due haste in the construction of said vessel, to enable said vessel to be delivered to the United States at the earliest possible date. The period of time necessary to complete the construction of said vessel is estimated to be fifteen (15) months, barring unforseen difficulties.

The Navy Department shall station at the construction site, during the construction of the vessel, an Inspector for Naval Aircraft, who shall represent the Navy Department and shall act as agent between the Navy Department and the Luftschiffbau Zeppelin. Said inspector may, during his absence and without regard to the reason for said absence, appoint an assistant to represent him, and said assistant shall have the same rights as the inspector himself. The Luftschiffbau Zeppelin shall provide office space (three rooms) as well as all necessary facilities for said inspector and his assistants, but shall not be liable for the personal expenses of said inspector and his staff. The inspector and his assistants shall have access to all places of manufacture of the airship and the engines, during working hours, for the purpose of supervising the construction of said airship and its parts. Furthermore, they shall have access to the places of manufacture of equipment and other parts, insofar as it shall be within the power of the Luftschiffbau Zeppelin to provide for said access. The inspector shall be provided information with respect to the kind of materials and the business firms from which the Luftschiffbau Zeppelin shall order material or equipment parts for said airship. The control system of the Luftschiffbau Zeppelin shall include the inspection of all materials, manufacturing processes and finished work...

...The Luftschiffbau Zeppelin shall determine the air-worthiness and operating safety of the vessel, by means of adequate test flights in Germany, prior to contemplating the delivery of the airship to the United States. The Navy Department shall reserve the right to designate a limited number of persons to observe the proper functioning, air-worthiness and operating safety of the airship during said test flights and delivery of said airship. The Luftschiffbau Zeppelin agrees to deliver the fully-equipped airship together with such spare parts as are customarily required in such airships in satisfactory condition to the Naval Air Station, Lakehurst, New Jersey, USA.

Delivery of said airship shall mean that said airship shall have landed and have been brought into the control of the landing crew. The airship shall thereafter be in the custody of the Department of the Navy, which shall thereafter assume responsibility for loss of or damage to said airship except in the event such damage or loss is proved to be due to the fault or negligence of the personnel of Luftschiffbau Zeppelin. As soon as possible following the landing of the airship the Navy Department shall surrender to Luftschiffbau Zeppelin a certificate of acceptance for the airship. The Department of the Navy agrees to facilitate the delivery of the airship to Lakehurst in every reasonable way and to provide a landing crew there. In the event the delivery of the airship at Lakehurst shall be deemed inadvisable or unfeasible due to unforseen circumstances, the Navy Department shall have the right to designate any other location within a radius of two hundred and fifty (250) statute miles of Lakehurst, and the Navy Department shall make the necessary arrangements at said location. It is hereby agreed that the Luftschiffbau Zeppelin shall deliver said airship to said alternate location as soon as the Navy Department has designated said location.

...The Luftschiffbau Zeppelin hereby assumes full liability for the airship against any and all risks until such time as said airship has been delivered to the Navy Department. In the event damage occurs, the Luftschiffbau Zeppelin shall undertake adequate repairs. In the event of total loss or damage to the point where repairs can no longer be made, the Luftschiffbau Zeppelin shall reimburse the German government for monies received and the Government of the United States may then demand payment of three million, thirty-one thousand, six hundred and sixty-five (3,031,665) gold marks as stipulated in the treaty of 26 June 1922 between the governments of Germany and the United States.

...The Luftschiffbau Zeppelin shall guarantee for a period of six (6) months, commencing on the day of formal acceptance of the airship by the United States, the proper construction, the quality of execution of works and material and the proper functioning of all parts and accessories of the airship. Any damage or defects which become apparent during this period of the time and which may be attributed to improper construction, poor execution of work or inferior material shall be eliminated by the Luftschiffbau Zeppelin at its own expense. An impartial investigation shall determine whether the Luftschiffbau Zeppelin will be held liable for any damage during this period.

...The government of the United States represented by the Department of the Navy shall conclude a special contract with the Luftschiffbau Zeppelin whereby the latter shall retain in the United States trained personnel as required for at least one-half of the aforementioned guarantee period.

...The government of the United States agrees to hold and save the Luftschiffbau Zeppelin harmless from all claims arising from patents issued in the United States and which may possibly be infringed upon through the construction and delivery of this airship. Patents or registered patterns issued by the German government shall be expressly excluded.

...The government of the United States shall assume responsibility for all import duties in the United States for said airship as well as all its parts or spare parts.

...Failure of the Luftschiffbau Zeppelin to comply with one of the provisions of this contract shall provide the government of the United States with sufficient grounds to request the government of Germany, by virtue of the protocol of June 26, 1922, to take steps necessary to guarantee the Luftschiffbau Zeppelin's compliance with the terms set forth herein. Should the German government not be in a position to guarantee compliance with this contract, the government of the United States may declare to the government of Germany that the execution of construction of said airship is unacceptable to the former and may demand from the government of Germany the payment of three million, thirty-one thousand, six hundred and sixty-five (3,031,665) gold marks in lieu of the previously specified airship, as stipulated by the protocol of 30 June 1921...

Luftschiffbau Zeppelin
Gesellschaft mit beschränkter Haftung
(signed) Dr. Hugo Eckener
p.p.a. Ernst A. Lehmann

Navy Department by L.S.
(signed) J. B. Upham
W. P. Beehler

Signed, sealed
and executed in the
presence of
(signed)
Landsdowne
Garland Fulton

Contract C:

... An experienced crew shall be provided by the Luftschiffbau Zeppelin to make possible an instructional demonstration. Said instructional demonstration shall be the best that Luftschiffbau Zeppelin is able to provide and shall have the purpose of training the personnel designated by the Navy Department to operate and mantain said airship in the safest and most effective way in the shortest possible time following acceptance of the airship by the Navy Department. The duration of said instructional demonstration shall at least in part coincide with the guarantee period of six (6) months assumed by the Luftschiffbau Zeppelin and set forth in paragraph 21 of the contract concluded between the Department of the Navy and the Luftschiffbau Zeppelin on 26 June 1922. Said training and demonstration shall further have the purpose of proving that said airship and, consequently, similar airships can indeed be operated in the safest and most effective way. In order to guarantee the safety of said airship, the Luftschiffbau Zeppelin shall furnish the following civilian personnel:

One (1) pilot
Three (3) Wheelsmen (qualified to navigate an airship)
Five (5) mechanics
One(1) radio-telegraph operator

... The members of the Luftschiffbau Zeppelin's demonstration crew shall be accorded a position identical to that accorded civilians of equivalent position in the service of the Navy Department.

... Responsibility for and control of the airship will be by Navy department personnel.

... The duration of said instructional demonstration shall be a period of three (3) months based on an estimated minimum three hundred (300) flight hours and thirty (30) flights. The government of the United States shall remunerate the Luftschiffbau Zeppelin for this service according to the following schedule: The Navy Department shall pay to the Luftschiffbau Zeppelin the sum of fifty thousand dollars ($50,000) per month at the end of each month for a period of three (3) months. The total sum of one-hundred and fifty thousand dollars ($150,000) shall represent full compensation for all services and expenditures by the Luftschiffbau Zeppelin. All aforementioned payments shall be made in U.S. dollars in the United States to a duly authorized representative of the Luftschiffbau Zeppelin. The Navy Department reserves the right to extend the demonstration period monthly for an additional three (3) months, if it deems nesessary. The length of said extension,should such be deemed necessary, shall be determined by the Navy Department and, if required, an agreement shall be made between the Navy Department and the Luftschiffbau Zeppelin in due time wherein the sum of ten thousand dollars ($10,000) shall be set forth as compensation for each additional month of the extension . . .

(Signed as in contract B)

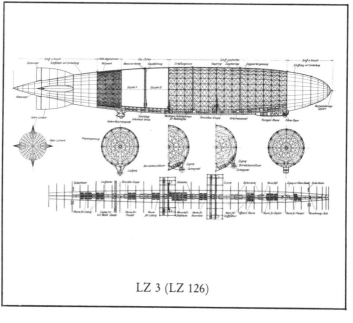

LZ 3 (LZ 126)

(Not part of the contract)

7.2 Agreement from September 19, 1923 between the Luftschiffbau Zeppelin, Friedrichshafen, and the Goodyear Tire and Rubber Company, Akron, Ohio*

The following agreement was concluded on September 19, 1923 between
Luftschiffbau Zeppelin GmbH, Friedrichshafen, Germany, hereinafter called ZEPPELIN, party of the first part,
and the Goodyear Tire and Rubber Company, Ohio, an Ohio corporation, Akron, Ohio USA, hereinafter called
GOODYEAR, party of the second part.

WHEREAS Zeppelin is engaged in the development and manufacture of rigid airships of a type commonly called zeppelin airships, and desires to promote the manufacture and sale of same in exclusively American territories as hereinafter defined and elsewhere to promote the manufacture and sale of such airships in said American territories, the parties agree as follows:

§ I.
Exclusively American territories shall mean and include the United States of America, its territories and island possessions, Mexico, Central America, Panama and all islands of the West Indies, with the exception of the possessions and protectorates of the British Empire.

§ II.
Goodyear shall form without delay a company, hereinafter called CORPORATION, chartered under the laws of any State of the United States of America of its choice, and which shall bear the name "The Goodyear Zeppelin Corporation" or another name of Goodyear's choice. However, the name must include the names Goodyear as well as Zeppelin. Said corporation shall be authorized to conduct the following business:
the manufacture, sale and operation of airships and aircraft of every

---

* Translated from the German (s. p. 219–229).

type as well as other related or ensuing business and activities as may be more precisely determined by Goodyear. Corporation shall, until further notice, be authorized to issue only nominal common stock to consist of 30,000 shares, which shall be considered fully paid and nonredeemable and of which Goodyear shall receive 20,000 shares and Zeppelin 10,000 shares. The exclusive voting rights of the corporation shall have their basis in said nominal common stock and no further shares shall be issued without the expressed consent of not less than 95 per cent of the combined shares.

§ III.

The corporation shall have nine (9) directors, six (6) of which shall be nominated by Goodyear, and three (3) by Zeppelin.

Corporation shall have a president and/or chairman of the Board of Directors, a vice-president, general manager, a secretary and treasurer, all of whom are to be nominated by Goodyear, as well as a vice-president and technical manager to be nominated by Zeppelin.

Goodyear and Zeppelin agree that directors shall, in future, be nominated as above and that, in the event the number of directors is increased, the members shall be nominated and elected proportionally: Goodyear – six (6), and Zeppelin – three (3).

§ IV.

The parties to the agreement shall organize in the United States, at the time the corporation is formed, a technical and general staff for the execution of temporary preparatory work, designs, cost estimates and projects for the manufacture and sale of Zeppelin airships, in such a manner as to promote and secure at the earliest possible time final contracts and orders for such vessels. For this purpose, Zeppelin shall make available to the corporation such suitable and experienced expert personnel as may become required to execute these preparations until such time as final contracts from the United States government or other seriously interested parties have been secured. The period of time just mentioned for such work is hereinafter called PREPARA-TION PERIOD.

§ V.

Goodyear agrees to provide the corporation (as initial payment for all common shares or in another manner of Goodyear's choosing) the fund required for all the corporation's expenditures during said preparation period, including salaries and travel expenses of the aforementioned expert personnel, and Goodyear shall provide to said corporation, at Goodyear's own expense, the necessary operating means and additional personnel as may be required to enable the corporation to execute its preparations to a reasonable extent. Furthermore, the corporation shall cooperate during the preparation period, through its legal staff, with an expert to be provided by Zeppelin, in order to secure all inventions, appliances, methods, processes and improvements pertaining to the construction and operation of airships (excepting engines), which have been used by Zeppelin or any of Zeppelin's subsidiary or related companies, as far as possible, through patents in the United States. This task shall be carried out expeditiously and the costs incurred shall be compensated as a portion of expenditures for the preparation period.

§ VI.

As soon as the corporation has promoted its work to the extent that either the government of the United States or any other seriously interested American party consents to conclude a final contract for the construction of one or more airships, the aforementioned preparation period shall be deemed terminated and the parties to this agreement shall proceed as follows:

1.) Zeppelin shall without delay:
a) transfer or cause to be transfered to the corporation, without forfeit of license, and in a form aproved by Goodyear's consultants, the rights to build and sell Zeppelin airships of every type;

b) grant or cause to be granted complete license or licenses for all patents and patent registrations whatsoever, related to the construction and operation of airships (excepting engines) and which are at present or will later be in the possession of Zeppelin or any subsidiary or associated companies, or to which they may have title, including in particular and without reservation all such patents in the Unites States of America;

c) notify or cause notification to the corporation without reservation all information pertaining to inventions, improvements, secret processes and methods which have been or will be applied prior to or after this point in time, or are at present in the possession of Zeppelin or any subsidiary or related companies and, furthermore, their experience in connection with the construction and operation of airships (excepting the construction of engines);

d) make available to the corporation, at corporation's own expense, the necessary expert and experienced personnel, which shall be in a position to execute successfully design, cost estimates and supervision of the construction and operation of airships and their essential parts (with the single exception of engines);

e) supply to the corporation at a reasonable price such special tools, devices, aids parts and pieces of equipment as Zeppelin may be in a position to supply, with the reservation that the corporation may procure same elsewhere should it so choose.

2.) Goodyear shall then immediately:

a) transfer to the corporation all unfinished orders and business pertaining to air navigation, as well as its existing aeronautical navigation organization and personnel and airship yard in Wingfoot Lake, Ohio, including the hangar, all appurtenant structures, including contents and furnishings and as much of Goodyear's property in Wingfoot Lake as may be required for the operation of said airship yard its reasonable expansion. However, Goodyear shall retain title to and control over all water rights and other rights of way which are at present available to the other Goodyear operations in the City of Akron;

b) convert the existing hangar in Wingfoot Lake to the (largest) possible size, or cause such conversion, and procure whatever aids may be required for the construction of such airships as it may be practical to build in said hangar;

c) make available to the corporation such additional funds in the form of an ordinary loan at the usual rate of interest, as my be required by the corporation as operating capital for the construction of such airships as may be built in the existing or converted hangar in Wingfoot Lake.

§ VII.

The rights and licenses to be granted by Zeppelin or which Zeppelin shall cause to be granted to the corporation, in pursuance of § VI of this agreement, shall be rights of the corporation exclusively in so far as they may pertain to construction and sale in exclusively American territories and to construction and sale for use in said exclusively American territories. Otherwise, such rights and licenses shall be deemed non-exclusive, as hereinafter defined, and, furthermore, the rights and the license to operate airships in the exclusively American territories shall not apply exclusively to the corporation.

The conclusion of agreements similar to those contained in this contract between Zeppelin and British interests is under consideration, according to which said British interests shall be awarded, as exclusively British territory, the entire British Empire with the exception of Canada. The corporation and said British interests shall each possess nonexclusive rights to construction and sale in Canada. However, no further rights or licenses für Canada shall be granted by Zeppelin to any other interests. The corporation agrees that, in the event such an agreement is concluded, it will refrain from the construction and sale of airships in, or their sale for use within the exclusively British territories and, as far as legally possible, shall impose corresponding restrictions on the purchasers of its airships. Upon the conclusion of any agreements between Zeppelin and said British interests, Zeppelin shall undertake to include in all such agreements a mutual understanding with said British interests, that said British interests shall refrain from the manufacture and sale of airships in, or their sale for operation in exclusively American territories and that the British interests shall, as far as legally permissible, impose corresponding restrictions on the purchasers of their vessels. Territories other than the exclusively American and exclusively British territories (if agreements thereto are concluded as mentioned above) and Canada shall be regarded as territories in which the corporation and said British interests may exercise their rights and licenses on a non-exclusive basis, with the exception that such non-exclusive rights and licenses in France, Spain and Italy shall not include the right to erect construction yards for the manufacture of airships within said countries. Zeppelin shall have the right to conclude additional exclusive agreements, similar to the present contract, pertaining to countries other than the exclusively

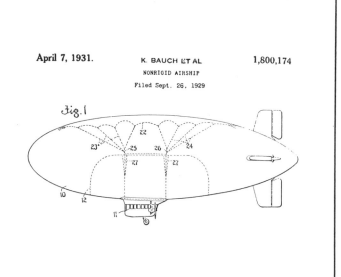

April 7, 1931.

K. BAUCH ET AL
NONRIGID AIRSHIP
Filed Sept. 26, 1929

1,800,174

Fig. 1

German engineers at the Goodyear-Zeppelin Corp. applied for patents for a number of investitions. Shown here is an excerpt from a patent specification granted to Kurt Bauch and Fritz Helma.

Die deutschen Ingenieure bei der Goodyear-Zeppelin Corp. meldeten zahlreiche Erfindungen zum Patent an. Hier der Ausschnitt aus einer Patentschrift, die Kurt Bauch und Fritz Helma erteilt wurde.

(Not part of the contract)

American and exclusively British territories and Canada and, in the event such exclusive agreements are concluded, the non-exclusive rights of the corporation and said British interests in the countries concerned shall be terminated on the condition that, upon the conclusion of further agreements (whether exclusive or non-exclusive), Zeppelin shall stipulate whithin the provisions of such agreements that the rights of the corporation in exclusively American territories are protected and recognized, and furthermore, that such agreements provide that the right to sell airships for international use shall at all times remain non-exclusive for all licenses other than Zeppelin.

The licenses and rights to be granted to the corporation under this contract, or to be acquired by same, shall be neither divisible nor transferable through expression of will or act of law, unless prior written consent from Zeppelin has been applied for and obtained.

All desings, drawings and data supplied by Zeppelin to Goodyear or to corporation shall be secret and Goodyear and the corporation shall take all necessary steps to maintain the secrecy of said data and provide access to same only to their own employees and personnel on a need-to-know basis, excepting the transfer of such data as is unavoidable in the course of the sale airships.

§ VIII.

As soon as a final contract for the construction of a Zeppelin airship larger than can be manufactured in the Wingfoot Lake hangar is obtained, Goodyear shall make all attempts to provide financing for the corporation, either through the sale of securities of the corporation or in another manner, to the extent required for the erection of a modern hangar and reasonable aids which shall be adequate for the proper construction of airships of a size up to cubic feet. However, it is agreed that Goodyear, by virtue of its voting majority in the corporation, may provide financing for the needs of the corporation by means of the sale of securities of the corporation in an amount not to exceed two million (2,000,000.00) dollars. No financing in excess of two million dollars may be taken without the consent of not less than ninety-five (95) per cent of the issued common stock.

Furthermore, it is agreed that all securities of the corporation made available for sale, including the above-mentioned two million dollars as well as any sum financed in excess of the above-mentioned two million dollars, as described above, shall in any case first be offered for sale to Goodyear and Zeppelin in proportion to their respective holdings of common stock, and at the current rate of sale on the American market. For this purpose, Goodyear shall designate its president and Zeppelin shall designate Mr. Vissering to be the recipients of such offers to sell securities and it is agreed that the corporation shall be free to dispose of said securities on the American market at the best price obtainable, in the event such offers are not accepted within ten (10) days.

In the event that firm orders for the construction of large-size airships are available, and that Goodyear, after being given reasonable opportunity to provide financing for the corporation, either by the sale of its securities or in another manner as described above, may not be in a position to provide same, or in the event that such financing cannot be obtained except through the sale of common stock issued originally to Goodyear and Zeppelin, Goodyear shall be deemed to have failed in its efforts to provide financing.

To the extent that Zeppelin possesses appliances, tools, material or pieces of equipment which may be required by the corporation for its operations, Zeppelin shall have the right to transfer ownership of such tools, appliances, material and pieces of equipment as payment for securities which shall be offered as described above, whereby such material, equipment, etc. shall be appraised for this purpose at the prime cost to Zeppelin less reasonable depreciation, or at the replacement cost in the United States, whichever is lower.

§ IX.

Goodyear agrees that it will at no time engage in the construction and operation of rigid airships in competition with the corporation, or with Zeppelin in the event the corporation is dissolved at a later date. On the other hand, Zeppelin agrees not to engage in the construction of rigid airships within the territory allotted to the corporation while the corporation is in existence.

§ X.

In the event that and as soon as Goodyear fails to provide financing for the corporation, as described above, Zeppelin shall have reasonable opportunity to obtain such financing, if it so desires. In the event that neither party is successful, the corporation shall, upon the motion of either party, be dissolved and liquidated, with the reservation, however, that Zeppelin shall, instead, have the right to acquire Goodyear's shares in said corporation at a reasonable price. In case the corporation is dissolved, it shall be agreed that all funds provided in the form of loans according to this contract be first repaid to Goodyear out of assets held by the corporation, and that all remaining assets shall be distributed to the shareholders in proportion to their respective holdings. All licenses, patents, etc., which may have been transfered to the corporation by Zeppelin, shall be returned and all patents received by the corporation as well as patents pending shall be transfered to Zeppelin. It is, however, agreed that no part of this agreement shall be construed or interpreted as preventing Goodyear from, in turn, engaging in aeronautical operations other than rigid airships in the event the corporation is dissolved.

§ XI.

In the event that differences of opinion between the two contract partners regarding the formulation and interpretation of any provisions of same shall arise, said differences shall be submitted to decision by three (3) arbitrators, one each to be named by Goodyear and Zeppelin and these two shall then name the third arbiter. In the event that the first two are not able to decide on the third arbiter, the latter shall be designated by a court of jurisdiction.

§ XII.

This agreement shall not become binding for either of the parties to the contract until it has been confirmed and approved by the members of the Board of Directors concerned.

Regarding this confirmation of the above, this contract has been executed by Goodyear and Zeppelin through their competent and duly authorized representatives on the aformementioned date and year.

Goodyear Tire & Rubber
Company, Ohio

Luftschiffbau Zeppelin GmbH
Friedrichshafen

From the "Pittsburgh Post Gazette" of September 9, 1936.
Aus „Pittsburgh Post Gazette" vom 9. September 1936.

7.3 Permit of October 11, 1935
for use of U.S. Navy facilities by the
airship LZ 129 "Hindenburg"

Revocable Permit

Whereas, the Luftschiffbau – Zeppelin, G.m.b.H. Friedrichshafen, Germany, represented in the United States by Mr. F. W. von Meister, 354 Fourth Avenue, New York City, and operating through its affiliate Deutsche Zeppelin-Reederei G.m.b.H., of Berlin, Germany, has outlined a proposal involving airship service to the United States for the Purpose of demonstrating the utility of airships as vehicles of commerce in foreign trade; and

Whereas, application has been duly submitted for permission to use without expense to the United States, airship terminal facilities at the Naval Air Station, Lakehurst, New Jersey, and at the Naval Reserve Aviation Base, Opa-Locka, Florida, in connection with this demonstration; and

Whereas, there are not available in the United States suitable privately owned terminals; and

Whereas, the granting of said permission under the conditions hereinafter enumerated will be in the public interest;

Now, therefore, by virtue of the authority vested in me by law as Secretary of the Navy, Permission is hereby granted to the aforesaid applicants, hereinafter referred to as Permittee, to use in connection with a series of Voyages to the United States by the airship LZ-129 the airship facilities hereinafter enumerated at the Naval Air Station, Lakehurst, New Jersey; at the Naval Reserve Aviation Base, Opa-Locka, Florida; and elsewhere as follows:

At Lakehurst, N. J.:

Shed space; mooring mast; ground handling facilities; landing crew comprising 90 men; storage space for 1.000.000 cubic feet hydrogen gas; gassing and refueling arrangements; weather service; policing arrangements; and such other facilities and services as are customarily required in the landing, mooring, handling, docking, and maintenance of an airship utilizing a terminal equipped as the Naval Air Station, Lakehurst, New Jersey, is at present equipped.

At Opa-Locka, Florida:
The expeditionary mooring mast and its attendant mooring equipment.

Elsewhere:

Services of up to seven (7) tank cars each equipped for the transportation of approximately 200.000 cubic feet of hydrogen gas.

Arrangements to make contact with Naval radio stations in accordance with an approved schedule for the purpose of obtaining weather reports and other communications of a non-commercial nature necessary to the safe and prudent navigation of the airship while enroute to and from the United States.

This Permit is granted subject to the following provisions and conditions.

1. The general premise on which this permit is founded is that the use of facilities herein described shall be at the risk of the Permittee and without expense to the United States, and wherever any financial outlay is required or any expense is incurred by the United States on account of the Permittee, it agrees to reimburse the United States therfore.

2. The period of occupancy under this permit shall not exceed six (6) months, beginning thirty (30) days after notification by the Permittee of readiness to begin the airship service herein described, unless this permit shall be extended in writing by the Secretary of the Navy, and this permit is subject to revocation at any time in the discretion of the Secretary of the Navy. It is anticipated that notification of readiness to begin service will be given on or about September 15, 1935, and that this permit will become operative thirty (30) days thereafter.

3. The Permittee agrees that the facilities made available to it will be used solely in connection with a series of twelve (12) round trips by the airship LZ-129 between the United States and Europe (or South America), said airship to carry passengers, mail and cargo on any or all such trips.

4. The Permittee agrees to furnish the Navy Department in advance of the date that this permit becomes operative a schedule showing the expected dates of arrival and departure of the airship and will keep the Navy Department and the Navy Department's representative at destination advised immediately of any changes in this schedule, and in particular will keep the Navy Department advised at least four days in advance of the definitely expected dates of arrival and departure of the airship. The intent of this proviso is to insure that the Navy Department is kept advised at all times, and as far in advance as practicable, of the date and hour of expected arrivals and departures of the airship.

5. The Permittee shall comply with all United States and local State laws, rules, and regulations and special instructions which may be issued by proper authority involved in the entering, operating and clearing of said airship while so engaged in commerce.

6. The Permittee will be given the privilege of ingress to and egress from the spaces covered by this instrument. While on the aforesaid Naval Station and Naval Base, the Permittee, its representatives and all passengers will comply with all existing Naval regulations and instructions.

7. The Permittee agrees to maintain at the Naval Air Station Lakehurst, and at the Naval Reserve Aviation Base, Opa-Locka, Florida for such periods as may be deemed expedient, before, during, and after arrivals of the airship LZ-129 a representative or representatives qualified and authorized to handle on behalf of the Permittee any questions or matters that may arise be they of a general or technical nature.

8. The permittee shall take all reasonable steps to insure that matters involving public relations are handled in a judicious manner. The Permittee agrees especially to avoid the giving out of information that might create in the public mind the impression that by reason of the permission herein granted, the Navy Department is responsible for any phase of the Permittee's activities or that Permittee is relying an government ownership of property and facilities as the basis for special consideration and special handling of any matters connected with its commercial activities.

9. The Permittee shall not undertake any alterations, repairs, or improvement to the aforesaid airship facilities without prior approval

of the Secretary of the Navy or his duly authorized representative, and that at the expiration of this permit it will surrender them in as good order and condition as they now are, or in a condition satisfactory to the Secretary of the Navy.

10. It is understood and agreed that for landings and dockings of the LZ-129 at the Naval Air Station Lakehurst, naval personnel up to ninety (90) men will be available as a landing-party, and at Opa-Locka the Permittee will make its own arrangements for landing party. If on account of the severity of weather or special conditions it is considered desirable to augment the landing party at the Naval Air Station, Lakehurst, the Permittee will make its own arrangements for the additional men required and will assure that said additional men are made available to the Commanding Officer, Lakehurst under Conditions satisfactory to that officer. Authority over naval personnel will be by naval officers and, if requested by the Permittee in each case, a naval officer will supervise (at Lakehurst) the landing and subsequent mooring or docking of the LZ-129 using methods customarily employed for naval airships, or as modified on request of the Permittee, but no responsibility of any sort can attach to naval personnel for any untoward incidents that may occur.

11. It is understood and agreed that the division of responsibility and interest between the Navy Department, the Permittee, and other interested agencies will be arranged by local representatives of the Department and the Permittee and specified in advance insofar as practicable so that appropriate lines of demarcation are understood by the representatives of all parties hereto.

12. The Permittee shall make its own arrangements for the procurement of fuel, hydrogen, consummable supplies, and for housing subsistence and shore transportation of passengers and crew.

13. The Permittee, having been informed in detail as to the dimensions and technical features of the existing landing, mooring, handling, docking, and refueling facilities now existing at the Naval Air Station, Lakehurst, and the Naval Reserve Aviation Base, Opa-Locka, accepts them as satisfactory for its purpose and agrees that the airship LZ-129 will be adapted to fit these existing facilities and that wherever adapters or special external fittings or appliances are required to make the airship LZ-129 fit the existing facilities, the Permittee will supply, in

advance, all such necessary adapters and external fittings and appliances.

14. Policing arrangements adequate to handle expected crowds of visitors, and satisfactory to the local representative of the Navy Department, will be arranged through cooperation with the Navy Department's representative and civic authorities. At Lakehurst, the Commanding Officer will make available for this purpose such personnel as are customarily available for policing duties and will prescribe and control the general policing procedure. At Opa-Locka, the Commanding Officer will prescribe a general procedure for policing but will not provide any personnel for policing purposes.

15. The Permission herein granted for use of tank cars is predicated upon approval being given by the appropriate regulatory authorities for the transportation of hydrogen gas in these cars. Tank cars will be made available to the Permittee at Lakehurst and will thereafter be routed and moved in accordance with prevailing Naval practice, between points designated and according to such schedule as the Permittee shall specify in writing. The Navy Department will keep records of freight and other charges incurred on account of these cars and the Permittee shall pay the total amount of such charges less the credit for liable earned by these cars. It is further stipulated that the Permittee shall not receive the benefit of any preferential freight rates that may accrue to the cars on account of the fact that their movements are under United States Government bills of lading but shall pay the freight rates that customarily would be charged if the cars were privately owned.

16. In agreeing to make available to the Permittee tank cars for transportation of hydrogen and storage space for up to 1.000.000 cubic feet of hydrogen at the Naval Air Station, Lakehurst, it is expressly understood that the United States assumes no responsibility in connection with any incidents that may arise on account thereof. Upon completion of their service with hydrogen, all tank cars, storage tanks, and service lines, shall be purged and restored to normal condition at the expense of the Permittee, and the Permittee assumes full responsibility for any damages that may result in the use of such tank cars including their restoration to their original conditions.

17. The Permittee agrees to keep the aforesaid facilities of the Naval

Air Station, Lakehurst, insured for five hundred thousand dollars ($ 500.000), and the aforesaid facilities at Opa-Locka insured for seventy-five thousand dollars ($ 75.000) during such periods as they are being used on account of the Permittee, against hazards of fire, explosion, and damage in a responsible insurance company or companies approved by the Secretary of the Navy. The policies shall contain no co-insurance clause, but shall be so written as to make all losses or returns, if any, payable to the Secretary of the Navy. The said insurance policy or policies shall be filed with the Judge Advocate General of the Navy.

18. The Permittee agrees to provide insurance, in an amount and with a company or companies satisfactory to the Secretary of the Navy, covering seven (7) railroad (hydrogen gas) tank cars against direct loss or damage from any external cause. The Policy or policies shall contain no co-insurance clause, but shall be so written as to make all losses or returns thereunder payable to the Secretary of the Navy. The said insurance policy or policies shall be filed with the Judge Advocate General of the Navy.

19. The Permittee agrees to provide liability insurance in an amount and with a company or companies satisfactory to the Secretary of the Navy, covering death, personal injury and property damage that may be substained in connection with the activities covered by this permit. The said insurance policy or policies shall be filed with the Judge Advocate General of the Navy.

20. The Permittee shall keep at all times a credit balance of at least five thousand dollars ($ 5.000) in a special deposit account with the Navy Department against which account shall be lodged charges for the use of the aforesaid facilities at the Naval Air Station, Lakehurst, and at the Naval Reserve Aviation Base, Opa-Locka, and their maintenance in a condition of readiness to receive the LZ-129, according to the following schedule:

For each day of 24 hours, prorated for a fraction thereof, the airship shed and mooring facilities at Lakehurst are held in readiness to receive the airship – One hundred dollars ($ 100.–). (Note: Charges shall be reckoned from the definitely designated dates and hours of arrival as specified to be furnished under § 4.)

For each day of 24 hours, prorated for a fraction therof, the airship is housed in the shed or is mooring at Lakehurst – Three hundred dollars ($ 300.–).

For each day of 24 hours, prorated for a fraction thereof, Opa-Locka mooring facilities are held in readiness – Thirty dollars ($ 30.–).

For each day of 24 hours, prorated for a fraction thereof, the airship is moored at Opa-Locka, – One hundred dollars ($ 100.–).

For each landing and each take-off at the Naval Air Station, Lakehurst, a ground crew service fee (covering 90 men) – Two hundred and fifty dollars $ 250.–).

For use of tank cars on a monthly basis, per car, per month (or fraction thereof) – Two hundred and fifty dollars ($ 250.–).

For use of gas storage space at Lakehurst, Twenty-five cents per 1000 cubic feet per month (or fraction thereof).

Freight charges for shipments of tank cars (less mileage credits to owner).

For any other expenditures, including power, light, repairs, alterations, etc., either to the airship or to government property on account of the airship, charges shall be on the basis of actual cost as determined by naval accounting procedure, plus a surcharge of twenty per cent (20%) of the total labor, material, and indirect charges; this surcharge being the estimated amount required to insure that there shall be no expense involved to the Government. The Permittee agrees that the operations under this permit shall not unduly interfere with naval activities on the Naval Air Station, Lakehurst, N. J., and the Naval Reserve Aviation Base, Opa-Locka, Florida.

22. No act or acts of the Permittee under this permit or any one in its behalf shall be construed or considered as giving it any title to or permanent interest in any property of the United States.

23. This permit is restricted and shall not be assigned or succeeded to in any manner without the consent of the Secretary of the Navy obtained beforehand, and in case of such assignment or succession so consented to, all of the foregoing provisions and conditions shall apply to such substituted Permittee.

24. The United States shall not under or by reason of this permit or by reason of anything contained herein incur any expense or liability

whatsoever, and the said Permittee will hold and save the Government harmless from and against any and all claims of any nature or kind that may arise from anything connected with or growing out of this permit not attributable to any act of the United States, its officers or agents.

25. In all matters of administrations in connection with this permit the Commanding Officer, Naval Air Station, Lakehurst, New Jersey, and the Commanding Officer, Naval Reserve Aviation Base, Opa-Locka, Florida, are hereby designated and empowered to act as the local representatives in their respective jurisdictions.

In witness whereof, I have hereunto set my hand and affixed the official seal of the Navy Department this
11[th.] day of October, 1935

UNITED STATES OF AMERICA
by Claude A. Swanson
Secretary of the Navy

This permit is also executed on behalf of the Luftschiffbau Zeppelin G.m.b.H. of Friedrichshafen, Germany, and the Deutsche Zeppelin-Reederei G.m.b.H. of Berlin, Germany, in acknowledgment of the acceptance of the terms and conditions therein set forth.

LUFTSCHIFFBAU ZEPPELIN G.m.b.H.
of Friedrichshafen, Germany
by Dr. Dürr, ppa. Lehmann
Geschäftsführer

by F. W. von Meister
Special United States Representative

DEUTSCHE ZEPPELIN-REEDEREI G.m.b.H.
of Berlin, Germany
Lehmann, ppa. Oesterle

7.4 Application for permission to fly the airship „Hindenburg" from Germany into United States territory in 1937

The Deutsche Zeppelin Reederei G.m.b.H. hereby respectfully requests permission to fly their Airship Hindenburg from Germany into United States territory in 1937 on a limited number of experimental demonstration flights. These flights are proposed in order to further explore meteorological conditions prevailing on the North Atlantic during the Spring, Summer and Fall Seasons. As outlined in the proposed time-table below, an attempt will be made to carry on a weekly round trip service during the months of August and September, for the purpose of determining if it will be possible to operate an airship of the Hindenburg type on a weekly turn-around over the distance involved.

The following information is furnished by the Applicants in reply to questions set forth by the United States Department of Commerce:

1. Q. Date information is submitted:
   A. February 8, 1937.
2. Q. Exact trade name of company:
   Deutsche Zeppelin-Reederei, Gesellschaft mit beschränkter Haftung.
3. Q. General Office address of company:
   A. Berlin W. 8, Unter den Linden 41
4. Q. Name, title, and post office address of the company official to whom correspondence in regard to experimental flights is to be addressed.
   A. F. W. von Meister, Vice President of American Zeppelin Transport, Inc., 354 Fourth Avenue, New York, New York, U. S. A., General U. S. Agents of the Applicants.
5. Q. Organization of company, to include kind of company, whether operating company, holding company, or other form of association; names of president, directors, and managing

officers, with citizenship of each; place where incorporated and where authorized to do business.

A. Applicants are a corporation (Gesellschaft mit beschränkter Haftung) organized and existing under the laws of Germany. Their business is ownership and operation of the zeppelin type airships.

Members of the Board of Directors:

Dr. Hugo Eckener, Chairman, Friedrichshafen a. B.
Ministerial-Dirigent A. Muehlig-Hofmann, Berlin
Director Martin Wronsky, Berlin

Management:

Ernst A. Lehmann, Manager, Friedrichshafen a. B.
Carl Christiansen, Manager, Magdeburg
Julius Oesterle, Prokurist, Friedrichshafen a. B.
Heinz M. Wronsky, Prokurist, Berlin

All members of the Board of Directors and of the Management are of German nationality.

Company was incorporated in Berlin and is authorized to do business in Berlin. A copy of the Certificate of Registration of Deutsche Zeppelin Reederei was furnished to the Department of Commerce under date of April 29, 1936 (marked Enclosure No. 1).*

6. Q. Approximate dates when the proposed flights are to be made between foreign territory and the United States, giving details as to schedules.

---

* Enclosures not published here

Trip No.	Leaves Frankfurt:	Arrives Lakehurst:	Leaves Lakehurst:	Arrives Frankfurt:
1	May 3, p.m.	May 6, a.m.	May 6, p.m.	May 9, a.m.
2	May 11, p.m.	May 14, a.m.	May 14, p.m.	May 17, a.m.
3	May 22, p.m.	May 25, a.m.	May 25, p.m.	May 28, a.m.
4	June 2, p.m.	June 5, a.m.	June 5, p.m.	June 8, a.m.
5	June 12, p.m.	June 15, a.m.	June 15, p.m.	June 18, a.m.
6	June 22, p.m.	June 25, a.m.	June 25, p.m.	June 28, a.m.
7	July 3, p.m.	July 6, a.m.	July 6, p.m.	July 9, a.m.
8	July 11, p.m.	July 14, a.m.	July 14, p.m.	July 17, a.m.
9	Aug. 13, p.m.	Aug. 16, a.m.	Aug. 16, p.m.	Aug. 19, a.m.
10	Aug. 20, p.m.	Aug. 23, a.m.	Aug. 23, p.m.	Aug. 26, a.m.
11	Aug. 27, p.m.	Aug. 30, a.m.	Aug. 30, p.m.	Sep. 2, a.m.
12	Sep. 3, p.m.	Sep. 6, a.m.	Sep. 6, p.m.	Sep. 9, a.m.
13	Sep. 10, p.m.	Sep. 13, a.m.	Sep. 13, p.m.	Sep. 16, a.m.
14	Sep. 17, p.m.	Sep. 20, a.m.	Sep. 20, p.m.	Sep. 23, a.m.
15	Sep. 28, p.m.	Oct. 1, a.m.	Oct. 1, p.m.	Oct. 4, a.m.
16	Oct. 8, p.m.	Oct. 11, a.m.	Oct. 11, p.m.	Oct. 14, a.m.
17	Oct. 19, p.m.	Oct. 22, a.m.	Oct. 22, p.m.	Oct. 25, a.m.
18	Oct. 30, p.m.	Nov. 2, a.m.	Nov. 2, p.m.	Nov. 5, a.m.

This proposed schedule is subject to change.

7. Q. Submit map on which is indicated the route, or routes, to be traversed and the terminals and intermediate stops thereon. Indicate portion of the route, or routes, to be navigated at night.

A. A map with scheduled routes was submitted by Applicants on April 29, 1936, and marked (Enclosure No. 3). The routes to be followed, however, in actual flight will depend upon weather conditions prevailing at the time of flight.

8. Q. Provide names of operating personnel who will engage in the experimental flights giving their airman certificate numbers or other designations.

A. The following is a list of the proposed crew of the Airship Hindenburg which, however, is subject to change in case of transfer or illness.

Name:	Position:
E. A. Lehmann	Captain of the ship

Officers

M. Pruss	Watch Officer
A. Sammt	Watch Officer
H. Bauer	Watch Officer
W. Ziegler	Navigator
M. Zabel	Navigator
F. Herzog	Navigator
K. Schoenherr	Chief Rudder Man
J. Geier	Chief Rudder Man
H. Gluud	Rudder Man
M. Schulz	Rudder Man
E. Huchel	Rudder Man
G. v. Mensenkampff	Rudder Man
L. Felber	Rudder Man
H. Lau	Rudder Man

Radio Officers

W. Speck	Chief Radio Officer
E. Hartwig	Radio Officer
G. Wieduwild	Radio Officer
E. Schweikard	Radio Officer

Sail Makers

L. Knorr	J. Freund	E. Spehl

Machinists

R. Sauter	Chief Flight Engineer
A. Groezinger	Second Flight Engineer
R. Halder	Machinist

J. Scheibmueller	Machinist
E. Schaeuble	Machinist
E. Dimmler	Machinist
G. Zettel	Machinist
R. Schaedler	Machinist
E. Bentele	Machinist
H. Rothfuß	Machinist
A. Deutschle	Machinist
W. Scheef	Machinist
A. Fischer II	Machinist
W. Banholzer	Machinist
W. Doebler	Machinist
H. Fiedler	Machinist
R. Moser	Machinist

Electricians

Ph. Lenz	G. Kunkel	J. Leibrecht

Stewards

H. Kubis	Chief Steward	
M. Henneberg	Steward	
M. Schulze	E. Nunnenmacher	Steward
F. Deeg	W. Balla	Steward
X. Maier	Cook	
A. Groezinger	Cook	
A. Stoeffler	Pastry Chef	
A. Rigger	Cabin Boy	

Crew's lists will become availabe upon each arrival of the Airship.

9. Q. List aircraft to be used, showing:
   (a) Ownership.
   (b) Airworthiness certificate or license number with international markings thereon.
   (c) Make, type, and model of aircraft.
   (d) Number and type of engines.
   (e) Number of crew and passenger capacity.

(f) Date of manufacture and brief general history.

A. (a) Deutsche Zeppelin-Reederei G.m.b.H.
(b) Airworthiness Certificate, issued by the Reich Air Ministry on March 20, 1936; License number: D-LZ 129.
(c) Dirigible, constructed by the Luftschiffbau Zeppelin, D-LZ 129.
(d) four 16 cylinder Daimler-Benz Diesel motors of approximately 1.100 HP each.
(e) Number of crew about 50; passenger capacity: 72.
(f) Built during 1932–1935. For complete data see technical description of the airship as submitted to the Department of Commerce under date of April 29, 1936 (marked Enclosure No. 4).

10. Q. State whether competent authority has issued necessary radio license, or licenses.
(a) List by location all radio ground facilities to be used in the United States.
(b) Is one or two-way radio installed in aircraft to be used?
(c) Is radio range beacon receiver installed in aircraft to be used?

A. (a) Refer to list attached with application filed April 29, 1936, marked (Enclosure No. 5).
(b) Two-way radio
(c) Yes

11. Q. Briefly describe weather service along route, or routes, to include sources and locations of reporting stations, frequency and method of collecting and disseminating weather reports.

A. From the European side, the airship will receive regularly the weather reports of the Hamburger Seewarte, Hamburg. The ship will also copy the standard Department of Agriculture and Navy Department weather broadcasts when approaching and leaving United States territory.

12. Q. Briefly describe the plan of operation to include personnel, aircraft, communications, weather service, if intentional instrument or overtop flying is contemplated, and such additional and related data as will assist the Bureau of Air Commerce to

coordinate the regulation of such flights with domestic air navigation and which will enable said Bureau to afford all possible aid at its disposal to the experimental flights to be conducted.

A. 18 experimental flights between Frankfurt a. M. and Lakehurst, New Jersey, are contemplated. The crew will number about 50, including one commander, 3 watch officers, 3 navigators, one chief engineer, one chief wireless officer, one medical doctor, one postal assistant, one chief steward and one chef.

Arrangements for landing and servicing at the United States Naval Air Station at Lakehurst, New Jersey, have been applied for and it has been informally indicated to the Applicant by the Navy Department that the Revocable Permit for the use of airship naval facilities will be extended by the Secretary of the Navy as soon as this application for permission to make the flights will have received approval by the United States Government. The Revocable Permit issued by the Secretary of the Navy covered technical questions, questions of liability, deposit accounts against which service charges are lodged, etc.

13. Q. State whether or not permission has been granted by the company's government for the proposed experimental flights.

A. Yes.

It is respectfully requested that this application may receive early consideration and that the Navy Department, as well as the Applicants, be informed of the action taken so that technical as well as commercial preparations for the safe and punctual carrying through of the proposed experimental demonstration service may be started as soon as possible.

New York, N. Y.
February 8, 1937

Respectfully submitted for
DEUTSCHE ZEPPELIN REEDEREI, G.m.b.H.
by AMERICAN ZEPPELIN TRANSPORT, INC.
General United States Agents
F. W. von Meister
Vice President

7.5 U.S. voyages of LZ 127 „Graf Zeppelin"

Oct.	11, 1928	Friedrichshafen–Lakehurst	Oct.	15, 1928
Oct.	29, 1928	Lakehurst–Friedrichshafen	Nov.	1, 1928

Aug.	1, 1929	Friedrichshafen–Lakehurst	Aug.	5, 1929
Aug.	7, 1929	Lakehurst–Friedrichshafen	Aug.	10, 1929
Aug.	23, 1929	Tokyo–Los Angeles	Aug.	26, 1929
Aug.	27, 1929	Los Angeles–Lakehurst	Aug.	29, 1929
Sept.	1, 1929	Lakehurst–Friedrichshafen	Sept.	4, 1929

May	28, 1930	Recife (Brazil)–Lakehurst	May	31, 1930
June	3, 1930	Lakehurst–Sevilla (Spain)	June	5, 1930

Oct.	21, 1933	Recife (Brazil)–Miami	Oct.	23, 1933
Oct.	24, 1933	Miami–Akron	Oct.	25, 1933
Oct.	26, 1933	Akron–Chicago	Oct.	26, 1933
Oct.	26, 1933	Chicago–Akron	Oct.	26, 1933
Oct.	28, 1933	Akron–Sevilla (Spain)	Oct.	31, 1933

7.6 U.S. voyages of LZ 129 „Hindenburg"

May	6, 1936	Frankfurt–Lakehurst	May	9, 1936
May	12, 1936	Lakehurst–Frankfurt	May	14, 1936

May	17, 1936	Frankfurt–Lakehurst	May	20, 1936
May	21, 1936	Lakehurst–Frankfurt	May	23, 1936

June 19, 1936	Frankfurt–Lakehurst	June 22, 1936
June 24, 1936	Lakehurst–Frankfurt	June 26, 1936
June 30, 1936	Frankfurt–Lakehurst	July 2, 1936
July 4, 1936	Lakehurst–Frankfurt	July 6, 1936
July 10, 1936	Frankfurt–Lakehurst	July 13, 1936
July 15, 1936	Lakehurst–Frankfurt	July 17, 1936
Aug. 5, 1936	Frankfurt–Lakehurst	Aug. 8, 1936
Aug. 10, 1936	Lakehurst–Frankfurt	Aug. 11, 1936
Aug. 16, 1936	Frankfurt–Lakehurst	Aug. 19, 1936
Aug. 20, 1936	Lakehurst–Frankfurt	Aug. 22, 1936
Sept. 17, 1936	Frankfurt–Lakehurst	Sept. 20, 1936
Sept. 22, 1936	Lakehurst–Frankfurt	Sept. 24, 1936
Sept. 26, 1936	Frankfurt–Lakehurst	Sept. 29, 1936
Oct. 1, 1936	Lakehurst–Frankfurt	Oct. 3, 1936
Oct. 5, 1936	Frankfurt–Lakehurst	Oct. 7, 1936
Oct. 9, 1936	Lakehurst–Lakehurst	Oct. 9, 1936
Oct. 10, 1936	Lakehurst–Frankfurt	Oct. 12, 1936
May 3, 1937*	Frankfurt–Lakehurst	May 7, 1937

* Scheduled voyages for 1937 cf. p. 133

LZ 127 "Graf Zeppelin" over New York (1928)
LZ 127 „Graf Zeppelin" über New York (1928)

8.
BIBLIOGRAPHY

Adams, H.: The Education of Henry Adams: An Autobiography (1918). Boston 1961, Houghton Mifflin.

Battles and Leaders of the Civil War, Vol. II. New York 1956, Castle Books.

Botting, D.: The Giant Airships. Alexandria, Virginia, 1980, Time Life Books.

Clausberg, K.: Zeppelin, die Geschichte eines unwahrscheinlichen Erfolges. München 1979, Schirmer/Mosel GmbH.

Cornish, J. J.: The Air Arm of the Confederacy. Richmond, Virginia, 1963, Richmond Civil War Centenial Committee.

Dick, H. G.: The Golden Age of the Great Rigid Airships. In „Inside the Control Car", Issue 27, Feb. 1979.

Eckener, H.: Im Luftschiff über Länder und Meere. München 1979, Wilhelm Heyne Verlag.

Eckener, H.: Zeppelin-Pläne für Nordamerika. In „Werkzeitschrift der Zeppelin-Betriebe" Nr. 4, 12/1936.

Hansen, Z.: The Goodyear Airships. Bloomington, Ill., 1977, Airship International Press.

Hildebrandt, H. (ed.): Zeppelin-Denkmal für das deutsche Volk. Stuttgart 1925, Germania-Verlag.

Holthusen, H. E.: Amerikaner und Deutsche – Dialog zweier Kulturen. München 1977, Verlag Georg D. W. Callwey.

Italiaander, R.: Graf Ferdinand von Zeppelin. Konstanz 1980, Verlag Friedrich Stadler.

Italiaander, R.: Hugo Eckener, ein moderner Columbus. Konstanz 1979, Verlag Friedrich Stadler.

Knäusel, H. G.: The Zeppelin History. Peoria, Ill., 1978, Lakeview Center for the Arts and Sciences.

Knapp, M., Link, W., Schröder, H. J., Schwabe, K.: Die USA und Deutschland 1918–1975. München 1978, Verlag C. H. Beck.

Lehmann, E. A.: Auf Luftpatrouille und Weltfahrt. Berlin 1936, Wegweiser Verlag.

Meyer, H. C., Gallup, S. V.: France Perceives the Zeppelin, 1924–1937. In „South Atlantic Quarterly", Winter 1979.

Meyers großes Personenlexikon. Mannheim/Zürich 1968, Bibliographisches Institut.

Miller, F. T.: The World in the Air, Vol. II. New York/London 1930, G. P. Putnam's Sons.

Moltmann, G.: Die Luftschiff-„Hindenburg"-Katastrophe und das Heliumproblem. In „Wehr-Wissenschaftliche Rundschau", 11. Jahrgg., Nov. 1961, Berlin/Frankfurt, Verlag E. S. Mittler & Sohn.

Piltz, Th. (ed.): Zweihundert Jahre deutsch-amerikanischer Beziehungen. München 1975, Heinz Moos Verlag.

Pochhammer, B.: ZR III, das deutsch-amerikanische Verkehrsluftschiff. Freiburg 1924, Theodor Fisher Verlag.

Samhaber, E.: Weltgeschichtliche Zusammenhänge – Perspektiven für die Zukunft. Gütersloh/Berlin/München/Wien 1976, Verlagsgruppe Bertelsmann GmbH.

Schiller, H. von: Zeppelinbuch. Leipzig 1938, Bibliographisches Institut AG.

Schiller, H. von: Zeppelin – Wegbereiter des Weltluftverkehrs. Bad Godesberg 1966, Kirschbaum Verlag.

Sheperd, J.: The Adams Chronicles, 1750–1900. Boston/Toronto 1975, Little, Brown and Company.

Smith, R. K.: The Airships Akron and Macon. Annapolis, Maryland 1965, Naval Institute Press.

ZR 3 "Los Angeles" over New York   ZR 3 „Los Angeles" über New York

Postal stamps of U.S. voyages of LZ 126, LZ 127 and LZ 129.
Poststempel verschiedener USA-Fahrten (LZ 126, LZ 127 und LZ 129).

9.
INDEX
OF NAMES

HANS G. KNÄUSEL

ZEPPELIN UND
DIE VEREINIGTEN STAATEN
VON AMERIKA

Ein bedeutendes Kapitel
deutsch-amerikanischer Beziehungen

1981
Friedrichshafen

Knäusel, H. G.: Zeppelin und die Vereinigten Staaten von Amerika –
Ein bedeutendes Kapitel deutsch-amerikanischer Beziehungen.
1. Auflage 1976
2. überarbeitete und erweiterte Auflage 1981
Engl. Übersetzung: M. O. McClellan
Herausgeber: Luftschiffbau Zeppelin GmbH
und Zeppelin-Metallwerke GmbH, Friedrichshafen
Alle Rechte vorbehalten.
Gesamtherstellung: Zeppelin-Druckerei, Friedrichshafen
Printed in Germany

ISBN 3-9800552-0-5 (Geb/iU)
ISBN 3-9800552-1-3 (Pb/iU)

Die Beziehungen zwischen den Vereinigten Staaten von Amerika und Deutschland haben eine lange Tradition. Mit kaum einem anderen Land verbindet die Amerikaner heute eine so herzliche Freundschaft wie mit der Bundesrepublik Deutschland. Die beiden Weltkriege unseres Jahrhunderts haben die guten Beziehungen zwar jeweils erheblich belastet, doch die freiheitsliebenden Amerikaner mit ihrem ausgeprägten Gerechtigkeitssinn waren jedesmal die ersten, die sich für eine rasche Normalisierung der Beziehungen einsetzten, weil sie die Deutschen nicht pauschal für Ereignisse verantwortlich machen wollten, die kleineren Gruppen anzulasten waren. Ein Mann wie Dr. Hugo Eckener beispielsweise genoß zwar im eigenen Lande bei den Regierenden kein Ansehen, doch um so mehr schätzten ihn die Amerikaner als Vertreter der Mehrheit der Deutschen, die nicht verantwortlich sein konnte für die Machenschaften der NSDAP. Dr. Eckener und seine Luftschiffe waren für Amerika ein Symbol für das friedliebende Deutschland und damit für Frieden und Freundschaft auf der Welt. Diese Schrift möchte jene Bedeutung der Zeppelin-Luftschiffahrt, die in einer kleinen Stadt, in Friedrichshafen am Bodensee, ihren Ursprung hatte, lebendig erhalten und dazu beitragen, das gegenseitige Verständnis zwischen den USA und Deutschland weiter zu vertiefen und die Bande der Freundschaft noch enger zu knüpfen.

Friedrichshafen, im Frühjahr 1981

Martin Herzog

Oberbürgermeister
der Stadt Friedrichshafen

Vorsitzender des Aufsichtsrates
der Luftschiffbau Zeppelin GmbH
und Zeppelin-Metallwerke GmbH

Willy Kaldenbach und *Heinrich Kollmann*

Geschäftsführer
der Luftschiffbau Zeppelin GmbH
und Zeppelin-Metallwerke GmbH

VORWORT

Als 1976 aus Anlaß des 200. Jahrestages der Vereinigten Staaten das Thema „Zeppelin und die USA" im Rahmen einer Friedrichshafener Ausstellung erstmals behandelt wurde, da wurde zugegebenermaßen die Komplexität der gestellten Aufgabe noch nicht voll erkannt. Doch viele Ratschläge und Hinweise vor allem aus den USA gaben den Anlaß, das seinerzeit als Beigabe zur Ausstellung erschienene Buch neu zu bearbeiten. Vor allem dem inzwischen verstorbenen F.W. von Meister verdankt der Autor zahlreiche Anregungen. Besonderer Dank gilt auch Captain Franklin D. Buckley von der US-Navy, der über die große Distanz durch geduldige Korrespondenz das Thema lebendig hielt, ebenso wie Henry Cord Meyer von der University of California, dessen eigene Arbeiten noch auf Veröffentlichungen warten und das Thema sicher weiter beleben werden. Doch auch in Deutschland waren es gewissenhafte Kenner und kritische Apologeten der Zeppelin-Geschichte, die erkannt haben, daß es heute nicht Sinn der Zeppelin-Geschichtsdarstellung sein kann, ausschließlich das Gesamtwerk in einer Überschau verbal und optisch zu präsentieren. Alfred Weber, der kluge und weitsichtige Privatgelehrte, war einer von ihnen, Hans von Schiller ebenso. Beide waren bei den ersten Vorbereitungen dieser Auflage behilflich, können sie nun aber nicht mehr erleben.

Hier kann nicht umfassend die Vielfalt der Beziehungen zwischen Deutschland und den USA auf dem Sektor Luftschiffahrt dargestellt werden, denn was – abgesehen von der frühen Begegnung des Grafen Zeppelin mit den Vereinigten Staaten – in den Jahren zwischen 1919 und 1939 an Kontakten stattfand, an Gedanken- und Erfahrungsaustausch, an persönlicher Begegnung, das läßt sich nicht auf ein paar Seiten komprimieren. Aber das Buch will anregen, sich mit der Geschichte auseinanderzusetzen und die Erträge und Erfahrungswerte eines ihrer Kapitel in die analytische Betrachtung des eigenen Handelns einzubeziehen. Die Zweisprachigkeit mag dabei helfen, den Zugang zum anderen Land zu erleichtern.

München/Erdweg, März 1981   *H. G. Knäusel*

INHALTSVERZEICHNIS

EINLEITUNG

Artikel, Schriften, Bücher über Zeppelin sind wohl zu Hunderten erschienen. Der Fülle weitere hinzuzufügen, bedeutet meist, sich in vielen Details zu wiederholen. Es gibt aber noch Bereiche, die bisher nicht behandelt oder nur am Rande erwähnt, teilweise sogar ganz vergessen wurden. Zwei Gründe können hierfür die Ursache sein: Entweder war das Thema noch nicht erkennbar, weil es eine historische Dimension besitzt, oder es wurde negiert, weil es zumindest zeitweise unangenehm war und verdrängt wurde. Zu letzteren zählt das hier behandelte Thema, das während der Zeit des Nationalsozialismus von Anbeginn mit Ressentiments beladen, spätestens ab 1938 am liebsten nicht nur aus den Archiven, sondern auch aus den Erinnerungen gestrichen worden wäre, hätte es dafür eine Möglichkeit gegeben. Was nach dem Ersten Weltkrieg für die gesamte Welt eine großartige Leistung war, nämlich die erfolgreiche Überführung von LZ 126 (ZR 3) in die USA, das war in Deutschland seit der Machtübernahme Hitlers im Jahre 1933 für die Nationalsozialisten eher ein Schandfleck in der Geschichte. Ein deutsches Luftschiff als Reparationsleistung! Der Versailler Vertrag wurde von Hitler rundweg abgelehnt, und in sein Weltbild paßten nicht die Bemühungen des amerikanischen Präsidenten Wilson, gegen die Einwände der übrigen Siegermächte einen gerechten Frieden zu schaffen, die Völker unter Einbeziehung Deutschlands in übernationaler Gesinnung zusammenzuführen. Kein anderes Land der Welt außer den USA war sich 1918 – wie 1945 wieder – der Aufgabe bewußt, daß man das deutsche Volk nach der Niederlage nicht pauschal verdammen und in eine ungewisse Zukunft entlassen dürfe. Heute weiß man, daß die Entwicklung in Europa und damit in der Welt mit ziemlicher Sicherheit einen anderen Verlauf genommen hätte, wenn sich nach 1918 alle Siegermächte jenen Vorstellungen Wilsons wenigstens hätten annähern können.

Zeppelin-Geschichte, das ist nicht nur die großartige Leistung eines genialen Erfinders, nicht nur die mit Stolz erfüllte, jubelnde Epoche des Kaiserreichs, als die ersten Luftschiffe mit fassungslosem Staunen am Himmel beobachtet wurden, das sind nicht nur die Konfettiparaden für Luftschiffbesatzungen auf dem Broadway. Zeppelin-Geschichte, das ist auch die Zeit des Ersten Weltkriegs, die Zeit der Weltwirtschaftskrise, die der Vorbereitungen Hitler-Deutschlands auf den Zweiten Weltkrieg – eine dramatische Spanne der Weltgeschichte. Innerhalb der großen weltgeschichtlichen Zusammenhänge mag das vorliegende Thema von untergeordneter Bedeutung sein, aber die Leistungen der deutschen Luftschiffer, die völkerverbindende Ausstrahlung ihrer Arbeit und die geradezu herzliche Freundschaft, die Luftschiffer in Amerika und Deutschland miteinander verband, haben auf ihre Weise Geschichte gemacht und sicher im politischen Bereich hier und da manch ungute Entwicklung gemildert. Auf jeden Fall waren Dr. Eckener und seine Leute ein Symbol für das Deutschland, das dem Nationalsozialismus ablehnend gegenüberstand, auch wenn man auf höheren Befehl ab 1934 das Hakenkreuz auf die Luftschiffe malte.

Die Wirkungen von Einzelleistungen im geschichtlichen Rahmen sind für den Beteiligten kaum erkennbar, doch hat nicht die Nachwelt die Pflicht, die Ereignisse auf ihren Tiefgang hin zu untersuchen, um daraus zu lernen? Woodrow Wilson legte 1919 sein Vierzehn-Punkte-Friedensprogramm dar, doch die Interessenkonflikte der europäischen Staaten einerseits und der Widerstand der Isolationisten im eigenen Land ließ das Programm scheitern; der schließlich unterzeichnete Versailler Vertrag wurde zur Basis für einen neuen Weltkonflikt. Unter solchen Aspekten gewinnt selbst das gesamthistorisch nur ausschnitthafte Kapitel des Luftschiffbaus an Bedeutung, denn selten waren – weder zuvor noch später – technische Entwicklung, politische und wirtschaftliche Entscheidungen sowie rein menschliche Begegnungen so intensiv miteinander verwoben wie in diesem Bereich. Die kleine Gruppe aktiver Luftschiffer und Luftschiffbauer auf beiden Seiten des Atlantiks konnte zwar den Gang der Geschichte nicht aufhalten, aber Karl Arnstein und Hugo Eckener, Charles E. Rosendahl und Hans von Schiller, Paul Litchfield und Willy von Meister und viele andere mehr haben sich mit den ihnen zur Verfügung stehenden Möglichkeiten dagegen gewehrt: Sie haben versucht, durch Freundschaft die Welt zusammenzuhalten.

Alles Geschehen auf unserer Welt beeinflußt unser persönliches Leben; die Bedeutung auch der – vermeintlichen – Randerscheinungen und damit die historische Position aller Beteiligten, vielleicht der eigenen Person, zu erkennen, ist die Aufgabe. Graf Ferdinand von Zeppelin als Beobachter im Sezessionskrieg – ein Zufall? Zunächst schon, aber von gravierender Bedeutung für seinen eigenen Lebensweg, später möglicherweise für eine ganze Epoche der Technikgeschichte! Der Wille eines Dr. Eckener, nach dem Ersten Weltkrieg ein Luftschiff zu bauen, um zunächst Arbeitsplätze zu erhalten, und die Chance, dies für die Vereinigten Staaten von Amerika tun zu können – gewiß kein Zufall, sondern die Realisierung der Erkenntnis einer Notwendigkeit, geboren aus historischen Fakten. Und so fügt sich eines zum anderen. Das langjährige Oberhaupt von Friedrichshafen und der um eine Generation jüngere Bürgermeister von Peoria, Illinois, Max Grünbeck und Richard E. Carver, werden Freunde, und die Freundschaft der „Zeppelin-Stadt" mit der „Stadt der Erdbewegung" wird besiegelt. Ein Zufall? Auch nicht, denn 20 Jahre zuvor hat ein in den Jahren der Luftschiffahrt erfahrener Mitarbeiter des Luftschiffbau Zeppelin in Friedrichshafen, Julius Oesterle, Nachfolger Eckeners in der Firmenleitung, die bestehenden Kontakte nach Amerika genützt und Verbindung zur Firma Caterpillar aufgenommen. Das Unternehmen, das einst weltberühmte Luftschiffe baute, vertritt nun in Deutschland die weltberühmte Firma auf dem Erdbewegungssektor. Die historische Bedeutung des Friedrichshafener Unternehmens gab mit den Ausschlag für die Entscheidung der amerikanischen Partner. Und die Entscheidung war der Beginn einer neuen beispiellosen Entwicklung, die auch der geschichtlichen Komponente des ehemaligen Luftschiffbaus einen neuen vitalen Aspekt verlieh. Und wenn heute als Folge ihrer geschichtlichen Tradition die relativ kleine Stadt Friedrichshafen eine wirklich aktive Partnerschaft zu der relativ kleinen amerikanischen Stadt Peoria unterhält, dann nimmt zwar nicht wie damals die ganze Welt Anteil an völkerverbindenden Ereignissen und Leistungen, aber ein paar Tausend Menschen haben die Chance, besseres Verständnis füreinander zu erwerben.

„Zeppelin und die Vereinigten Staaten von Amerika" ist ein Thema, das im wesentlichen mit dem absoluten Tiefpunkt der deutschen Geschichte zusammenfällt, aber wenn die Beschäftigung mit der Geschichte auch nur einen Sinn hat, dann den, daß es aufgrund vielschichtiger Begegnungen nie wieder zu einer so sinnlosen und tragischen Auseinandersetzung zwischen den USA und Deutschland kommen kann, wie schon zweimal in diesem Jahrhundert, sondern daß es fortan wie bei Hugo Eckener und seinen Mitarbeitern die positiven persönlichen Begegnungen sein werden, die das Miteinander bestimmen.

Der deutsche Teil dieses Buches
enthält nur wenige Illustrationen.
Es wird auf den
englischen Teil verwiesen.
Die erläuternden Texte dort
sind in Englisch und Deutsch.
Im Namens- und Ortsregister
sind die Abbildungen im
englischen Teil berücksichtigt
und durch *Kursivsatz* besonders
gekennzeichnet.

1.
ERFAHRUNGEN
MIT AMERIKA

1.1 Graf Zeppelin begegnet Präsident Lincoln

Als Graf Ferdinand von Zeppelin 1863 im Alter von 25 Jahren in die USA ging, da war er für dieses Land noch ein Unbekannter; ein paar Jahrzehnte später kannte den Namen Zeppelin jeder Amerikaner.

Seit 1861 erschütterte der Bürgerkrieg das Land. Graf Zeppelin wollte als Beobachter teilnehmen, um Erfahrungen zu sammeln. Als Berufssoldat interessierten ihn die damals neuartigen Methoden der Kriegsführung.

Die Erlaubnis, sich innerhalb der Truppen der Nordstaaten bewegen zu dürfen, wurde ihm als einem von insgesamt nur vier ausländischen Beobachtern von Präsident Lincoln erteilt, der den jungen Deutschen sogar zu einer Audienz empfing. In seinen Erinnerungen notierte Graf Zeppelin über die Begegnung mit dem amerikanischen Präsidenten: „Der Präsident sprach seine lebhafte Befriedigung über mein Kommen und meine Zwecke aus und wünschte mir guten Erfolg für meine Studien. – Bevor mir die Audienz gewährt wurde, hatte der Präsident angeordnet, Erkundigungen über mich einzuziehen. Durch die Güte des Herrn von Schleiden, des hanseatischen Gesandten, besitze ich als wertvolles Autograph ein von Lincoln an den Staatssekretär des Auswärtigen und den Kriegssekretär Stanton gerichtetes kurzes Schreiben, worin er fragt, ob die über mich eingezogenen Erkundigungen die Gewährung meiner Bitte um einen Paß zur Armee gestatten würden. Diesen Paß, der mir volle Bewegungsfreiheit unter den Armeen der Nordstaaten gab, erhielt ich denn auch. Einen solchen Paß haben während des ganzen Krieges außer mir nur der Herzog von Joinville, der Herzog von Chartres und der Graf von Paris erhalten."

Bald nach der Begegnung mit Lincoln begab sich Graf Zeppelin zu einer Brigade unter Generalmajor Butterfield innerhalb der Potomac-Armee, die damals General Hooker befehligte.

Es waren nicht etwa geruhsame Wochen in der Etappe. Graf Zeppelin nutzte die Möglichkeiten, die ihm der Militärpaß der Potomac-Armee durch aktive Teilnahme am Geschehen eröffnete, wobei er mehrfach in durchaus ernste Situationen kam und nur mit Glück und draufgängerischem Geschick sein Leben rettete. Für alle Fälle trug Graf Zeppelin nach eigenem Bekunden heimlich „einen warmen Empfehlungsbrief an den General Lee von dessen reizender Nichte, die ich in Philadelphia kennengelernt hatte", in der Tasche, denn hätten ihn die Soldaten der Südstaaten bei seinen Erkundungsritten gefangen genommen, man hätte ihn wohl, wie er selbst schreibt, „kurzerhand erschossen oder an einem Baum aufgeknüpft".

Zeppelin lernte auch Carl Schurz kennen. Das Bild, das er von diesem berühmten General der Nordarmee gewann, ist interessanterweise nicht identisch mit dem, wie es heute in amerikanischen und deutschen Chroniken oft gezeichnet wird. Von den militärischen Fähigkeiten Schurz', der nach der Revolution von 1848 aus Deutschland nach Amerika gekommen war und es bereits 1877 im Kabinett von Präsident Hayes zum Innenminister brachte, hielt Zeppelin damals jedenfalls nicht viel. Hier ist anzumerken, daß Carl Schurz, der 1906 starb, seine historische Bedeutung erst später als Journalist erlangte. Zeppelin, selbst noch ein junger Mann, lernte also nur den relativ jungen Schurz kennen.

1.2 Ballonaufstieg in Amerika

Im August 1863 nahm Zeppelin an dem Aufstieg mit einem Fesselballon in der Nähe von St. Paul, Minnesota, also nicht im Kampfgebiet, teil. Die Verwendung von Beobachtungsballons war ihm von beiden Seiten der Fronten her sicher bekannt, denn sowohl die Nord- als auch die Südstaaten setzten diese ein. Hier in St. Paul wurde möglicherweise der Grundstein für seine späteren Arbeiten gelegt. Als Soldat dachte er zunächst daran, den Fesselballon intensiver für militärische Zwecke zu nützen; geradezu ideal erschien ihm der Verwendungszweck als Beobachtungsstation. Der Gedanke, den Ballon fahrbar und lenkbar zu machen, ihn eventuell auch anders zu konstruieren, kam ihm vielleicht auch schon, belegt ist dies nicht. Lediglich Gedanken darüber, durch Anbringung eines festen Ruders den Ballon zu stabilisieren, werden in einem Brief geäußert[1]. Im übrigen hatte im

---

[1] Brief vom 19. August 1863 aus St. Paul, Minn. (vgl. Italiaander: F. Graf von Zeppelin, Verlag Stadler, Konstanz 1980, S. 29).
Eine systematische Analyse der etwa 25 Briefe, die Graf Zeppelin aus Amerika schrieb, könnte hier vielleicht eine endgültige Klärung schaffen.

Juni 1863 Solomon Andrews, ein Arzt aus Perth Amboy, New Jersey, mit seinem Luftschiff Aereon I gelenkte Flüge unternommen, ein Ereignis, das auch Graf Zeppelin bekannt gewesen sein dürfte.

Nach dem Aufenthalt bei der Armee ergab sich für Graf Zeppelin noch die Gelegenheit, eine Expedition in das Quellgebiet des Mississippi zu begleiten. Nach zeitgenössischen Schilderungen standen die Abenteuer, die er dabei erlebte, denen im Frontgebiet der Potomac-Armee in nichts nach.

Ein Bravourstück besonderer Art sei noch erwähnt, weil es offenbar typisch für den jungen Grafen war. Beim Besuch der Niagara-Fälle hatte er beobachtet, daß ein Stück Holz, das er ins Wasser warf, von einem Wasserwirbel immer wieder auf einen Felsen zutrieb. Daraufhin sprang er selbst ins Wasser und wurde in der gleichen Richtung an den Felsen getrieben und hatte nun einen großartigen Blick auf das Innere der Wasserfälle.

Nach einem halben Jahr Amerikaaufenthalt kehrte Graf Zeppelin im November 1863 nach Deutschland zurück.

1.3 Analyse einer Begegnung

Die positive Haltung Lincolns gegenüber dem jungen Zeppelin ist interessant, wenn man einmal die zeitgeschichtliche Situation jener Jahre betrachtet. Von der geradezu schwärmerischen Verehrung Deutschlands durch die Amerikaner um die Wende vom 18. zum 19. Jahrhundert war nicht mehr viel übriggeblieben; sie sollte nach 1870 für Jahrzehnte ganz verschwinden. Die Zeit war vorüber, als ein John Quincy Adams, späterer sechster Präsident der Vereinigten Staaten, Wielands Oberon übersetzte, als es in intellektuellen Kreisen selbstverständlich war, Goethe und Schiller zu lesen. Deutschland hatte sich verändert. Nach der kulturellen Blüte der Goethezeit war es in eine Phase kultureller Langeweile gesunken. Die politischen Zustände hatten eine kleinmütige, dürftige Dimension angenommen, die dem fortschrittlichen, noch jungen und dynamischen Drang nach persönlicher Freiheit, aber auch nach politischer Stärke der Amerikaner zuwiderlaufen mußte. Gerade der Bruderkrieg war ja (für die Nordstaaten) die verzweifelte Dokumentation dieser Haltung, der Wille, Freiheit und Stärke durch die Einheit der Nation zu bewahren.

Die Wandlung in Deutschland blieb den Amerikanern nicht verborgen. Tief enttäuscht schildert der im gleichen Jahr wie Graf Zeppelin geborene Henry Adams[2] in seiner Selbstbiographie „Die Erziehung des Henry Adams" die geistig engen und sozial ärmlichen Zustände, wie er sie auf seiner Europareise 1858/60 in Deutschland antraf. Das kaiserliche Deutschland mit nationalistischem Gehabe und Weltmachtansprüchen kündigte sich bereits an und wurde vor allem von den amerikanischen Intellektuellen scharf abgelehnt[3].

Aus diesem Deutschland kam Graf Zeppelin, der sich natürlich sehr über die ungemein legere Haltung und den unkonventionellen Umgangston des Präsidenten wunderte. Analysiert man die Erinnerungen Zeppelins über die Begegnung mit Lincoln einmal genauer, dann kann man ahnen, daß dieser sich wohl ein wenig über den steifen Auftritt des Bittstellers amüsiert haben mag, der wegen einer für einen Präsidenten eher belanglosen Kleinigkeit, nämlich der Bitte, als Beobachter tätig sein zu dürfen, im feierlichen Anzug mit Zylinder erschienen war. Doch mit kluger Einsicht paßte sich Graf Zeppelin sofort der fremden Lebensart an, und so hatte er auch keinerlei Probleme, sich im Umgang mit seinen rauhbeinigen Kampfgefährten in der Potomac-Armee zurechtzufinden. Trotzdem verlor er nicht seine Bindung an die europäische Geisteshaltung, was beispielsweise in der zuvor erwähnten kritischen Beurteilung von Carl Schurz zum Ausdruck kommt. Die Kritik bezog sich darauf, daß ein deutscher Offizier mangelnde soldatische Fähigkeiten durch Eitelkeit kaschierte, ein Vorgang, der im freizügigen Amerika auch heute noch eher Amüsement als Verwunderung oder gar Mißbilligung hervorrufen würde.

---

[2] Henry Adams (1838–1918), Enkel von Quincy John Adams (s. o.).

[3] Bis zum Krieg gegen Frankreich 1870 vollzog sich endgültig die Loslösung. Nicht mehr Berlin, Paris war jetzt die geistige und kulturelle Metropole in Europa, auch für die Amerikaner. Sicher kein Zufall ist die zwar nicht bedeutungsvolle, aber doch interessante Feststellung, daß die übrigen drei von Präsident Lincoln akzeptierten Kriegsbeobachter Franzosen waren (vgl. S. 164).

Verfolgt man die Vita des Grafen Zeppelin weiter, so kann unschwer gesagt werden, daß seine Begegnung mit Amerika einen großen Einfluß auf ihn ausgeübt und sein späteres Denken und Handeln mitbestimmt hat.

1.4 New York als Reiseziel schon 1895 geplant

Ob es, wie oft angenommen wird, ein Erlebnis im Krieg 1870–71 gegen Frankreich war – er beobachtete, wie wichtige Persönlichkeiten aus dem belagerten Paris mit Freiballons ausflogen – oder eine Veröffentlichung des preußischen Generalpostmeisters v. Stephan zum Thema der Postbeförderung per Luft[4], das Thema, lenkbare Ballons zu bauen, hat ihn schon während seiner Militärdienstzeit nachweislich beschäftigt. In seinem Tagebuch findet sich unter dem 25. 4. 1874 eine Eintragung über die Idee eines Ballonfahrzeuges.

Unmittelbar nach seiner Freistellung vom Militärdienst im November 1890 beginnt er, den Gedanken, lenkbare Luftschiffe zu bauen, konsequent weiterzuverfolgen. Ab 1892 werden die konstruktiven Arbeiten in seinem Auftrag von Theodor Kober soweit vorangetrieben, daß es schon 1895 zur Erteilung eines Patents für einen „Luftfahrzug" kommt. Wenn auch die späteren „Zeppeline" in einigen Details von den in dieser Patentschrift fixierten Vorstellungen abwichen, das Grundprinzip – starres Gerippe mit Außenhülle und mehreren innenliegenden Traggaszellen – blieb bis zu den letzten Zeppelin-Luftschiffen erhalten und erwies sich in der langen Reihe der zur Ausführung gelangten Luftschiffsysteme als sinnvoll. Allein das starre System des Grafen Zeppelin gestattete damals den Bau größerer, leistungsfähiger Luftschiffe.

Daß Zeppelin nicht nur an die militärische Verwendung späterer Luftschiffe dachte, wie oft behauptet wird, geht eindeutig aus einer aus dem Jahre 1895 stammenden Tagebucheintragung hervor, in der er

---

[4] Heinrich v. Stephan war Begründer des Weltpostvereins (1874) und hatte 1873 eine Schrift mit dem Titel „Weltpost und Luftschiffahrt" verfaßt.

Pläne für den Transport von Passagieren und Fracht in Luftschiffen u.a. nach New York skizzierte. Diese Idee war allerdings zu dieser Zeit nicht neu. U.a. hatten auch schon mehrere Amerikaner, wie beispielsweise John Wise (1843) oder T.S.C.Lowe (um 1850), den Gedanken der Atlantiküberquerung mit Ballonfahrzeugen geäußert; teilweise wurden sogar praktische Versuche unternommen, die allerdings alle fehlschlugen.

1.5 Der populäre Graf

Am 2. Juli 1900 erhob sich das erste Zeppelin-Luftschiff vom Bodensee. Für die Beziehungen zu den Vereinigten Staaten ergeben sich in den Anfangsjahren der Luftschiffahrt zunächst wenig Anhaltspunkte, doch das Wirken des Grafen Zeppelin blieb in Amerika nicht unbeachtet. Durch das Unglück bei Echterdingen im Jahre 1908, bei dem das Luftschiff LZ 4 nach einer viel bewunderten Dauerfahrt durch ein Unwetter am Boden zerstört wurde, erlangte er in den USA schon eine beachtliche Popularität. Vor allem die zahlreichen deutschen Clubs und Vereine in den großen Städten, insbesondere in New York und Chicago, trugen hierzu erheblich bei, war doch für sie Graf Zeppelin eine Symbolfigur für das Vaterland, das man einst zwar verlassen, aber nicht vergessen hatte. Alle wichtigen Ereignisse dort wurden natürlich mit Spannung verfolgt, und so wie überall in Europa erregte das Luftschiff auch in Amerika die Gemüter.

Auszeichnungen durch die Amerikaner in Form von Ehrenmitgliedschaften, Einladungen und Dankschreiben für die dem deutschen Volk und damit den Deutschen in Amerika erwirkte weltweite Anerkennung sind in großer Zahl feststellbar. Besonders die deutschen Veteranenvereine trieben geradezu einen Kult mit dem Grafen, dem diese überschwengliche Zuneigung keineswegs immer behagte, und sicherlich nicht allein aus Zeitmangel hat er sich nur äußerst selten persönlich für die Ehrungen bedankt, sondern dies durch seine Mitarbeiter erledigen lassen.

AERO CLUB OF COLUMBUS

MEMBER FEDERATION OF AMERICAN AERO CLUBS

AUGUST 29, 1908	INTERNATIONAL BALOONING CHAMPIONSHIP FOR BOARD OF TRADE TROPHY COLUMBUS DRIVING PARK

Columbus, Ohio,   Aug. 8, 1908.

Eing.g. 20 AUG. 1908.
Erledigt. *15. Aug. Zf. Drukkwch*
Rud.

The Hon. Count Zeppelin,

Friedrichshafen,

Germany.

Honored Sir:-

      In the name of this organization and the citizens
of this community, we take this opportunity of expressing
to you our deep regret and heartfelt sympathy in the time of
your great misfortune.

      We can realize what a great loss to you and the
world in general the destruction of your great work has been
and we note with satisfaction and great pleasure how quick
your country was to appreciate your value.

      And now allow us to add our heartiest congratulations
on the very wonderful flight you made. This we consider the
greatest of all aeronautic achievements yet attained.

      Success be with you and may you have all the good
fortune in the world and do even greater deeds than the
wonderful ones you have already done in the past.

      Very Cordially Yours,

Aero Club of Columbus,
per Herman Hoster

Following the crash of the LZ 4 in 1908, Count Zeppelin received many letters
from the United States, encouraging him to continue his efforts in spite of the
setback (see also pp. 24–28).

*Nach dem Unglück von LZ 4 im Jahre 1908 erhielt Graf Zeppelin viele Briefe
auch aus den USA, in denen er ermuntert wurde, seine Arbeit trotz des
Rückschlages fortzusetzen (s. a. S. 24–28).*

170

2.
DIE ZEIT
NACH DEM ERSTEN WELTKRIEG

2.1 Die „Shenandoah"
wird in den USA gebaut

Weltweite Verbindungen, der Gedankenaustausch mit Luftschiff-konstrukteuren anderer Länder werden durch den Ersten Weltkrieg verhindert. Ein nicht eben gewünschter indirekter Kontakt zu den USA ergibt sich, als das Marineluftschiff L 49 (LZ 96)[5] am 20. Oktober 1917 wegen Brennstoffmangels in der Nähe von Bourbonne/Frankreich notlanden muß und den Streitkräften der Alliierten fast unbeschädigt in die Hände fällt. Das Schiff wurde zerlegt und in allen Einzelheiten vermessen. Nach dem Krieg baute man in den USA die „Shenandoah", wobei die Pläne von LZ 96 zum großen Teil berücksichtigt wurden. Graf Zeppelin, der am 8. März 1917 starb, erlebte diesen ersten konkreten Niederschlag seiner Idee in den USA allerdings nicht mehr.

Die „Shenandoah" mit der Typenbezeichnung ZR 1 wurde in den USA im September 1923 in Dienst gestellt und in erster Linie als Versuchsschiff eingesetzt. Insbesondere wurden Versuche zur Verbesserung der Lande- und Ankertechnik (hier speziell am Hochmast) durchgeführt. Die „Shenandoah" war das erste Luftschiff, das mit dem unbrennbaren Helium als Auftriebsgas gefahren wurde.

Im September 1925 geriet die „Shenandoah" in einen Sturm und brach in der Luft in zwei Teile. C. E. Rosendahl, der als Navigator an Bord war und sich später einen Namen als Kapitän der „Los Angeles" machte, gelang es, die eine Hälfte des Schiffs mit einem Teil der Besatzung notzulanden. Trotz dieses Unfalls war es gerade Rosendahl, der sich für den Bau von Luftschiffen in den Vereinigten Staaten einsetzte. Rosendahl unterhielt auch besonders enge und freundschaftliche Kontakte zu den Luftschiffern in Deutschland.

2.2 LZ 124 kann nicht gebaut werden

Nach Kriegsende 1918 mußten die in Deutschland noch vorhandenen Luftschiffe an die Alliierten ausgeliefert werden. Das Interesse an den Schiffen war so groß, daß damit ein – wenn auch nur geringer –

---

[5] LZ mit fortlaufender Nummer stand für sämtliche Projekte, die vom Luft-

Teil der Deutschland auferlegten Reparationslasten beglichen werden konnte. Auch die Vereinigten Staaten zeigten sich interessiert, doch schien der Plan für den Bau eines Großluftschiffs zunächst daran zu scheitern, daß man der Überführung über den Atlantik keine Chancen gab. Hier aber beginnt ein Kapitel der deutsch-amerikanischen Beziehungen, das trotz des Zweiten Weltkriegs, trotz des Dritten Reichs mit all den schwerwiegenden Ereignissen bis heute das freundschaftliche Verhältnis beider Staaten mitgeprägt hat.

Für Dr. Hugo Eckener, den Leiter des Luftschiffbau Zeppelin in Friedrichshafen, galt es nach dem Krieg zunächst, vor allem die Arbeitsplätze der Zeppelin-Mitarbeiter zu erhalten, was nur möglich war, wenn man aus dem Ausland den Auftrag zum Bau eines Großluftschiffes erhielt. Der Bau großer Luftfahrzeuge war aber in Deutschland verboten, die Mittel für den Bau waren ohnehin nicht vorhanden. Pläne für ein 100 000-m³-Luftschiff, die in den ersten Jahren nach dem Krieg Oberst William S. Hensley im Auftrag einer amerikanischen Reederei zusammen mit den Friedrichshafener Luftschiffbauern zu realisieren suchte, scheiterten an den Bestimmungen des Versailler Vertrages[6]. Obwohl Hensley, der im Jahre 1919 den Rückflug von R 34 aus den USA nach Europa als Beobachter mitgemacht hatte (s. S. 174), ein Luftschiff ausschließlich zur Post-, Fracht- und Passagierbeförderung im Atlantikverkehr vorsah und der Bau bereits vertraglich gesichert war, wurde die Genehmigung von den Alliierten nicht erteilt. Mit der Bautypennummer LZ 124 verschwanden die Zeichnungen als „Projekt Hensley" in der Schublade. Die einzige Hoffnung für den Fortbestand des Luftschiffbau Zeppelin konnte daher nur der Auftrag der Regierung eines Siegerstaates sein.

---

schiffbau Zeppelin bearbeitet wurden. Von insgesamt 131 Projekten kamen von 1900 bis 1938 119 zur Ausführung. Die Marine gab ihren Schiffen andere Nummern, denen ein L vorangestellt war.

[6] Gesetz über den Friedensschluß zwischen Deutschland und den alliierten und assoziierten Mächten vom 16. Juli 1919; Artikel 198, Abs. 4: „Kein Lenkluftschiff darf unterhalten werden." Dieses Verbot wurde zwar eingeschränkt und betraf nicht Luftschiffe bis 30 000 m³ Inhalt (vgl. Pochhammer, ZR III, das deutsch-amerikanische Verkehrsluftschiff, S. 110. Freiburg 1924), doch schloß diese Größenordnung den Einsatz als Weltverkehrsmittel ohnehin aus.

2.3 LZ 126, das Amerika-Luftschiff

Ein Chicagoer Fabrikant namens Harry Vissering war eine Schlüsselfigur bei der Entwicklung der deutsch-amerikanischen Zusammenarbeit auf dem Luftschiffsektor. Als guter Freund von Präsident Harding verstand er es, in Washington den Gedanken zu vertiefen, daß man in den USA aus dem Luftschiffgeschäft heraus sei, wenn nicht eine Zusammenarbeit mit den deutschen Luftschiffern zustande käme. Vissering konnte auch Paul W. Litchfield von Goodyear für das Thema interessieren und zwischen diesem und Dr. Eckener vermitteln. Und schließlich waren noch zahlreiche andere Fürsprecher da, allen voran Commander Rosendahl und Konteradmiral Moffet von der Navy, denen es zu verdanken ist, daß die Regierung der Vereinigten Staaten für die Summe von drei Millionen Mark als Anrechnung auf die laut Versailler Vertrag zu erbringende Reparationsleistung den Auftrag zum Bau eines Luftschiffs schließlich erteilte (Auszüge aus dem Vertrag siehe Anhang 7.1). Allerdings drohte das Projekt zunächst daran zu scheitern, daß die Überführung des Schiffs nur auf dem Luftweg möglich war und weder die deutsche Regierung hierfür die Genehmigung erteilen, noch eine Versicherungsgesellschaft das Risiko tragen wollte.

Eckener ging aufs Ganze. Er setzte das gesamte Vermögen des Luftschiffkonzerns als Sicherheit ein und erhielt dann doch die Genehmigung. Einen Risikofaktor ließ man dabei völlig außer acht. Die Vereinigten Staaten hatten sich vorbehalten, die Annahme des Schiffes nach seiner Ankunft in Lakehurst verweigern zu können, wenn es nicht alle Bedingungen erfüllte [s. Anhg. 7.1]. Man vertraute in Friedrichshafen also voll und ganz auf die Erfahrungen, die man in über 20 Jahren gesammelt hatte.

LZ 126 mit der amerikanischen Bezeichnung ZR 3 war für die Friedrichshafener das erste Luftschiff, das für Langstrecken- und Überseebetrieb mit Passagieren gebaut werden mußte. Eckener war sich der ungeheuren Verantwortung bewußt, die er mit dem Auftrag übernahm. Zu den wenigen Vorbildern für Langstreckenfahrten zählten die Afrikafahrt von LZ 104 (L 59), das 1917 nonstop 6750 km zurückgelegt hatte, und die Fahrt des britischen Luftschiffs R 34 im Jahre 1919. R 34 hatte in einer für damalige Verhältnisse sensationellen

Fahrt den Atlantik in beiden Richtungen überquert. Das Konstruktionsprinzip von R 34 war dem Zeppelin-Prinzip gleich; es unterschied sich nur in wenigen technischen und konstruktiven Details. Die Zwischenlandung in den USA erfolgte auf dem Roosevelt Field in Mineola auf Long Island bei New York.

Das neue Schiff der Friedrichshafener Werft mußte nicht nur technisch bis dahin nie gestellten Anforderungen genügen, es sollte auch eine zukunftsträchtige Aufgabe erfüllen: Glückte die Atlantiküberquerung, dann waren die Allwettertauglichkeit, die Tauglichkeit für Langstreckenverkehr und damit für Eckener und den Luftschiffbau in Friedrichshafen die Möglichkeit erwiesen, Zeppelin-Luftschiffe in größerem Rahmen für den Weltluftverkehr einzusetzen. Für alle späteren Luftschiffbauten mußte ZR 3 im Hinblick auf Zuverlässigkeit und Sicherheit maßgebend werden, ein Vorhaben, das den Zeppelin-Ingenieuren unter der erfahrenen Leitung von Dr. Ludwig Dürr auch voll gelang.

Die Typenbezeichnung „ZR" bewies übrigens, daß auch in den USA das Luftschiffsystem des Grafen Zeppelin als richtig anerkannt wurde, denn Z stand (inoffiziell) für Zeppelin und R für rigid = starr. Und nach ZR 1 „Shenandoah", das ja in wesentlichen Teilen ein nachgebautes Zeppelin-Luftschiff war, und einem für die USA nicht zum Einsatz gelangten britischen Starrluftschiff[7] sollte ZR 3 der dritte „Zeppelin" für die Amerikaner werden.

2.4 Atlantik-Überquerung
mit politischer Wirkung

Mit dem Bau von LZ 126 konnte 1922 begonnen werden. Die US-Navy hatte in den Friedrichshafener Werken ein eigenes Büro, das „Office of Inspector of Naval Aircraft" unter Leitung von Garland

---

[7] R 38 sollte als ZR 2 von den USA übernommen werden, stürzte aber im August 1921 bei einer Versuchsfahrt ab, wobei 16 von 17 Amerikanern an Bord ums Leben kamen. Dieses Unglück dämpfte zunächst den Enthusiasmus der Amerikaner für den Luftschiffbau; zu dieser Zeit befand sich in der Naval Aircraft Factory in Philadelphia ZR 1 im Bau.

Fulton, eingerichtet und überwachte die Arbeiten. Spezielle Motoren wurden von Maybach entwickelt und in endlosen Testläufen für die neue und ungewöhnliche Aufgabe erprobt. Die zukünftige Besatzung absolvierte intensive Schulungen. Schon nach rund eineinhalbjähriger Bauzeit fand am 27. August 1924 die erste Probefahrt statt, wobei sich bereits zeigte, daß die errechneten Leistungsdaten eingehalten werden konnten. Und trotzdem herrschte großes Bangen, ob die für den Oktober vorgesehene Fahrt über den Atlantik klappen würde, an der ja alle Hoffnungen für den Bestand der Friedrichshafener Betriebe und für die konsequente Weiterentwicklung der zukunftsorientierten Luftschiffidee hingen.

Am 12. Oktober 1924 stieg LZ 126 zu der alles entscheidenden Fahrt über den Atlantik auf. Die 85 Stunden bis zur Landung in Lakehurst sind in zahlreichen Berichten geschildert worden. Als Gäste nahmen vier US-Offiziere an der Reise teil, die später für den Einsatz des Schiffs in den USA mitverantwortlich sein sollten[8].

Die Atlantiküberquerung gelang ohne schwerwiegende Zwischenfälle. Als das Luftschiff über dem New Yorker Hafen kreiste, wurde es von einem Höllenlärm der Feuersirenen der Stadt und aller Sirenen der im Hafen liegenden Seeschiffe begrüßt. Auf dem Landeplatz in Lakehurst bei New York hatten sich so viele Tausende von Menschen eingefunden, um dem Landemanöver beizuwohnen, so daß man kaum noch in die große Halle einfahren konnte.

Dr. Eckener und die Offiziere wurden zu einem offiziellen Empfang von Präsident Coolidge nach Washington ins Weiße Haus gebeten. Der Präsident der Vereinigten Staaten erkannte die Bedeutung des Ereignisses. Für ihn war die Überführung mehr als nur eine großartige technische Leistung. Er bezeichnete das Luftschiff als Friedensboten, mit dem Deutschland nach den Jahren des Krieges wieder Aufnahme in den Kreis der Völkergemeinschaft finden würde. ZR 3 „Los Angeles", wie LZ 126 fortan hieß, hatte somit nicht nur eine allgemeine technische und für den Luftverkehr in Deutschland wirtschaftlich bedeutungsvolle Aufgabe erfüllt, es hatte auch eine unerwartete politi-

---

[8] Als Gäste waren an Bord: Captain G. W. Steele, Cdr. J. H. Klein, Lt. Cdr. S. J. Kraus (Navy) und Major G. Kennedy (Army).

sche Funktion übernommen, die die Beziehungen zwischen Deutschland und den Vereinigten Staaten von Amerika für viele Jahre nachhaltig beeinflussen sollte. Als bei einer Filmvorführung über die Atlantikfahrt von ZR 3 von den begeisterten amerikanischen Zuschauern spontan das Deutschlandlied gesungen wurde, schien für die Amerikaner der nur wenige Jahre zurückliegende Krieg vergessen. Nach zahlreichen Feierlichkeiten unternahm Dr. Eckener mit Kapitän Ernst Lehmann und Navigationsoffizier Hans von Schiller eine Reise durch die Staaten, um Kontakte zu knüpfen und den geplanten Welt-Luftschiffverkehr vorzubereiten.

Interessant und erwähnenswert ist, daß neuere Veröffentlichungen über das Deutschland der 20er Jahre das Phänomen der Begeisterung der Amerikaner und die spätere Zusammenarbeit auf dem Luftschiffsektor völlig negieren. Selbst spezielle Untersuchungen, wie Knapp, M. (u.a.): Die USA und Deutschland 1918–1975[9], erwähnen die großartige Leistung Dr. Eckeners und seiner Mitarbeiter ebensowenig wie die geradezu euphorische Begeisterung der Amerikaner für das deutsche Luftschiff und die sich daran knüpfenden vielschichtigen politischen und wirtschaftlichen Vorgänge. Wenn man allein die zahllosen namhaften Ehrungen bedenkt, die Dr. Eckener zuteil wurden und die heutigen Autoren nicht verborgen geblieben sein können, dann ist die Nichterwähnung des Luftschiffbaus und seiner verdienstvollen Aktivitäten im Rahmen der vielfältigen Beziehungen zwischen Amerika und Deutschland jener Jahre unverständlich.

Von der Mannschaft blieb ein Teil in den USA zurück, um die amerikanische Besatzung der „Los Angeles" einzuweisen, oder – wie Kapitän Lehmann, der in Akron, Ohio, bei Goodyear blieb – um die Beziehungen für eine Zusammenarbeit zu vertiefen. Damals profitierten die deutschen Luftschiffer viel von den Amerikanern, die großzügig Mittel in Versuche mit der „Shenandoah" zur Verbesserung der Landetechnik investiert hatten. Man hatte ja in Deutschland immer

---

[9] Knapp, Link, Schröder, Schwabe: Die USA und Deutschland 1918–1975. München 1978, C. H. Beck'sche Verlagsbuchhandlung. Beck'sche Schwarze Reihe Nr. 177. Untertitel: Deutsch-amerikanische Beziehungen zwischen Rivalität und Partnerschaft.

wieder Schiffe verloren, weil nur ungenügende Landeeinrichtungen zur Verfügung standen. Das Landen am Mast, das für die großen Luftschiffe der zwanziger und dreißiger Jahre eine wichtige Technik wurde, hatten die Amerikaner mit der „Shenandoah" bereits weit entwickelt.

2.5 Zeppelin und Goodyear

Am 19. September 1923 wurde ein Abkommen zur Gründung der Goodyear-Zeppelin-Corporation unterzeichnet [s. Anhang 7.2], die später einige namhafte Ingenieure aus Friedrichshafen, an ihrer Spitze Dr. Karl Arnstein, beschäftigen sollte. Zwei Drittel des Unternehmens gehörten der Goodyear Rubber and Tire Co., ein Drittel dem Luftschiffbau Zeppelin. Sämtliche Patente des Zeppelin-Luftschiffbaus und aller Tochtergesellschaften wurden an Goodyear übertragen. Umgekehrt konnten die Friedrichshafener sämtliche Luftschiffpatente von Goodyear nützen[10]. Von diesen Vereinbarungen waren lediglich die Motoren ausgenommen. Goodyear stellte der Gesellschaft die Werksanlagen einschließlich Personal in Wingfoot Lake, Ohio, zur Verfügung. Für die „Zeppeliner", die zu Goodyear gingen, war dies nach dem Krieg eine einzigartige Chance, an der Luftschiffentwicklung unter günstigen Bedingungen weiterzuarbeiten.

Zu den wichtigen Persönlichkeiten, die dem Luftschiff in den Vereinigten Staaten Geltung verschafften, zählte zweifellos Dr. Karl Arnstein, der Vizepräsident der Goodyear-Zeppelin-Corporation wurde und dieser als leitender Ingenieur bis zu seiner Pensionierung im Jahre 1957 angehörte. Ab 1939 nannte sich die Firma Goodyear Aircraft Corporation.

Mehrere starre Luftschiffe wurden damals bei Goodyear projektiert, doch erst 1928 konnte ein Vertrag mit der US-Navy zum Bau

---

[10] Letzte Veröffentlichung hierzu: H. G. Dick, The Golden Age of the Great Rigid Airships. Inside the Control Car, Febr. 1979, Issue 27, S. 1. – Die Angaben der Beteiligungsverhältnisse in den diversen Quellen schwanken, was auf nachträgliche Änderungen des Vertrags bzw. von Teilen daraus zurückzuführen ist.

zweier Großluftschiffe unterzeichnet werden, wenige Tage bevor LZ 127 „Graf Zeppelin" seine erste Reise in die USA unternahm. Der „Akron" und der „Macon" (Typenbezeichnung ZRS-4 und ZRS-5) war allerdings kein glückliches Schicksal beschieden; sie gingen schon 1933 bzw. 1934 verloren, wobei insgesamt 75 Menschenleben zu beklagen waren. Fast schicksalhaft könnte man die Tatsache werten, daß der Untergang der „Akron" im Atlantik von einem deutschen Schiff, der „Phoebus" entdeckt und um die Welt gefunkt wurde. Von der 76 Mann starken Besatzung konnte die "Phoebus" nur vier bergen; einer davon starb an Bord des Schiffes.

Dr. Eckener nutzte stets seine Aufenthalte in den USA, um die Beziehungen auszubauen. Die Werft in Friedrichshafen mußte schließlich weiterbeschäftigt werden. Der Erfolg von ZR 3 „Los Angeles" war allein noch keine Garantie für den Fortbestand des Unternehmens.

Eckener, der von der Zukunft eines weltweiten Luftschiffverkehrs überzeugt war, versuchte damals, eine gemeinsame deutsch-amerikanische Luftfahrtgesellschaft ins Leben zu rufen. Eine solche Gesellschaft schien ihm Voraussetzung für den Bau von Passagierluftschiffen in größerer Stückzahl zu sein. Doch Dr. Eckener hatte bald erkannt, daß seine Bemühungen so rasch nicht zum Erfolg führen würden. Und so suchte er einen anderen Weg.

Anmerkung: Überraschenderweise drängten nach anfänglicher Zurückhaltung später auch Hermann Göring und das Reichsluftfahrtministerium Dr. Eckener, eine amerikanische „Luftschiffverkehrsgesellschaft" zu gründen. Der Reichsminister der Luftfahrt schreibt per Eilboten am 28. September 1936 an Dr. Eckener:
„Ich bin damit einverstanden, daß Sie Ende dieses Monats nach den Vereinigten Staaten von Nordamerika mit dem Luftschiff „Hindenburg" fahren, um mit den beteiligten amerikanischen Kreisen Fühlung aufzunehmen in der Frage einer Zusammenarbeit zwischen der Deutschen Zeppelin-Reederei G.m.b.H. und einer noch zu gründenden amerikanischen Luftschiffverkehrsgesellschaft. Ich habe davon Kenntnis genommen, daß es sich nur um eine unverbindliche Aussprache über die in Ihrem Schreiben näher angeführten Punkte handeln soll, bitte jedoch von Verhandlungen über Postbeförderung abzusehen, da diese den beteiligten Postverwaltungen vorbehalten bleiben müssen. Von dem Ergebnis Ihrer Besprechungen bitte ich mir nach Ihrer Rückkehr einen schriftlichen Bericht einzusenden."

2.6 Die Zeppelin-Eckener-Spende

Obwohl der Erfolg des ZR 3 auch bei der deutschen Bevölkerung nachhaltig gewirkt hatte, war die Reichsregierung nach wie vor skeptisch und zunächst nicht bereit, Mittel für den Bau eines weiteren Großluftschiffs zur Verfügung zu stellen, da man die Zukunft des Luftverkehrs schon damals eher beim Flugzeug sah. Graf Zeppelin selbst hatte für diese Auffassung Jahre zuvor schon Argumente geliefert, denn auch er sah eine große Zukunft des Flugzeugs voraus und hatte den Bau von Flugzeugen bereits vor dem Ersten Weltkrieg angeregt.

Dr. Eckener beschritt deshalb einen anderen Weg. Monatelang ging er mit der Besatzung von ZR 3 auf eine Tournee, zeigte Lichtbilder von der Reise über den Atlantik und sammelte in der als „Zeppelin-Eckener-Spende" bekannt gewordenen Aktion rund 2½ Millionen Mark. Damit konnten etwa 30 % der Kosten für den Bau von LZ 127 gedeckt werden. Für die deutsch-amerikanischen Beziehungen sollte dieses Schiff von großer Bedeutung werden, wie es überhaupt Weltruhm erlangte und das erfolgreichste Luftschiff aller Zeiten wurde. LZ 127 „Graf Zeppelin" war im Grunde das Luftschiff, das die Faszination der „Zeppeline" bewirkte, die bis in unsere Tage nicht abgeklungen ist.

(s. a. Seite 48)

Der Reichsausschuß für die

Zeppelin ⋅ Eckener ⋅ Spende

stellt folgende Verkaufswerte zur Verfügung

Abzeichen aus Seidenband mit Bronzeeinfassung in erstklassiger Ausführung mit Anstecknadel, zum Verkauf bei Straßensammlungen, in Restaurants, Hotels, Cafés, bei geselligen Veranstaltungen usw.
Verkaufspreis per Stück Mk. 1.—

Offizielle Postkarte des Reichsausschusses mit Bildnis des Grafen Zeppelin oder Dr. Eckeners (nach Wahl) zum Verkauf bei Straßensammlungen usw. . . . . Verkaufspreis per Stück Mk. 0.10

Abzeichen in einfacher Ausführung, Messing versilbert, zum Verkauf bei Straßensammlungen usw. wie oben . . . . Verkaufspreis per Stück Mk. 0.20

Offizielle Spendenmarke in der Ausführung von Briefmarken, zum Vertrieb bei Behörden, Industriebetrieben, Verkehrsgesellschaften usw. Abzug vom Wochenlohn, Monatsgehalt, durch Kleben von Marken auf die Lohnbeutel. Verkauf an den Kassen der Warenhäuser, erstklassiger Kaufhäuser und Spezialgeschäfte . . . . Verkaufspreis per Stück Mk. 0.10

3.
OHNE HELIUM
KEINE LUFTSCHIFFAHRT?

3.1 Erste Amerikafahrt des „Graf Zeppelin"

Vier Jahre nach der unvergessenen Fahrt des ZR 3 über den Atlantik startete LZ 127 zu seiner ersten Fahrt in die USA. An Bord befand sich auch ein alter Freund des Zeppelin-Luftschiffbaus, Charles E. Rosendahl, der auf dieser Reise weitere Erfahrungen sammeln wollte. Auch Presse und Rundfunk waren mit von der Partie. Lady Drummond Hay, die Tochter des amerikanischen Zeitungsverlegers Hearst, lieferte Reportagen und Schlagzeilen und stand als einzige Frau an Bord des Schiffes selbst im Mittelpunkt.

Die mit viel Enthusiasmus vorbereitete Reise lief nicht ohne Probleme ab. Eine Windboe hatte über dem Atlantik die untere Bespannung am linken Höhenruder teilweise zerstört. Der Rest der Bespannung konnte während der Fahrt zwar notdüftig befestigt, die Fahrt aber nur mit stark reduzierter Geschwindigkeit fortgesetzt werden. Dem Gelingen des Gesamtunternehmens tat dieser Zwischenfall aber keinen Abbruch, im Gegenteil, die Fahrt bekam einen dramatischen Aspekt, der natürlich von den an Bord befindlichen Presseleuten gern aufgegriffen und entsprechend verbreitet wurde.

Der Empfang in den USA übertraf den von ZR 3 noch erheblich. Im Triumphzug wurde die Besatzung durch New York geleitet. Die Stadt ließ sich die Gelegenheit nicht entgehen, eine Konfettiparade zu veranstalten, eine Ehre, die ja nur wenigen berühmten Persönlichkeiten zuteil wurde. Es folgten ein Empfang bei Bürgermeister Jimmy Walker und ein Besuch bei Präsident Coolidge in Washington. Die geplante Rundreise des „Graf Zeppelin" nach Cleveland, St. Louis und Chicago mußte zwar wegen schlechten Wetters abgesagt werden, doch Dr. Eckener, der Chicago einen Höflichkeitsbesuch abstattete, wurde trotzdem ungemein herzlich empfangen. In Detroit traf er sich mit Henry Ford, mit Walter Chrysler und mit Managern des General Motors-Konzerns, um Fragen des Luftverkehrs zu erörtern. Auf dieser Reise wurde Eckener wie bei fast allen späteren USA-Aufenthalten erstmals von F. W. von Meister begleitet, der wenig später in New York ein Büro eröffnete und die Interessen des Luftschiffbau Zeppelin in den USA bis zum Ende der Zusammenarbeit wahrnahm[11].

Damals kannte jedes Kind in Amerika nicht nur den Namen Zeppelin, sondern auch Dr. Eckener. Wo immer er und die Mannschaft von

LZ 127 auftauchten, kannte die Begeisterung keine Grenzen. Über keine andere Zeppelin-Fahrt – wenn man mal von der Weltfahrt, die ein Jahr später stattfand, absieht –, ja wohl über kaum ein anderes Zeitereignis wurde in der amerikanischen Presse soviel berichtet. Hatte man bei der Überführung von ZR 3 möglicherweise in erster Linie die technisch-sportliche Leistung der Atlantikfahrt bewundert, so waren es jetzt vorwiegend freundschaftliche Aspekte, die die Haltung der Amerikaner gegenüber den Luftschiffern aus Deutschland kennzeichneten.

Eine Begebenheit von der Rückfahrt soll nicht unerwähnt bleiben. Bei einem Kontrollgang durch das Schiff stöberte Hans von Schiller einen blinden Passagier auf, einen knapp 19jährigen Amerikaner, der wohl als einziger blinder Passagier aller Zeiten Weltruhm erlangte. Bei seiner Ankunft in Deutschland hat er angeblich sogar Autogramme gegeben; jedenfalls beweisen zeitgenössische Fotos, daß er zumindest stürmisch gefeiert wurde.

3.2 „Graf Zeppelin" auf Weltfahrt

Die erfolgreiche Amerikafahrt ermunterte nicht nur die Friedrichshafener Zeppeliner zu neuen Taten. Der Zeitungsverleger Willam Randolph Hearst sicherte sich für eine geplante Erdumrundung das Monopol für die Berichterstattung auf der ganzen Welt, wodurch die Finanzierung eines solchen Unternehmens kein Problem darstellte. Und auf zahlreichen Fahrten hatte man inzwischen genug Erfahrungen

---

[11] F. W. (Willy) von Meister war auch Vizepräsident der American Zeppelin Transport Inc., die eine Gründung von Goodyear-Zeppelin und der German Zeppelin Transport Co. war. Letztere unterhielt zwangsläufig enge Beziehungen zum Luftfahrtministerium in Berlin. Nach dem Überfall auf Pearl Harbor wurden alle Akten der Firma, die sich seit 1938 bei von Meister befanden, beschlagnahmt. Anfang der 60er Jahre wurde das meiste Material vernichtet, weshalb heute viele wichtige Unterlagen, die Beziehungen zwischen den USA und Deutschland im Zusammenhang mit der Luftschiffahrt betreffend, fehlen und interessante Details nicht mehr ermittelt werden können.

gesammelt, um sich an ein derartiges Projekt heranwagen zu können. Für Hearst ging der amerikanische Journalist Karl von Wiegand mit auf Weltreise, der seither stets engen Kontakt zu Dr. Eckener hielt.

Nur drei Zwischenlandungen waren auf der Fahrt um die Erde vorgesehen. Die Bedingung, die der Verleger Hearst für seinen Anteil der Finanzierung stellte, war der Start an der Freiheitsstatue in New York. Und so fuhr LZ 127 zunächst von Friedrichshafen nach New York, um dort am 7. August 1929 die Reise um die Welt – zumindest aus amerikanischer Sicht – offiziell zu beginnen. Am 10. August 1929 war man wieder in Friedrichshafen und startete am Morgen des 15. August ein zweites Mal, diesmal Richtung Osten. Daß dies für die Deutschen der offizielle Beginn der Weltreise war, dafür hatten die an Bord befindlichen amerikanischen Gäste volles Verständnis.

Nach der Zwischenlandung in Tokio, die für die Japaner wie für Fahrgäste und Besatzung ein unvergeßliches Erlebnis war, ging es mit Ziel Los Angeles auf den schwierigsten Teil der Reise, die Luftfahrt über die größte Wasserfläche der Erde, den Stillen Ozean, den noch kein Mensch auf diesem Wege nonstop überquert hatte.

Nach 68 Stunden war die amerikanische Westküste erreicht. Das Schiff hätte an sich einige Stunden früher ankommen müssen. Auf die besorgte Frage F. W. von Meisters, der Dr. Eckener in San Francisco erwartete, antwortete dieser: „Aber, Herr von Meister, wenn zum ersten Mal in der Weltgeschichte ein Luftschiff über den Pazifik fliegt, sollte es dann nicht bei Sonnenuntergang über dem Golden Gate erscheinen?"[12] Ein gelungener psychologischer Trick, denn „. . . seine Kalkulation war vollkommen richtig. Dem ‚Graf Zeppelin' wurde ein tumultartiger Empfang bereitet."[13]

Bei der Weiterfahrt entlang der Küste wurde die für den Empfang des Luftschiffes festlich illuminierte Villa des die Reise im wesentlichen finanzierenden Verlegers Hearst gesichtet.

---

[12] Nach einer Niederschrift, die Henry Cord Meyer, Professor für Geschichte an der University of California, Irvine, Ca., am 15. 9. 1979 über ein Gespräch mit F. W. von Meister kurz nach dessen Tod gemacht hat.

[13] ebd.

Los Angeles war nur Haltepunkt; man wollte rasch weiter, und erstmals schien LZ 127 einer Katastrophe nahe, doch Dr. Eckener meistert die Situation. Hans von Schiller, als wachhabender Offizier an Bord, schildert die Situation[14]:

„Als wir am Abend starten wollen, ist die Temperatur erheblich höher als erwartet. Wir müssen noch allen überflüssigen Proviant und Wasserballast von Bord geben. Endlich scheint es zu gehen, die Haltemannschaft stößt das Schiff hoch. Wir steigen aber schon in 20 Meter Höhe nicht mehr weiter und müssen alle Motoren mit äußerster Kraft anlaufen lassen, um das Schiff dynamisch zu heben. Wir nehmen Fahrt auf – und erblicken 1 km vor uns eine gut 40 Meter hohe Hochspannungsleitung! Durch den Druck des Höhensteuers senkt sich das Heck hinten und berührt den Boden, daß Gras und Kraut aufwirbeln und sich die Unterkante der Stabilisierungsfläche verfängt. Doch wir fahren weiter. Dr. Eckener ist die Ruhe selbst. Gelassen sagt er zu seinem Sohn am Höhensteuer: ‚Knut, halt ihn gerade!' Und dicht vor dem Hindernis: ‚Jetzt nimm ihn hoch!' Die Spitze des Zeppelins überspringt die Leitung. Wir bangen um das Achterteil. Doch als das Schiff mit der Mitte den Draht passiert hat, kommt die ruhige Anweisung Eckeners: ‚Und jetzt leg ihn wieder gerade!' Und haarscharf schaffen wir es."

Die Navy war übrigens untröstlich darüber, daß sechs Mann der Besatzung mit dem Zug nach Lakehurst fahren mußten, weil man versehentlich zu wenig Wasserstoffgas in Los Angeles bereitgestellt hatte.

Obwohl die Zeppelin-Mannschaft nun schon daran gewöhnt war, begeistert empfangen zu werden, übertraf dieser Empfang nach der Weltumrundung in New York alles bisher Erlebte. Der „Zeppelin" hatte – so schien es – für alle Zeiten die Lüfte erobert. Die Technik feierte einen Triumph, der beispiellos war. Die Wertschätzung, die man der Besatzung zuteil werden ließ, dokumentierte sich u. a. in der Verleihung der „Freedom of City", des Bürgerrechts durch New Yorks Bürgermeister Jimmy Walker.

---

[14] Hans v. Schiller: Zeppelin – Wegbereiter des Luftverkehrs. Kirschbaum-Verlag, Bad Godesberg 1966. 1. Aufl. S. 97 (Anm.: 2. überarbeitete und erweiterte Auflage in Vorbereitung).

3.3 Schlüsselwort „Helium"

Dr. Eckener blieb zu Verhandlungen in den USA, während LZ 127 unter Kapitän Lehmann die Heimreise nach Friedrichshafen antrat.

Wichtigster Verhandlungsgegenstand in diesen Jahren der großen Erfolge von LZ 127 – u.a. fand 1931 die berühmt gewordene Forschungsfahrt in die Arktis statt, an der auch zwei Amerikaner teilnahmen[15] – war die Lieferung des unbrennbaren Heliums, über das damals nur die Vereinigten Staaten in größeren Mengen verfügten. Für den Ausbau eines weltweiten Luftschiffverkehrsnetzes mußte der Sicherheit der Luftschiffe oberste Priorität eingeräumt werden. Was heute keine Luftfahrtbehörde genehmigen würde, war in den dreißiger Jahren aber noch möglich; man beförderte Passagiere über weite Strecken unter Verwendung des hochexplosiven Wasserstoffs als Traggas. Man war sich aber auch darüber im klaren, daß dies nur ein vorübergehender Zustand sein konnte, der langfristig nicht zu verantworten war. LZ 129 „Hindenburg" wurde dann bereits auch als Heliumschiff projektiert. Als man mit den Bauarbeiten 1934 begann, hatte man noch die feste Hoffnung, das Helium aus den USA – nicht zuletzt wegen der guten gegenseitigen Beziehungen auf dem Luftschiffsektor – geliefert zu bekommen. Die Bemühungen Dr. Eckeners, der deutschen und amerikanischen Mitarbeiter der Goodyear-Zeppelin-Corporation und der Niederlassung der Deutschen Zeppelin-Reederei in den USA, hier vor allem ihres Repräsentanten, F.W. von Meister, waren jedoch vergebens. Die politische Entwicklung in Deutschland bestimmte schließlich die Entscheidung der Amerikaner, das unbrennbare Traggas nicht zu liefern, eine Entscheidung, die zwar aus politischen Überlegungen verständlich war, aber wenig später schwerwiegende Folgen haben sollte.

So wurde LZ 129 dann doch für Wasserstoffbetrieb gebaut. Man vertraute weiter auf die guten Erfahrungen, die man mit LZ 127 gemacht hatte. Außerdem war LZ 129 technisch dem nun schon

---

[15] Lt. Commander E. H. Smith von der Navy und Lincoln Elsworth, Polarforscher aus New York.

betagten LZ 127 in vieler Hinsicht weit überlegen, so daß man nach ausgiebigen Probefahrten noch 1936 den fahrplanmäßigen Liniendienst aufnahm.

3.4 Zeppeline im Liniendienst zwischen Europa und Amerika

Seit Ende August 1932 fuhr LZ 127 „Graf Zeppelin" regelmäßig nach Südamerika. Im Oktober 1933 wurde dabei auf einer Rückreise den USA nochmal ein Besuch abgestattet. In Miami, Florida, Akron, Ohio, und Chicago, Illinois, wurde Station gemacht. In die Vereinigten Staaten, in das Land, wo es seine größten Erfolge gefeiert hatte, ist „Der Graf", wie man LZ 127 damals oft kurz nannte, danach nicht mehr gekommen.

Die sehr guten, in vieler Hinsicht freundschaftlichen Beziehungen zwischen den Friedrichshafener Zeppelinern und der US-Navy fanden vielfältig dokumentierten Niederschlag. So wurde am 11. Oktober 1935 ein Abkommen unterzeichnet, das der Deutschen Zeppelin-Reederei GmbH, Berlin, die Nutzung der technischen Einrichtungen für das im Bau befindliche LZ 129 auf dem Flugfeld von Lakehurst und der Marine-Basis in Opa-Locka, Florida, sicherte (siehe Anhang 7.3, Seite 230). Gegen geringe Gebühren war gewährleistet, daß LZ 129 in Lakehurst die Halle, den Landemast, Lager für rund 30000 m^3 Wasserstoffgas zum Nachfüllen mit den erforderlichen Fülleinrichtungen, Tankwagen etc. benutzen konnte. Außerdem stand für jeden Lande- und Startvorgang eine Haltemannschaft von 90 Mann gegen eine Gebühr von nur 250 Dollar zur Verfügung, ein wahrhaft freundschaftlicher Preis. Würde LZ 129 irgendwo sonst in den USA landen, dann war vereinbart, daß bis zu sieben Tankwagen die Gas- und Treibstoffversorgung sicherstellten. Auch die Funkeinrichtungen der Flughäfen durften genutzt werden.

Am meisten überrascht, daß man die Lagerung von Wasserstoff in größeren Mengen erlaubte. Alle großen amerikanischen Luftschiffe wurden ja von Anfang an aus Sicherheitsgründen ausschließlich mit Helium gefüllt. Auch ZR 3 war sofort nach seiner Ablieferung an die

US-Navy mit Helium gefüllt worden. Die Unterstützung, die die US-Navy den Zeppelinern auch in diesem Punkt gewährte, ist Ausdruck des hervorragenden Verhältnisses, das amerikanische und deutsche Luftschiffer unterhielten.

Die erste USA-Reise, die LZ 129 „Hindenburg" durchführte, fand im Mai 1936 statt und ging wie auch die späteren direkt nach Lakehurst. Insgesamt elfmal fuhr das größte jemals im Passagierdienst eingesetzte Luftschiff diese Strecke, und trotzdem war jede Ankunft – wie überall, wo Zeppeline auftauchten – stets ein Ereignis, das zahlreiche Zuschauer sowie Foto- und Filmreporter anlockte. Eine Unmenge selbst heute noch nicht vollständig bekannten Bildmaterials zeugt von dem über Jahre anhaltenden Interesse an den Luftschiffen, das seinesgleichen sucht. Im Juli 1936 schreibt Göring, der Reichsminister für Luftfahrt, an die Zeppelin-Reederei in Berlin:

„Einer aus New York ergangenen Anregung zufolge bitte ich um Mitteilung, ob es möglich ist, anläßlich einer der nächsten Nordamerikafahrten das Luftschiff „Hindenburg" in den Tagesstunden über New York kreuzen zu lassen. Bisher soll „Hindenburg" immer nur in Zeiten der Dunkelheit New York überfahren haben, so daß der Bevölkerung keinerlei Gelegenheit gegeben war, das so viel bewunderte Luftschiff zu sehen. Wie mir mitgeteilt wird, verspricht man sich von einer mehrstündigen Kreuzfahrt über die Stadt propagandistische Vorteile.
Ich kenne die Berechtigung des Antrages schon aus dem Grunde an, weil die amerikanische Marine in zuvorkommender Weise den Luftschiffhafen Lakehurst zur Verfügung gestellt hat."

Selbst die Katastrophe von Lakehurst am 6. Mai 1937, bei der LZ 129 verbrannte, änderte nichts an dem allgemeinen Interesse für Luftschiffe, das bis heute anhält. Das tragische Ende dieses Schiffs wurde in allen Einzelheiten im Bild festgehalten. Die auf Tonträgern gespeicherte Reportage des amerikanischen Rundfunkreporters Herbert Morrison ist eines der dramatischsten Zeugnisse des modernen Journalismus, die es gibt.

Mit dem Untergang von LZ 129 „Hindenburg" war die Aera der Passagier-Luftschiffahrt beendet. Zwar wurde in Friedrichshafen LZ 130 noch fertiggebaut, zum Einsatz für die Passagierbeförderung kam es jedoch nicht mehr; lediglich Test- und Beobachtungsfahrten wurden durchgeführt. Das in fast neunjährigem ununterbrochenem Einsatz bewährte LZ 127 „Graf Zeppelin" wurde nach dem Lakehurst-Unglück außer Dienst gestellt.

3.5 Die Heliumfrage wird zum Politikum

Der amerikanische Kongreß beschäftigte sich in ausführlichen Debatten schon seit 1925 mit Helium. Erstmals am 3. März 1925 wurde per Gesetz die Ausfuhr drastisch eingeschränkt. Debatten zu diesem Thema folgten immer wieder in den Jahren danach. Nach dem Lakehurst-Debakel war eine große Mehrheit der Amerikaner dafür, Dr. Eckener durch die Lieferung von Helium die Fortführung seines Werks zu ermöglichen, doch die Entwicklung lief anders.

Nur eine Woche nach der Katastrophe in Lakehurst legte Innenminister Harold L. Ickes dem Kabinett in Washington eine Anfrage aus Deutschland vor. Rund 300 000 m^3 Helium für das im Bau befindliche LZ 130 wollte man kaufen, aber das Kabinett befürchtete, Deutschland könne das Gas bzw. die Luftschiffe für Kriegszwecke verwenden. Präsident Roosevelt, Eckener und seiner Idee stets wohlgesonnen, ließ deshalb durch eine fünfköpfige Sonderkommission, die der Innenminister vorschlug, das Heliumthema weiter beraten. Neben Ickes, der später zu einem der schärfsten Gegner einer Heliumlieferung an Deutschland wurde, waren sich die der Kommission angehörenden Außenminister Cordell Hull, Handelsminister Daniel C. Roper, Kriegsminister Harry H. Woodring und Marineminister Claude A. Swanson in wenigen Tagen darüber einig, unter gewissen Voraussetzungen dem Präsidenten zu empfehlen, Helium „für die Verwendung im kommerziellen Luftschiffverkehr zwischen den Vereinigten Staaten und anderen Ländern" zu verkaufen[16]. Die Empfehlung wurde Roosevelt bereits am 25. Mai 1937 zugeleitet, als die ganze Welt noch unter

---

[16] Verwendungsmöglichkeiten für wissenschaftliche Zwecke waren u. a. ebenfalls berücksichtigt.

dem Eindruck des Unglücks von Lakehurst stand. Sie enthielt natürlich den Hinweis darauf, daß Vorkehrungen zu treffen seien, die die
militärische Verwendung des Heliums ausschließen sollten und stellten
humanitäre Überlegungen in den Vordergrund, „…um Wirtschaft
und Wissenschaft zu fördern, menschliche Leiden zu mindern, das
Leben von Luftschiffpassagieren zu schützen und so die internationale
Freundschaft zu stärken."[17] Roosevelt leitete den Vorschlag der Kommission umgehend befürwortend an die zuständigen Ausschüsse des
Kongresses weiter. Eckener, der sich zur Untersuchung des Unglücks
in jenen Wochen in Amerika aufhielt, sagte sogar vor den Militäraus-
schüssen von Senat und Repräsentantenhaus aus und versuchte zu
bekräftigen, daß eine militärische Verwendung des Heliums nicht in
Frage käme. Bei diesen Anhörungen soll es sich um die ersten überhaupt gehandelt haben, die diese Ausschüsse mit einem Ausländer
durchführten.

Die Sache schien gut zu laufen. Die deutsche Botschaft in Washington schickte am 7. Dezember 1937 folgendes Telegramm an das
Auswärtige Amt in Berlin:

1) Amerikanische Regierung übersandte soeben Note, wonach sie
   der Deutschen Zeppelin-Reederei G.m.b.H. für 1937 erteilte
   Einfluggenehmigung auf 1938 überträgt und für Luftschiff LZ
   130 achtzehn Einflüge genehmigt.

2) Nach gestern erfolgter Veröffentlichung State Departement ist
   American Zeppelin-Transport Inc. New York als Vertreterin der
   Deutschen Zeppelin-Reederei G.m.b.H. Frankfurt a/M. auf
   Grund Einstimmigkeit Empfehlung aller Mitglieder Munition-
   kontrollbehörde und des Innenministers ein Quantum von
   17 900 000 Kubikfuß Helium zugeteilt worden, das bis zum
   31. Oktober 1938 auf Grund besonderer Ausfuhrerlaubnisse
   ausgeführt werden kann. Nach Angabe Mellons handelt es sich
   bei dem noch zu beantragenden Ausfuhrhandel um eine reine
   Formalität.

---

[17] Nach Moltmann, G.: Die Luftschiff-„Hindenburg"-Katastrophe und das
Heliumproblem. Wehrwissenschaftliche Rundschau, 11/1961.

Warum dieses Telegramm allerdings erst am 24. Dezember 1937 an die Deutsche Zeppelin-Reederei in Frankfurt weitergeleitet wurde, bleibt unklar. Diese Verzögerungstaktik der Berliner Ministerien wird fortgesetzt, denn erst am 15. Januar 1938 geht bei der Zeppelin-Reederei die vollständige Originalabschrift dieser bedeutsamen Note ein, die in Berlin wesentlich früher vorgelegen haben muß. Der Begleitbrief zur Note hat folgenden Wortlaut:

„In der Anlage wird Abschrift einer Note übersandt, mit der das amerikanische Staatsdepartement der Deutschen Botschaft in Washington mitteilt, daß die der Deutschen Zeppelin-Reederei für 1937 erteilte Einfluggenehmigung auf 1938 übertragen wird und 18 Einflüge des Luftschiffes LZ 130 während des Jahres 1938 genehmigt werden. Ich bitte, von den Bedingungen der Note Kenntnis zu nehmen.

In einer Veröffentlichung des amerikanischen Staatsdepartments vom 6. Dezember 1937 über Ausfuhrgenehmigung von Waffen, Munition und sonstigem Kriegsmaterial (implements of war) wird auch Helium aufgeführt. Es heißt dort:

„On the joint recommendation of all of the members of the National Munitions Control Board and the Secretary of the Interior, an allotment of 17,900,000 cubic feet of helium gas, the exportation of which may be authorized by license during a period of one year after November 1, 1937, was granted on November 23, 1937, to American Zeppelin Transport, Incorporated, New York, as Agent for Deutsche Zeppelin-Reederei G.m.b.H., Frankfort on the Main, Germany, in accordance with paragraphs (6) and (7) of the Regulations Governing the Exportation of Helium Gas. No licenses have as yet been applied for or issued under this allotment."

Auf Grund der für einen begrenzten Zeitraum befristeten Ausfuhrgenehmigung muß angenommen werden, daß auch in Zukunft mit Erteilung der Exportlizenzen nur von Fall zu Fall gerechnet werden kann."

Die Note der Einfluggenehmigung in die USA für LZ 130, vom State Department in Washington am 7. Dezember der Deutschen Botschaft zugestellt, lautete[18]:

---

[18] Department of State, Washington, D.C., Aktenzeichen 811.79662 LZ-130/8

„Der Secretary of State übermittelt hiermit Sr. Exzellenz, dem deutschen Botschafter, seine besten Empfehlungen und bezieht sich auf den vorangegangenen Schriftwechsel bezüglich des Antrags der Deutschen Zeppelin-Reederei GmbH, hinsichtlich der Durchführung experimenteller Transatlantikfahrten mit dem Luftschiff LZ-130 während des Jahres 1938.

Der Secretary of State freut sich, dem deutschen Botschafter mitteilen zu können, daß der Secretary of Commerce die der Deutschen Zeppelin-Reederei GmbH bisher erteilte provisorische Genehmigung auf das Jahr 1938 ausgedehnt hat. Diese Verlängerung basiert auf den im Antrag gemachten Angaben und Darstellungen sowie folgenden Bedingungen:

(1) Die Gesamtzahl der zwischen Frankfurt/M und Lakehurst, New Jersey, geplanten Hin- und Rückfahrten ist auf 18 beschränkt. Vor jedem Fahrtantritt in US-Hoheitsgebiet ist dem US-Handelsministerium ein Fahrplan mit ungefähren Daten der geplanten Fahrt zwischen dem Ausland und den Vereinigten Staaten einzureichen.

(2) Die in dieser Genehmigung bedachten Fahrten unterliegen den Bedingungen des zwischen den Vereinigten Staaten und Deutschland am 1. Juni 1932 in Kraft getretenen Luftfahrtabkommens.

(3) Es wird zur Auflage gemacht, daß sich das hiermit erteilte Privileg auf die Navigation des Luftschiffs LZ-130 erstreckt, und zwar in direktem Flug von einem Ort in Deutschland nach Lakehurst, New Jersey, und zurück. Die dabei benutzte Fahrtroute ist über US-Hoheitsgebiet aufs kürzeste zu beschränken, es sei denn, daß Witterungsverhältnisse oder andere Vorkommnisse eine Änderung dieser Fahrtroute erforderlich machen.

(4) Diese Genehmigung wird unter der Voraussetzung erteilt, daß amerikanischen Luftfahrtunternehmen nach ordnungsgemäßer Antragstellung seitens dieser Regierung Einflugs- und Wartungsprivilegien für deutsches Hoheitsgebiet eingeräumt werden, und zwar gleichwertig mit denen, die dem deutschen Luftfahrtministerium seitens der US-Regierung bereits gewährt wurden bzw. hiermit werden.

(5) Ferner wird zur Bedingung gemacht, daß vor Aufnahme des kommerziellen Fahrgastverkehrs zwischen den US und Deutschland eine angemessene Zahl von Probefahrten durchzuführen ist."

Ende 1937 wurden die ersten Heliumladungen auf den Weg nach Deutschland gebracht. Doch als dann am 13. März 1938 Hitler Österreich annektierte, brach das von Eckener geduldig und beharrlich aufgebaute gute Verhältnis zu den USA schlagartig zusammen. Am 14. März 1938 schon verabschiedete das Repräsentantenhaus ein Gesetz, wonach entgegen der 1937 gegebenen Zusage dem Deutschen Reich kein Helium geliefert werden durfte[19]. Zwar versuchte Eckener noch, direkt von Präsident Roosevelt eine Zusage für die Lieferung des Heliums zu bekommen, doch Roosevelt waren durch die Entscheidungen der Heliumkommission und des Kongresses die Hände gebunden. Die Dramatik jener Wochen und Monate schildert Eckener selbst sehr eindrucksvoll in seinem Buch „Im Luftschiff über Länder und Meere"[20]. Ein deutsches Frachtschiff, das im Frühjahr 1938 bereits im texanischen Hafen Galveston lag, um Helium an Bord zu nehmen, mußte unverrichteter Dinge zurückkehren.

Gewiß bedauerte die große Mehrheit der Amerikaner die Entscheidung, denn Dr. Eckener und seine Mitarbeiter konnten ja nun ihr viel bewundertes und gerade auch in Amerika geliebtes Werk nicht fortsetzen, aber wegen des aggressiven Gebarens Hitler-Deutschlands fand die Entscheidung bei den Amerikanern mehrheitlich doch Zustimmung. Die Zeitungen berichteten täglich über die Auseinandersetzungen, und nicht zuletzt wegen der Heliumsdiskussion wurde die sich zuspitzende politische Situation in Europa von ganz Amerika mit viel Aufmerksamkeit verfolgt.

---

[19] „. . . the sale of helium gas to the German Reich shall be prohibited." Gesetz vom 14. März 1938, H. R. 9855. (Original s. S. 85.)

[20] Heyne-Taschenbuch 5582, München 1979, Seite 271 ff. (leicht gekürzter Nachdruck der Originalausgabe von 1949, Verlag Chr. Wolff, Flensburg), mit Vorwort von R. Italiaander und einigen zusätzlichen Kommentaren.

3.6 Dr. Eckener
Mittler zwischen Deutschland
und Amerika

Eine Tatsache, die damals im Ausland und insbesondere in den USA weit mehr bekannt war als in Deutschland, waren die Spannungen zwischen Dr. Hugo Eckener und den Nationalsozialisten. Mit Beharrlichkeit weigerte er sich, in den Anfangsjahren des NS-Regimes die Luftschiffe für propagandistische Zwecke einzusetzen oder beispielsweise die Luftschiffhalle in Friedrichshafen für eine nationalsozialistische Massenveranstaltung zur Verfügung zu stellen. Die Gestapo verlangte 1933 von ihm, öffentlich eine Erklärung für Hitler abzugeben (nachdem er noch 1932 eine Rundfunkrede zu Gunsten von Reichskanzler Heinrich Brüning gehalten hatte), was er jedoch ebenso ablehnte wie eine „Zustimmungserklärung" zum Einmarsch der deutschen Truppen ins Rheinland im März 1936. Und unverhohlen war 1936 auch seine Mißbilligung der Propagandafahrten von LZ 127 und LZ 129 zu den Olympischen Spielen in Berlin. Nicht verhindern konnte er, daß ab 1934 „Graf Zeppelin" mit dem Hakenkreuz auf den Stabilisierungsflächen fahren mußte, was – ebenso wie später bei der „Hindenburg" – gelegentlich zu Mißfallensäußerugen in den USA geführt hatte. Daß Eckener später nach eigenem Bekunden, um die Luftschiffsache nicht aufs Spiel zu setzen, gelegentlich nachgeben mußte, lag allein in der Pression durch die Nationalsozialisten begründet.

Seine ablehnende Haltung gegenüber dem Naziregime hatte schließlich zur Folge, daß Hitler die Absetzung Eckeners verlangte. Diese Absicht ließ sich jedoch nicht zuletzt wegen seiner Popularität in den USA nicht durchsetzen. Der deutschen Presse und dem Rundfunk wurde aber verboten, seinen Namen weiterhin zu nennen. Der amerikanische Botschafter in Berlin, William E. Dodd, informierte sein Land regelmäßig ausführlich über diese internen Vorgänge in Deutschland, wie u.a. aus Akten des State Department in Washington[21] oder

---

[21] Z.B. Botschaftsbericht aus Berlin vom 14. 4. 1936, Akz. 862.00/3594.

aus Unterlagen der Roosevelt Library, New York[22], hervorgeht. Man kann jedenfalls davon ausgehen, daß Präsident Roosevelt genau über die Rolle Eckeners innerhalb Nazideutschlands informiert war, was schließlich auch sein betont herzliches Verhältnis zu Eckener erklärt. Die vorerwähnte Roosevelt Library enthält u. a. auch eine private Empfehlung, Eckener nach Amerika zu holen, um ihn für den eigenen Luftschiffbau zu gewinnen[23].

Die amerikanische Botschaft in Berlin empfahl, Eckener bei seiner ersten Landung mit der „Hindenburg" in Lakehurst 1936 besonders herzlich zu empfangen, was ja auch geschah und nach der Verbannung Eckeners aus den Massenmedien einer Brüskierung des Hitler-Regimes gleichkam. Alle Ehrungen, die Eckener nach der Machtübernahme Hitlers 1933 in den USA erfuhr, sind somit auch unter diesem hochpolitischen Gesichtspunkt zu sehen. Das heißt zwar nicht, daß Eckeners Leistung in den USA als reines Politikum ausgenutzt wurde, doch hatten weite Kreise Amerikas, die scharfe Kritik an Hitlers Politik übten, hier eine willkommene Gelegenheit, Hitler selbst bloßzustellen. Vor diesem Hintergrund ist dann auch die ungemein große öffentliche Anteilnahme an der Lakehurst-Katastrophe und der sich anschließenden Helium-Diskussion zu sehen.

Eine Episode, die Eckeners Wertschätzung durch Präsident Roosevelt verdeutlicht, hat F. W. von Meister wiedergegeben[24]. Während des Aufenthalts in den USA im Oktober 1933 erhielt Dr. Eckener eine Einladung vom Weißen Haus „zum Tee mit der Gattin des Präsidenten". Man war einigermaßen überrascht. Als man zum verabredeten Zeitpunkt ins Weiße Haus kam, empfing ihn der Präsident sehr herzlich und bat um Verständnis für das ungewöhnliche Arrangement, denn nur so sei es möglich gewesen, ihn allein sprechen zu können, „ohne den Nazi-Botschafter einladen zu müssen".

---

[22] Z. B. Brief an R. W. Moore vom 18. 4. 1936, Official File 523.

[23] Off. File 2275; Brief von J. Mesmer an Präs. Roosevelt, 18. 5. 1936.

[24] s. Fußnt. 12, Seite 184.

THE UNITED STATES OF AMERICA

PORT SANITARY STATEMENT,

U. S. PUBLIC HEALTH SERVICE.

Port of _PHILADELPHIA, PA_

Vessel: _Ger. Airsaip „Graf Zeppelin"_

Bound from _PHILADELPHIA, PA_ to _Friedrichshafen, Germany_

Number of cases of and deaths from the following-named diseases reported during the two weeks ending _Oct. 20_, 192_8_

DISEASES.	NUMBER OF CASES.	NUMBER OF DEATHS.	REMARKS. (Any condition affecting the public health existing in the port to be stated here, including operations in rodent examination and extermination.)
Cerebro-spinal Meningitis (epidemic)	1	1	PHILA., PA., Population
Cholera, Asiatic			No epidemic of disease,
Diphtheria	72	5	
Measles	6		
Plague			
Poliomyelitis (acute anterior) (poliomyelitis)	2		
Scarlet Fever	51		
Smallpox			
Typhoid Fever	9	1	
Typhus Fever			
Yellow Fever			
TOTALS	141	7	

Vessel last fumigated at _New Airship_ , 19

Given under my hand and seal this ____ day of _Oct._ , 192_8_

H. M. Manning
Surgeon, U. S. Public Health Service.
Sanitary Inspector

During their flights to the United States, LZ 127 "Graf Zeppelin" and LZ 129 "Hindenburg" were treated as seagoing vessels in the processing of formalities (see also p. 206).

LZ 127 „Graf Zeppelin" und LZ 129 „Hindenburg" wurden bei ihren Fahrten in die USA auch bei der Abwicklung der Formalitäten wie Seeschiffe behandelt (s. a. S. 206).

196

4.
DIE ZUKUNFT
DER LUFTSCHIFFAHRT
IST OFFEN

4.1 Der Krieg setzt ein Ende

Mit dem Ausbruch des Zweiten Weltkriegs wurden die bis zuletzt guten Beziehungen der Luftschiffer in Europa und Amerika für Jahre abgebrochen. An eine Weiterentwicklung des Luftschiffbaus war nicht zu denken. Im Frühjahr 1940 wurden LZ 127 und LZ 130 abgewrackt, die Luftschiffhallen in Frankfurt, einst stolzer Ausgangspunkt für vielfältige Kontakte und friedliche Zusammenarbeit mit Amerika, wurden gesprengt[25].

Ein alter Freund der Friedrichshafener Zeppeliner, der amerikanische Journalist Karl von Wiegand, wurde im Herbst 1940 als einer der letzten Vertreter der USA von Hitler empfangen. Von Wiegand hatte 1929 im Auftrag des Verlegers W. R. Hearst an der Weltfahrt von LZ 127 „Graf Zeppelin" teilgenommen, unterhielt seither enge persönliche Kontakte zu Dr. Eckener und vielen Luftschiffern und kannte wie kaum ein anderer ausländischer Journalist die Verhältnisse im damaligen Deutschland. Bei seinem Besuch wollte er Hitler davor warnen, nach dem Frankreichfeldzug seine Eroberungspolitik fortzusetzen, weil dies mit Sicherheit die Vereinigten Staaten zum Eingreifen in den Krieg veranlassen würde, doch Hitler schlug die Bedenken in den Wind[26].

Die Zusammenarbeit zwischen dem ehemaligen Luftschiffbau in Friedrichshafen und der Firma Goodyear war durch den Krieg zwar beendet worden, doch die freundschaftlichen Bande bestanden weiter. Nur zwei Beispiele über weiterbestehende Kontakte:

Dr. Eckener reiste bereits im Mai 1947 nach Amerika, um der Goodyear Aircraft Corporation beratend zur Seite zu stehen. Mit vielen Freunden aus besseren Tagen, wie T. G. W. Settle, traf er dabei

---

[25] Zu dieser Zeit (1939/40) wurde übrigens auch ZR 3, das 1932 aus dem Fahrbetrieb der Navy ausgeschieden war, abgewrackt. („Los Angeles" unternahm Fahrten bis zum 30. Juni 1932. Sie wurde zur Einsparung der Betriebskosten während der Wirtschaftskrise außer Dienst gestellt. Von 1934 bis 1936 diente sie noch für Ankerungsexperimente [Buckley, F.D.].)

[26] vgl. Samhaber, E.: Weltgeschichtliche Zusammenhänge. Gütersloh 1976, S. 9.

zusammen. Und im Beisein von Dr. Max Grünbeck, dem Oberbürgermeister der Stadt Friedrichshafen, wurden 1955 in der Kirche der U.S. Naval Air Station in Lakehurst von Paul W. Litchfield, dem Präsidenten der Goodyear Aircraft Corporation, drei Glasfenster übergeben, die die Geschichte der Luftfahrt darstellen und u. a. auch LZ 127 „Graf Zeppelin" zeigen.

4.2 Die Luftschiffidee ist noch lebendig

Nach dem Kriege waren es dann die modernen Flugzeuge, die einer Wiederbelebung des Luftschiffgedankens zunächst entgegenstanden. Sie waren zuverlässig, schnell und vor allem größer geworden mit Reichweiten, die sie auch für Langstreckenverkehr brauchbar machten. Trotzdem ist bis heute der Ruf nach neuen Luftschiffen nicht verstummt.

Enorm ist die Zahl der Vereine und Gruppen, die sich noch mit der Weiterentwicklung des Luftschiffs beschäftigen. Die Realisten unter ihnen wissen, daß bislang noch vieles trotz moderner technischer Möglichkeiten gegen den Neubau von Luftschiffen spricht, insbesondere gegen eine kommerzielle Verwendung. Zumindest weiß man, daß es unrealistisch ist, dort anknüpfen zu wollen, wo man vor nunmehr über 40 Jahren aufgehört hat. Daß es aber unabhängig von dieser Einschätzung sinnvoll sein kann, sich mit Luftschiffproblemen zu beschäftigen, das zeigen die Arbeiten beispielsweise des American Institute of Aeronautics and Astronautics (AIAA), das u. a. Veranstaltungen unter dem Motto „Conference on Lighter-Than-Air Technology" durchführt. Mit Fragen der Luftschiffahrt beschäftigt sich auch die Lighter-Than-Air Society, die in Akron/Ohio ihren Sitz hat. Die Gesellschaft gibt ein Mitteilungsblatt heraus, das neben eigenen Arbeiten der Mitglieder durch die Wiedergabe historischer Ereignisse und durch die Erwähnung des zahlreichen in aller Welt nach wie vor neu erscheinenden Schrifttums das Thema Luftschiff lebendig erhält. Die Zusammenarbeit mit deutschen Vereinigungen, beispielsweise der Deutschen Gesellschaft für Luft- und Raumfahrt (DGLR), wird intensiv betrieben.

Bei all diesen Arbeiten ist ein Gesichtspunkt wichtig: Das strukturelle Konzept des Zeppelin-Luftschiffs, nämlich starres Gerippe mit außen aufliegender Hülle und innenliegenden, flexiblen Traggaszellen, hatte sich zwar in den 20er und 30er Jahren bewährt und war als beste und brauchbarste Lösung akzeptiert. Diese Anerkennung führte aber wohl dazu, daß man sich bei allen weiterführenden Projekten zunächst nicht von diesem Grundkonzept lösen konnte, weshalb auch trotz vielfältiger Anstrengungen kaum eines der Projekte über das Reißbrettstadium hinausgekommen ist. Auch die in den sechziger Jahren intensiv begonnenen Arbeiten an sogenannten Hybridluftschiffen, einer Kombination aus konventionellem Luftschiff und dem Helikopterprinzip, haben sich nur wenig und selten ganz von der Fixierung auf den ehemaligen „Zeppelin" lösen können. Allerdings beginnen sich in den letzten Jahren Projekte bemerkbar zu machen, die neue Wege gehen und die vor allem die wirtschaftliche Realisierbarkeit im Auge haben. Daß es dabei – sollten größere Projekte anstehen – wieder zu deutsch-amerikanischer Zusammenarbeit kommen wird, ist nicht schwierig zu prognostizieren.

4.3 Friedrichshafen – noch heute Zeppelinstadt

Wohl keine Stadt von der Größe Friedrichshafens (rund 50 000 Einwohner) außerhalb der USA ist den Amerikanern so bekannt oder war es zumindest zur Zeit der Zeppelin-Luftschiffe. Viele kommen jedes Jahr aus Amerika, um sich im Zeppelin-Museum umzusehen, viele finden den Weg zum ehemaligen Werftgelände des Luftschiffbau Zeppelin, wo sich heute die Werksanlagen der Zeppelin-Metallwerke und der weltberühmten Zahnradfabrik Friedrichshafen (ZF) befinden, zwei bedeutende Nachfolgeunternehmen des ehemaligen Luftschiffbaus. In Gesprächen mit alten Mitarbeitern der Firmen werden da manche Erinnerungen ausgetauscht. Historiker vom anderen Kontinent finden sich ein, um das interessante Kapitel der Zeppelin-Geschichte an Ort und Stelle zu studieren und nach neuen Erkenntnissen zum besseren Verständnis der gemeinsamen deutsch-amerikanischen Zeppelin-Epoche zu suchen.

Die engen Bindungen, die zwischen dem Luftschiffbau Zeppelin und den Vereinigten Staaten vor dem Kriege bestanden, wurden 1954 erneuert. Damals übernahmen die Zeppelin-Metallwerke die Vertretung für die Caterpillar Tractor Company in der Bundesrepublik Deutschland. Als ein Ergebnis der engen geschäftlichen Beziehungen beider Firmen wurde 1976 Friedrichshafen Schwesterstadt von Peoria im US-Bundesstaat Illinois, dem Sitz der Caterpillar Tractor Company. Eine große Ausstellung über die Geschichte der Zeppelin-Luftschiffe, die von den Zeppelin-Metallwerken im Auftrag der Sister City-Kommission der Stadt Friedrichshafen in Peoria gezeigt wurde[27], hat nicht nur den Bürgern Peorias das Thema Luftschiffbau nahegebracht. Die Ausstellung fand ein weites Echo in den USA. Die Städtepartnerschaft zwischen Friedrichshafen und Peoria hat bisher zwei Ehrenbürgerschaften ergeben[28], die – verfolgt man ihre Entstehung – letztendlich auf die Zeppelin-Vergangenheit der Stadt Friedrichshafen zurückzuführen sind und das Thema „Zeppelin und die USA" weitertragen.

"Peoria Journal Star" of August 31, 1976.
„Peoria Journal Star", 31. August 1976.

---

[27] „The Zeppelin History". Ausstellung mit Bildern und Dokumenten von 1863 bis 1938 im Lakeview Center for the Arts and Sciences, Peoria, Illinois, 20. Januar bis 26. Februar 1978. Broschüre zur Ausstellung vom Autor.

[28] 1977 Dr. Max Grünbeck, Oberbürgermeister der Stadt Friedrichshafen von 1948 bis 1977 und Initiator der Partnerschaft;
1980 Willy Kaldenbach, Geschäftsführer der Luftschiffbau Zeppelin GmbH und der Zeppelin-Metallwerke GmbH.

October 15, 1928 edition of the German-language "New Yorker Staats-Zeitung", which, like many other American newspaper, devoted its entire front page to the arrival of LZ 127 "Graf Zeppelin" (also see p. 52 and pp. 56–59).

Die Ausgabe vom 15. Oktober 1928 der deutschsprachigen „New Yorker Staatszeitung", die wie viele amerikanische Zeitungen die ganze Titelseite ausschließlich der Ankunft von LZ 127 „Graf Zeppelin" widmete (s. a. S. 52 und S. 56–59).

5.
NEUERE LUFTSCHIFFLITERATUR
ZUM THEMA
„ZEPPELIN UND DIE USA"

Daß es eine innige Verzahnung zwischen dem technischen Fortschritt und der gesellschaftlichen Entwicklung gibt, ist längst bekannt. Das Kapitel über die völkerverbindende Wirkung von Zeppelin-Luftschiffen während der 20er und 30er Jahre muß aber noch geschrieben werden. In der deutschen wie in der amerikanischen Geschichte des zwanzigsten Jahrhunderts wird dieses Thema einen bedeutenden Platz einnehmen. Einige neuere Veröffentlichungen nehmen sich zwar des Themas an, doch bislang gibt es keine umfassende wissenschaftliche Untersuchung. Bekannt ist aber, daß in Irvine an der University of California Henry Cord Meyer, Professor für neuere Geschichte, an dem Thema arbeitet[29]. Von Meyer liegt auch eine vergleichende Studie der vier Zeppelin-Baustädte Friedrichshafen, Cardington, Howden und Akron und damit über die technischen und sozialpolitischen Einwirkungen des Luftschiffbaus in der modernen Industriegesellschaft als Vortragsmanuskript vor[30].

Die Biographien von R. Italiaander über Graf Zeppelin[31] und Hugo Eckener[32] schildern ausführlich die wichtigsten bekannten Begegnungen dieser beiden bedeutendsten Luftschiffer mit Amerika. Das komplexe Buch von K. Clausberg[33] widmet gleich das erste Kapitel der entscheidenden Begegnung mit den USA, der Überführung von ZR 3.

---

[29] s. Zeitschrift South Atlantic Quarterly, Winter 1979, Seite 107. Fußnote: „Henry Cord Meyer ... is studying the political manipulation of airship technology and operation in Germany, England and the United States from 1919 to 1939."

[30] Henry Cord Meyer: The social impact of an emerging technology: The rigid airship in western society, 1900–1936. Das Manuskript war Gegenstand einer Diskussion auf dem „First Annual Irvine [Cal.] Seminar on Social History and Theory" (1978). Hierzu Tonbandaufzeichnung des Kommentars von Professor Todd Laporte, Berkeley-University, bei H. C. M.

[31] Rolf Italiaander: Ferdinand Graf von Zeppelin, Reitergeneral, Diplomat, Luftschiffpionier. Konstanz 1980, Verlag Friedrich Stadler.

[32] Rolf Italiaander: Hugo Eckener, ein moderner Columbus. Konstanz 1979, Verlag Friedrich Stadler.

[33] Karl Clausberg: Zeppelin, die Geschichte eines unwahrscheinlichen Erfolges. München 1979, Schirmer/Mosel-Verlag.

Und schlägt man in Neuerscheinungen amerikanischer Verlage nach, dann wird man stets finden, daß mit Hochachtung von den deutschen Luftschiffpionieren und deren Einfluß auf den Luftschiffbau in den USA gesprochen wird, wie beispielsweise bei R. K. Smith[34] in seinem hervorragenden Werk über die US-Schiffe Akron und Macon oder bei Z. Hansen[35], der über die Geschichte der Goodyear-Luftschiffe eine ausführliche Würdigung des Zeppelin-Luftschiffbaus nicht vermissen läßt. Schließlich dürfte auch D. Bottings Time-Life-Buch[36] die Luftschiff-Ära wieder einem breiten Publikum nahebringen, wobei auch hier die deutsch-amerikanische Zusammenarbeit in den 20er und 30er Jahren ein zentrales Thema bildet.

American landing crew   *Amerikanische Bodenmannschaft*

[34] Richard K. Smith: The Airships Akron and Macon. Annapolis, Maryland (USA) 1965, United States Naval Institute.

[35] Zenon Hansen: The Goodyear Airships. Bloomington, Illinois (USA) 1977, Airship International Press.

[36] Douglas Botting (ed.): The Giant Airships. Alexandria, Virginia (USA) 1980, Time-Life Books Inc. (Anm.: Deutsche Ausgabe in Vorbereitung).

Clearance

The United States of America

DEPARTMENT OF COMMERCE
BUREAU OF NAVIGATION

CLEARANCE OF VESSEL TO A FOREIGN PORT

[Arts. 137, 151, 159, 160, 161, 162, 163, 168, 169, and 170, Customs Regulations, 1923; Section 4201, Revised Statutes]

District of _____PHILADELPHIA_____

Port of _____PHILADELPHIA_____

These are to certify all whom it doth concern:

That _____Hugo Eckener_____

Master or Commander of the _____German aircraft GRAF ZEPPELIN_____

burden _____—_____ Tons, or thereabouts, mounted with _____no_____

Guns, navigated with _____40_____ Men, _____foreign_____

_____German_____ built, and bound for _____

_____Friedrichshafen, Germany_____

with passengers and having on board _____

MERCHANDISE AND STORES,

hath here entered and cleared his said vessel, according to law.

Given under our hands and seals, at the Customhouse of _____PHILADELPHIA_____

_____, this _____15th_____ day of _____October_____

one thousand nine hundred _____twenty eight_____, and in the _____153rd_____

year of the Independence of the United States of America.

_____
11—4804
Comptroller of Customs.
DEPUTY COMPTROLLER

_____
Acting DEPUTY Collector of Customs.

6.
ZEITTAFEL

1863   Graf Zeppelin geht in die USA und nimmt als Beobachter am Sezessionskrieg teil.

      Audienz bei Präsident Lincoln.

      Begegnung mit Carl Schurz.

      Teilnahme an Ballonaufstieg bei St. Paul, Minnesota.

      Teilnahme an Expedition Quellgebiet des Mississippi.

1873   Heinrich von Stephan (Gründer des Weltpostvereins, 1874) veröffentlicht Schrift zum Thema „Weltpost und Luftschifffahrt".

1874   Erste Eintragung über ein Ballonfahrzeug in Graf Zeppelins Tagebuch.

1895   Tagebucheintragung des Grafen Zeppelin über Pläne, mit Luftschiffen Passagiere, Post und Fracht nach New York zu transportieren.

      Erteilung des Patents für einen „lenkbaren Luftfahrzug" an Graf Zeppelin.

1900   Erster Aufstieg eines Zeppelin-Luftschiffs.

1908   LZ 4 geht nach Dauerfahrt verloren; Spende des deutschen Volkes; Beginn des Aufstiegs des Zeppelin-Konzerns. Zahlreiche Ehrungen des Grafen Zeppelin in den USA.

1917   Das deutsche Marineluftschiff L 49 (LZ 96) fällt den Alliierten Streitkräften fast unbeschädigt in die Hände. Es wird in allen Details vermessen und dient später in den USA als wesentliche Vorlage für den Bau von ZR 1 „Shenandoah".

1919   Das britische Luftschiff R 34 überquert den Atlantik in beiden Richtungen.

      In Friedrichshafen versucht William S. Hensley LZ 124 zu bauen; das Projekt scheitert am Versailler Vertrag.

1920   Dr. Eckener verhandelt mit den USA wegen des Baus eines Zeppelin-Luftschiffs als Reparationsleistung.

1921 R 38 (ZR 2) stürzt bei Versuchsfahrt ab; 16 Amerikaner kommen ums Leben.

1922 Vertrag zwischen dem Luftschiffbau Zeppelin und der US-Navy über die Lieferung eines Zivilluftschiffes (LZ 126 = ZR 3).

1923 ZR 1 „Shenandoah" wird in Dienst gestellt.

Gründung der Goodyear-Zeppelin-Corporation; gegenseitige Nutzung aller Patente vereinbart.

1924 LZ 126 wird in die USA überführt. Als ZR 3 „Los Angeles" bis 1932 (1936) als Versuchsschiff in Betrieb.

1925 Shenandoah-Unglück; C. E. Rosendahl kann eine Hälfte des Schiffes notlanden und einen Teil der Besatzung retten.

Beginn der Helium-Debatten im amerikanischen Kongreß.

1928 Erste Fahrt von LZ 127 „Graf Zeppelin" nach Lakehurst, New Jersey.

1929 Weltfahrt des LZ 127, im wesentlichen vom amerikanischen Zeitungsverleger Hearst finanziert; offizieller Start in Lakehurst; Route führt über Friedrichshafen, Tokio, Los Angeles zurück nach Lakehurst, weiter nach Friedrichshafen.

Verhandlungen Dr. Eckeners in den USA über die Lieferung von Helium; Versuche zur Bildung einer deutsch-amerikanischen Luftschiffahrtsgesellschaft.

1931 ZRS-4 „Akron" wird in Dienst gestellt.

Forschungsfahrt von LZ 127 in die Arktis, an der neben drei russischen und einem schwedischen auch zwei amerikanische Wissenschaftler teilnehmen.

1933 ZRS-4 „Akron" stürzt ab; 3 Überlebende von deutschem Schiff geborgen.

ZRS-5 „Macon" in Dienst gestellt.

LZ 127 besucht Miami, Akron und Chicago.

1935 ZRS-5 „Macon" geht verloren.

Umfangreiches Abkommen zwischen der US-Navy und der deutschen Zeppelin-Reederei über Nutzung der Einrichtungen in Lakehurst, N. J., und Opa-Locka, Florida, durch LZ 129.

1936 LZ 129 „Hindenburg" nimmt regelmäßigen Passagierdienst nach Lakehurst, N. J., auf.

1937 LZ 129 verbrennt bei Landemanöver in Lakehurst; Ende der Passagierluftschiffahrt.

Positive Empfehlung der sogenannten Heliumkommission unter Innenminister H. L. Ickes an Präsident Roosevelt, Helium an Deutschland zu liefern; erste Heliumlieferungen Ende des Jahres.

1938 Gesetz vom 14. März stoppt Heliumlieferungen an Deutschland.

1940 ZR 3 „Los Angeles" in den USA, LZ 127 und LZ 130 in Deutschland werden abgewrackt.

1954 Die Zeppelin-Metallwerke, Nachfolgebetrieb des Luftschiffbau Zeppelin, übernehmen die Vertretung für die Produkte der amerikanischen Firma „Caterpillar" in der Bundesrepublik Deutschland.

1976 Friedrichshafen wird Schwesterstadt von Peoria/Illinois, USA.

Aus Anlaß des 200. Unabhängigkeitstages Ausstellung in Friedrichshafen zum Thema „Zeppelin und die USA".

1978 Ausstellung in Peoria, Ill., zum Thema „The Zeppelin History".

7.
ANHANG

7.1 Auszüge aus den Verträgen
zum Bau von ZR 3 (LZ 126) vom 26. Juni 1922
zwischen dem Luftschiffbau Zeppelin, Friedrichshafen,
und dem Navy Department, United States Navy.

Vertrag B:

... Der Luftschiffbau Zeppelin wird ein starres Luftschiff in der Weise und auf Grund der Bedingungen, welche in folgendem dargelegt sind, erbauen und wird dieses Luftschiff in jeder Hinsicht vollständig und in zufriedenstellendem Zustand an die Marineluftschiffstation *Lakehurst*, New Jersey, Vereinigte Staaten, abliefern.

Die Bezeichnung „vollständiges Luftschiff", wie sie in diesem Vertrag gebraucht wird, soll ein vollständiges Luftschiff bedeuten in Übereinstimmung mit den vom Navy Department genehmigten Baubeschreibungen und in jeder Hinsicht fahrbereit, einschließlich Maschinengondeln, Führergondel, Passagiergondel mit Küche und Speiseraum-Ausstattung, aller notwendigen und üblichen Navigationsinstrumente, F.-T.-Anlage, Maschinen-Ausrüstung, einschließlich solcher Werkzeuge und Reserveteile, welche üblicherweise auf Fahrten mitgeführt werden.

Das Schiff soll ein Zivilluftschiff sein und eine Einrichtung zur Beförderung von etwa 20 Passagieren außer der eigentlichen Besatzung enthalten. Die Hauptabmessungen und Leistungen des Schiffes sollen ungefähr folgende sein:

Länge		200 Meter
Größter Durchmesser		28 Meter
Höhe		32 Meter
Rechnungsmäßiges Gas-Fassungsvermögen		70,000 m^3
Gesamt-Auftrieb	mit Wasserstoff bei 760 mm Luftdruck	
		81,850 kg
Leergewicht	0° C Temp.; 0,1 spez. Gasgewicht;	
	60 % rel. Luftfeuchtigkeit	41,850 kg

Nutzlast   40,000 kg

Mindestgeschwindigkeit in jedem Fall 70 amerikanische Meilen
(statue miles) (112,6 km) pro Stunde durch ruhige Luft in einer Höhe
von 1000 Metern.

Maschinenleistung   2000–2250 rechnungsmäßige PS
zu leisten durch Luftschiffmotoren des besten erhältlichen Typs. Das
Luftschiff soll nach Form, Konstruktion und Material vom modern-
sten Typ sein, wie die L 70 und Nordstern-Klassen, insoweit abgeän-
dert, so es nötig oder wünschenswert befunden wird infolge von
Verbesserungen seit der Fertigstellung dieser Klassen, so daß das
Luftschiff die neuesten Gedanken und Erfahrungen im Luftschiffbau
verkörpern soll. Es soll so entworfen werden, daß es reichlich stark für
seinen Zweck ist, aber gleichzeitig soll alles unnötige Gewicht vermieden werden. Es soll gute Manövriereigenschaften in der Luft unter
verschiedenen Belastungszuständen haben. Die Ausrüstung und Einrichtungen im ganzen Luftschiff sollen so entworfen und ausgeführt
werden, daß ein Maximum an Gefahrlosigkeit hinsichtlich der Verwendung von Wasserstoffgas und der bei Luftschiffmotoren üblichen
Brennstoffe erreicht wird. Besondere Vorkehrungen sollen getroffen
werden, um die Feuergefahr in jeder Hinsicht zu entfernen. Besondere
Verstärkungen sollen im Bug des Schiffes eingebaut und Anschlüsse
vorgesehen werden, welche ein Festmachen des Schiffes an einen
Ankermast gestatten. . . .

. . . Alle Vertragsparteien verpflichten sich, pflichtschuldigen Eifer
beim Bau dieses Schiffes anzuwenden, damit seine Ablieferung an die
Vereinigten Staaten zum frühesten erreichbaren Zeitpunkt stattfinden
kann. Es ist geschätzt, daß der Bau des Schiffes in 15 Monaten
fertiggestellt sein kann, wenn nicht unvorhergesehene Schwierigkeiten
auftreten.

Das Navy Department wird während des Baues des Luftschiffes auf
der Bauwerft einen Inspektor für Marine-Luftfahrzeuge stationieren,
welcher das Navy Department vertreten und die Vermittlungsstelle
zwischen diesem und dem Luftschiffbau Zeppelin bilden soll. Der
Inspektor kann sich bei etwaiger Abwesenheit ohne Rücksicht auf den
Grund seiner Abwesenheit durch einen von ihm zu bezeichnenden
Assistenten vertreten lassen, welcher dieselben Rechte haben soll wie

der Inspektor selbst. Der Luftschiffbau Zeppelin wird für den Inspektor und seine Assistenten Bureau-Räumlichkeiten (drei Räume) und alle erforderlichen Erleichterungen beschaffen, er hat jedoch nicht für die persönlichen Ausgaben des Inspektors oder seines Stabes aufzukommen. Der Inspektor und seine Assistenten sollen während der Arbeitsstunden zu allen Stellen, wo das Luftschiff und die Motoren hergestellt werden, Zutritt haben zwecks Überwachung des Baues dieses Luftschiffes und seiner Teile. Ferner sollen sie Zutritt haben zu den Stellen, wo die Ausrüstung und andere Teile hergestellt werden, soweit es in der Macht des Luftschiffbau Zeppelin liegt, ihnen den Zutritt zu verschaffen. Der Inspektor soll Kenntnis erhalten über die Art des Materials und über die Firmen, bei welchen der Luftschiffbau Zeppelin Material oder Ausrüstungsteile für dieses Luftschiff bestellt. Das Kontrollsystem des Luftschiffbau Zeppelin soll sich auf die Prüfung aller Materialien, Herstellungsverfahren und Fertig-Arbeiten erstrecken . . .

. . . Der Luftschiffbau Zeppelin soll durch zureichende Probefahrten in Deutschland die Lufttüchtigkeit und Betriebssicherheit des Schiffes feststellen, bevor die Überführung nach den Vereinigten Staaten in Betracht gezogen wird. Das Navy Department soll das Recht haben, eine beschränkte Anzahl von Personal zur Beobachtung des richtigen Arbeitens, der Lufttüchtigkeit und Betriebssicherheit des Schiffes während der Probefahrten und der Überführung des Schiffes zu bezeichnen. Der Luftschiffbau Zeppelin erklärt sich bereit, das vollständige Luftschiff zusammen mit den üblichen zum Schiff gehörenden Reserveteilen in zufriedenstellendem Zustand in der Marine-Luftschiffstation Lakehurst, New Jersey, Vereinigte Staaten, abzuliefern.

Ablieferung des Luftschiffes soll bedeuten, daß das Luftschiff gelandet und in die Hände des Landungstrupps gelangt ist. Von diesem Zeitpunkt an ist das Luftschiff in der Obhut des Navy Department und dieses übernimmt von diesem Zeitpunkt ab die Verantwortung für Verlust oder Beschädigung des Schiffes, ausgenommen, wenn solcher Schaden oder Verlust nachweislich auf Nachlässigkeit oder Verschulden des Personals des Luftschiffbau Zeppelin zurückzuführen ist. Sobald als angängig, soll nach erfolgter Landung das Navy Department dem Luftschiffbau Zeppelin einen Verwahrungsschein für das Luftschiff aushändigen. Das Navy Department erklärt sich bereit, die Überführung des Luftschiffes nach Lakehurst in jeder vernunftmäßigen Weise zu erleichtern und eine Landungsmannschaft dort bereitzustellen. Falls die Ablieferung des Luftschiffes in Lakehurst infolge von unvorhergesehenen Umständen nicht ratsam oder unausführbar erscheinen sollte, so kann das Navy Department irgend einen anderen Ort innerhalb eines Radius von 250 amerikanischen Meilen von Lakehurst bezeichnen. Dort wird das Navy Department die nötigen Vorkehrungen treffen. Es wird hierdurch vereinbart, daß, sobald das Navy Department diesen Ort bezeichnet, das Luftschiff durch den Luftschiffbau Zeppelin dorthin abgeliefert werden muß...

... Der Luftschiffbau Zeppelin übernimmt hiermit die volle Haftung für das Luftschiff gegen jegliche Gefahr bis zum Zeitpunkt seiner Ablieferung an das Navy Department. Im Falle von Beschädigungen wird der Luftschiffbau Zeppelin angemessene Reparaturen vornehmen. Im Falle des Totalverlustes oder Havarie bis zur Reparaturunfähigkeit hat der Luftschiffbau Zeppelin der deutschen Regierung die empfangenen Geldbeträge zurückzuerstatten und die Regierung der Vereinigten Staaten kann dann ihrerseits von der deutschen Regierung die Zahlung von 3 031 665 Goldmark entsprechend dem Vertrag zwischen der deutschen Regierung und der amerikanischen Regierung vom 26. Juni 1922 verlangen...

... Der Luftschiffbau Zeppelin gibt eine allgemeine Garantie für einen Zeitraum von 6 Monaten, gerechnet vom Tage der formellen Übernahme des Luftschiffes durch die Vereinigten Staaten, für die sachgemäße Konstruktion, Güte der Arbeitsausführung und des Materials und das richtige Arbeiten aller Teile und Zubehör des Luftschiffes. Alle Schäden, welche sich innerhalb dieses Zeitraumes herausstellen und welche auf unsachgemäße Konstruktionen, schlechte Arbeitsausführung oder schlechtes Material zurückzuführen sind, müssen vom Luftschiffbau Zeppelin auf seine Kosten beseitigt werden. Eine unparteiische Untersuchung wird feststellen, ob der Luftschiffbau Zeppelin für irgendwelche Schäden, die sich während dieser Periode herausstellen, verantwortlich ist.

Die Regierung der Vereinigten Staaten, vertreten durch das Navy Department, wird einen Sondervertrag mit dem Luftschiffbau Zeppelin abschließen, wodurch dieser ein fachmäßiges Personal, wie erforderlich, in den Vereinigten Staaten während wenigstens der Hälfte der früher erwähnten Garantie-Periode behalten wird . . .

. . . Die Regierung der Vereinigten Staaten verplichtet sich, den Luftschiffbau Zeppelin schadlos zu halten gegenüber allen Ansprüchen aus Patenten, die in den Vereinigten Staaten erteilt sind und durch den Bau und die Ablieferung dieses Luftschiffes verletzt werden. Patente oder Schutzmuster, die von der deutschen Regierung erteilt sind, werden ausdrücklich ausgenommen . . .

. . . Die Regierung der Vereinigten Staaten übernimmt die Verantwortung für die Bezahlung aller Einfuhrzölle in den Vereinigten Staaten für das Luftschiff sowie für alle seine Teile oder Ersatzteile.

Wenn der Luftschiffbau Zeppelin eine der Bestimmungen dieses Vertrages nicht erfüllt, so ist für die Regierung der Vereinigten Staaten genügender Anlaß gegeben, die deutsche Regierung auf Grund des Abkommens vom 26. Juni 1922 aufzufordern, die nötigen Schritte zu tun, um die Erfüllung der Vertragsbestimmungen durch den Luftschiffbau Zeppelin sicherzustellen. Ist die deutsche Regierung nicht in der Lage, die Erfüllung des Vertrages sicherzustellen, so kann die Regierung der Vereinigten Staaten der deutschen Regierung erklären, daß die Bauausführung des Luftschiffes für sie unannehmbar ist, und kann auf Grund des Protokolls vom 30. Juni 1921 von der deutschen Regierung Zahlung von 3 031 665 Goldmark anstelle des oben beschriebenen Luftschiffes fordern . . .

· Luftschiffbau Zeppelin
Gesellschaft mit beschränkter Haftung
gez. Dr. Hugo Eckener
ppa. Ernst A. Lehmann
Navy Department by L. S.
gez. J. B. Upham
W. P. Beehler

gezeichnet, gesiegelt
und ausgeführt in
Gegenwart von
gez.:
Lansdowne,
Garland Fulton.

Vertrag C:

... Um die unterweisende Vorführung zu gewährleisten, stellt der Luftschiffbau Zeppelin eine erfahrene Besatzung zur Verfügung. Die unterweisende Vorführung soll die beste sein, die der Luftschiffbau Zeppelin zu gewährleisten in der Lage ist mit dem Ziele, das vom Navy Department bezeichnete Personal in den Stand zu setzen, dieses Luftschiff in sicherster und wirksamster Weise zu führen und zu unterhalten und zwar in möglichst kurzer Zeit nach Übernahme des Schiffes durch das Navy Department. Die Dauer dieser unterweisenden Vorführung soll wenigstens teilweise mit der vom Luftschiffbau Zeppelin in Paragraph 21 des am 26. Juni 1922 zwischen dem Navy Department und dem Luftschiffbau Zeppelin geschlossenen Vertrages übernommen Garantie von 6 Monaten zusammenfallen. Die Ausbildung und Vorführung sollen das weitere Ziel haben, zu beweisen, daß dieses Luftschiff und demzufolge auch ähnliche Luftschiffe, in sicherster und wirksamster Weise geführt werden können. Um die Sicherheit des Luftschiffes zu gewährleisten, soll der Luftschiffbau Zeppelin das folgende Civil-Personal stellen:

Einen (1) Führer,

Drei (3) Steuerleute (mit Befähigung zum Steuern eines Luftschiffes),

Fünf (5) Monteure,

Einen (1) F.-T.-Mann

... Den Angehörigen der Luftschiffbau-Zeppelin-Vorführungsbesatzung wird die gleiche Stellung eingeräumt wie sie Civilisten gleichwertiger Art im Dienste des Navy Department gewährt wird ...

... Die Verantwortlichkeit für das Luftschiff und seine Kontrolle hat das Personal des Navy Department.

Die Dauer dieser unterweisenden Vorführung soll drei (3) Monate betragen bei schätzungsweise wenigstens dreihundert (300) Fahrtstunden und dreißig (30) Fahrten. Die Regierung der Vereinigten Staaten entschädigt den Luftschiffbau Zeppelin für diese Dienste in folgender Weise: Das Navy Department zahlt dem Luftschiffbau Zeppelin je Dollar 50,000.00 am Ende jeden Monats für einen Zeitraum von drei

(3) Monaten. Die Gesamtsumme von $ 150,000.00 soll die volle Entschädigung für alle Leistungen und Auslagen des Luftschiffbau Zeppelin darstellen. Alle vorgenannten Zahlungen erfolgen in Dollars in den Vereinigten Staaten zu Händen eines ordnungsmäßig bevollmächtigten Vertreters des Luftschiffbau Zeppelin. Das Navy Department hat das Recht, die Vorführungszeit monatweise um drei (3) weitere Monate zu verlängern, wenn es ihr erforderlich erscheint. Die Dauer der Verlängerung, wenn eine solche überhaupt nötig erscheint, wird vom Navy Department bestimmt und zu gegebener Zeit soll nötigenfalls ein Abkommen zwischen dem Navy Department und dem Luftschiffbau Zeppelin getroffen werden, worin die Summe von $ 10,000.00 als Vergütung für jeden weiteren Monat der Verlängerung festgesetzt werden soll . . .

(gezeichnet wie Vertrag B)

ZR 3 after landing in Lakehurst October 15, 1924.
ZR 3 nach der Landung in Lakehurst am 15. Oktober 1924.

7.2 Abkommen zwischen der Luftschiffbau Zeppelin GmbH und der Goodyear Tire and Rubber Company vom 19. September 1923

Abkommen.
-.-.-.-.-.-.-.-.

Folgendes Abkommen wurde geschlossen am 19. Sept.1923

zwischen Luftschiffbau Zeppelin G.m.b.H. Friedrichshafen,
Deutschland (im folgenden "Zeppelin" genannt) 1.Vertragspartei

und Goodyear Tire & Rubber Company, eine Ohio-
Gesellschaft, Akron,Ohio .... (im folgenden "Goodyear"
genannt), 2.Vertragspartei.

-.-.-.-

nachdem Zeppelin die Entwicklung und Herstellung von
Starrluftschiffen des weiterhin als Zeppelin-Luftschiffe be-
kannten Typs betrieben und ... ungehabt hat, die Herstellung und den
Verkauf solcher Luftschiffe in ... schliesslich amerikanischen
Gebieten (wie später definiert) ... zu fördern,

und nachdem sowohl Goodyear, wie Zeppelin den Bau und
den Verkauf solcher Schiffe im besagten amerikanischen Gebiet zu
fördern wünschen, kommen die Parteien wie folgt überein :

§ I.

Das ausschliesslich amerikanische Gebiet soll bedeuten
und einschliessen: die Vereinigten Staaten von Amerika, ihre
Territorial- & Inselbesitzungen, ..., Mittelamerika, Panama
und alle westindischen Inseln ... der Besitzungen und
... des ...

II.

Goodyear ... Verzug unter den Gesetzen eines Staates
der Vereinigten Staaten von Amerika nach ihrer Wahl eine Gesellschaft bilden (im folgenden als "Gesellschaft" genannt), mit dem
Namen "Goodyear-Zeppelin-Gesellschaft", oder einem anderen nach
Bestimmung von Goodyear, welcher jedoch die Namen sowohl von Goodyear,
als auch Zeppelin enthalten muss. Diese Gesellschaft soll
zur Vornahme folgender Geschäftshandlungen berechtigt sein :
Herstellung, Verkauf & Betrieb von Luftschiffen und Luftfahrzeugen

jeder Art und anderen verwandten oder sich ergebenden Geschäften
und Betätigungen nach näherer Bestimmung durch Goodyear. Die
Gesellschaft soll bis auf Weiteres nur zur Ausgabe von nominellen Stammanteilen berechtigt sein, welche aus 3o ooo Anteilen
bestehen, welche als voll bezahlt und nicht kündbar gelten
sollen und von welchen Goodyear 2oooo Anteile und Zeppelin
1oooo Anteile erhalten soll. Die ausschliesslichen Stimmrechte
der Gesellschaft sollen in solchen nominellen Stammanteilen
ruhen und keine weiteren Anteile sollen ausgegeben werden ohne
die Zustimmung von nicht weniger als 95 % der Anteile.

§ III.

Die Gesellschaft soll 9 Direktoren haben, von welchen
6 von Goodyear und 3 von Zeppelin aufgestellt werden.

Die Gesellschaft soll einen Präsidenten u./oder Vorsitzenden des Aufsichtsrates, einen Vizepräsidenten, allgemeinen
Geschäftsführer, einen Schriftführer und Schatzmeister, diese
von Goodyear aufzustellen und einen Vizepräsidenten und technischen Geschäftsführer, von Zeppelin aufzustellen, haben.

Goodyear und Zeppelin kommen überein, dass sie in Zukunft
Aufsichtsräte und Direktoren wie oben ernennen werden und dass
im Falle einer Vergrösserung des Aufsichtsrats die Mitglieder
desselben aufgestellt und gewählt werden sollen, im Verhältnis
von 6 von Goodyear und 3 von Zeppelin.

§ IV.

Die Vertragsparteien werden nach Bildung der Gesellschaft
für dieselbe einen technischen und allgemeinen Stab in den
Vereinigten Staaten organisieren, zur Ausführung von vorläu-
figen Vorbereitungsarbeiten, Entwürfe, Kostenanschläge und
Projekte für den Bau und Verkauf von Zeppelin-Luftschiffen,
derart, dass endgültige Bestellungen und Verträge für solche
Schiffe gefördert und zum frühestmöglichen Zeitpunkt gesichert

./.

werden. Zu diesem Zweck stellt Zeppelin der Gesellschaft solche
geeigneten und erfahrenen Sachverständigen zur Verfügung,wie
sie nötig sein werden, um diese Vorbereitungsarbeit fortlaufend
durchzuführen, bis endgültige Verträge von der Amerikanischen
Regierung oder anderen ernsthaften Interessenten gesichert sind.
Der eben erwähnte Zeitraum für solche Arbeiten ist im Folgenden
"die Vorbereitungsperiode" genannt.

§ V.

Goodyear verpflichtet sich, der Gesellschaft (als Anzahlung
für sämtliche Stammanteile oder in anderer Weise nach Wahl von
Goodyear), die notwendigen Mittel zu liefern für alle Ausgaben
derselben während der Vorbereitungsperiode, eingeschlossen
Gehälter und Reiseausgaben der oben erwähnten Sachverständigen,
und Goodyear soll ferner der besagten Gesellschaft (zu lassen
von Goodyear) die erforderlichen Arbeitsmöglichkeiten und weiteres Personal stellen, um die Gesellschaft instand zu setzen,
ihre Vorbereitungsarbeiten in angemessenem Umfange durchzuführen. Ferner soll die Gesellschaft während der Vorbereitungsperiode vermittels ihrer juristischen Sachverständigen zusammen-
arbeiten mit einem von Zeppelin zu stellenden Sachverständigen,
um alle Erfindungen, Vorrichtungen, Methoden, Verfahren und
Verbesserungen auf dem Gebiet des Baues und Betriebs von Luftschiffen (ausgenommen den Motor) welche bisher von Zeppelin
oder irgendwelchen Tochter- oder verwandten Gesellschaften
benutzt wurden, soweit als möglich durch Patente in den Vereinigten Staaten sicher zu stellen. Diese Arbeit soll beschleu-
nigt durchgeführt werden und die Kosten derselben sollen als
Teil der Ausgaben für die Vorbereitungsperiode bezahlt werden.

§ VI.

Wenn und sobald die Gesellschaft ihre Arbeiten soweit gefördert hat, dass entweder die Regierung der Vereinigten Staaten

./.

oder irgendwelche anderen ernsthaften amerikanischen Interessen-
tenbereit sind, einen endgültigen Vertrag für den Bau von einem
oder mehreren Luftschiffen abzuschliessen, dann soll die vorerwähnte Vorbereitungsperiode als beendigt gelten und die Vertragsparteien sollen wie folgt verfahren :

1.) Zeppelin soll daraufhin ohne Verzug:

a) der Gesellschaft (in einer von Goodyear's Beratern gut-
geheissenen Form) ohne Lizenzabgaben das Recht zum Bau und
Verkauf von Zeppelin-Luftschiffen jeder Art übertragen, oder
Uebertragung veranlassen,

b) eine vollständige Lizenz oder Lizenzen für jegliche
Patente und Patentanmeldungen erteilen, oder die Erteilung
veranlassen, welche sich beziehen auf den Bau und Betrieb
von Luftschiffen (ausgenommen den Motor) und welche jetzt
oder später im Besitz von Zeppelin oder irgendwelcher Toch-
ter- oder nahestehenden Gesellschaften sind, oder an welche
sie Rechte haben, einschliesslich besonders und ohne Ein-
schränkung alle derartigen Patente in den Vereinigten
Staaten von Amerika,

c) der Gesellschaft uneingeschränkt mitteilen oder Mitteilung veranlassen von allen Erfindungen, Verbesserungen,
Geheimverfahren und Arbeitsweisen, welche vor oder nach die-
dem Zeitpunkt angewendet, oder im Besitz von Zeppelin oder
irgendwelcher Tochter- oder nahestehenden Gesellschaft sich
befinden, ferner ihre Erfahrungen in Verbindung mit dem
Bau und Betrieb von Luftschiffen (ausgenommen Bau von Motor),

d) der Gesellschaft auf deren Kosten das erforderliche
sachverständige und erfahrene Personal zur Verfügung zu
stellen, welches imstande ist, mit Erfolg die Arbeiten des
Entwurfs, Kostenanschlags und der Leitung des Baues und Betriebs von Luftschiffen und deren wesentlichen Teilen,

./.

(mit alleiniger Ausnahme des Motors) durchzuführen,

  e) der Gesellschaft zu angemessenem Preis solche Sonder-
werkzeuge, Vorrichtungen, Hilfsmittel, Teile und Ausrü-
stungsgegenstände zu liefern, welche Zeppelin zu liefern
imstande ist, mit dem Vorbehalt, dass die Gesellschaft sich
solche nach ihrer Wahl auch anderweitig beschaffen kann.

2.) Goodyear soll daraufhin umgehend :

  a) der Gesellschaft alle ihre bis dahin unausgeführten,
die Luftfahrt betreffenden Aufträge und Geschäfte übertragen
ferner ihre bestehende aeronautische Luftfahr+Organisation
und Personal und ihre Luftschiffwerft in Wingfoot-Lake,Ohio,
einschliesslich der Halle, alle zugehörigen Gebäude samt
Inhalt und Ausrüstung und soviel von Goodyears Grundeigen-
tum in Wingfoot-Lake, als erforderlich sein wird, für den
Betrieb der besagten Luftschiffwerft und deren angemessene
Erweiterung; es sollen jedoch Goodyear vorbehalten bleiben
alle Wasserrechte, Wegerechte und deren Kontrolle, welche
z.Zt. wesentlich für die anderen Goodyear-Betriebe in der
Stadt Akron sind,

  b) die bestehende Halle in Wingfoot-Lake bis zu der mög-
lichen Grösse umbauen, oder den Umbau veranlassen und die
nötigen Hilfsmittel für den Bau solcher Luftschiffe beschaffen, welche zweckmässigerweise in dieser Halle gebaut
werden können,

  c) der Gesellschaft in der Form eines gewöhnlichen Dar-
lehens zum üblichen Zinssatz solche weiteren Geldbeträge
zur Verfügung stellen, welche die Gesellschaft als Betriebs-
kapital benötigt, zum Bau von solchen Schiffen, welche in
der vorhandenen oder umgebauten Halle in Wingfoot-Lake gebaut werden können.

.￼/.

6

§ VII.

Die Rechte und Lizenzen, welche Zeppelin erteilen soll, oder deren Erteilung an die Gesellschaft Zeppelin veranlassen soll, im Verfolg von § VI dieses Abkommens, sollen ausschliesslich Rechte für die Gesellschaft sein , soweit sie sich auf Bau und Verkauf in dem ausschliesslich amerikanischen Gebiet und auf Bau und Verkauf zum Gebrauch in dem erwähnten ausschliesslich amerikanischen Gebiet beziehen. Im Uebrigen sollen solche Rechte und Lizenzen als nicht ausschliesslich gelten, wie später definiert, und ferner soll das Recht und die Lizenz zum Fahrbetrieb mit Luftschiffen in dem ausschliesslich amerikanischen Gebiet nicht als ausschliesslich für die Gesellschaft gelten.

Der Abschluss von Vereinbarungen, ähnlich denen dieses Vertrags zwischen Zeppelin und britischen Jnteressenten ist in Aussicht genommen, wonach solchen britischen Jnteressenten das gesamte Britische Reich mit Ausnahme von Canada als ausschliesslich britisches Gebiet zugesprochen werden soll. Die Gesellschaft und die erwähnten britischen Jnteressenten sollen jeder ein nicht ausschliessliches Recht zum Bau und Verkauf zum Gebrauch in Canada haben, aber keine weiteren Rechte oder Lizenzen für Canada sollen von Zeppelin an irgendwelche weiteren Jnteressenten vergeben werden. Die Gesellschaft verpflichtet sich für den Fall, dass solche Abkommen abgeschlossen werden, dass sie für sich selbst auf den Bau und Verkauf von Luftschiffen oder deren Verkauf zum Gebrauch innerhalb des ausschliesslichen britischen Gebietes zu verzichten und soweit dies gesetzlich möglich, dahingehend Beschränkungen den Käufern ihrer Luftschiffe aufzuerlegen. Beim Abschluss jeglicher Vereinbarungen zwischen Zeppelin und besagten britischen Jnteressenten unternimmt Zeppelin das in solchen Vereinbarungen ein auf Gegenseitigkeit beruhendes Abkommen von Seiten der britischen Jnteressenten eingeschlossen wird, welches besagt, dass solche

./.

britischen Jnteressenten auf den Bau und Verkauf von Luftschiffen
oder deren Verkauf zum Betrieb in dem ausschliesslich amerikanischen Gebiet verzichten und dass die britischen Jnteressenten,
soweit gesetzlich zulässig, entsprechende Beschränkungen den
Käufern ihrer Schiffe auferlegen. Andere Gebiete als das ausschliesslich amerikanische Gebiet und das ausschliesslich britische Gebiet (wenn Abkommen darüber, wie oben erwähnt, abgeschlossen wird) und Canada sollen als Gebiete gelten, innerhalb
deren die Gesellschaft und besagte britische Jnteressenten ihre
Rechte und Lizenzen auf einer nicht ausschliesslichen Basis aus-
nützen können, mit der Ausnahme, dass solche nicht ausschliesslichen Rechte und Lizenzen in Frankreich, Spanien und Jtalien
nicht das Recht einschliessen zur Errichtung von Bauwerften zur
Herstellung von Luftschiffen innerhalb der genannten Länder.
Zeppelin soll das Recht haben, weitere ausschliessliche Abkommen, ähnlich dem vorliegenden Vertrag abzuschliessenm, mit Be-
zug auf andere Länder als die ausschliesslichen amerikanischen
und britischen Gebiete und Canada und wenn solche ausschliesslichen Abkommen abgeschlossen werden, sollen die nicht ausschliesslichen Rechte der Gesellschaft und der besagten britischen Jnteressenten in den betreffenden Ländern erlöschen: Voraussetzung ist dabei, dass beim Abschluss weitere Abkommen
(seien sie ausschliesslich, oder nicht ausschliesslich) Zeppelin
dafür Sorge trägt, durch die Bedingung solcher Abkommen die Rechte der Gesellschaft in dem ausschliesslichen amerikanischen
Gebiet weitgehend zu schützen und deren Anerkennung zu bewirken:
und ferner dass solche Abkommen vorsehen, dass das Recht, Luftschiffe zum internationalen Gebrauch zu verkaufen, stets für alle
Lizenznehmer als Zeppelin als nicht ausschliesslich aufrecht erhalten bleibt.

     Die Lizenzen und Rechte, welche der Gesellschaft nach
diesem Vertrage zu erteilen, oder von ihr zu erwerben sind,

.∕.

sollen nicht teilbar und nicht übertragbar durch Willensäusserung
oder Gesetzesakt sein, ohne dass zuvor die schriftliche Ein-
willigung von Zeppelin eingeholt und erteilt ist.

Alle Entwürfe, Zeichnungen und Jnformationen, welche
Zeppelin an Goodyear oder die Gesellschaft übermittelt, sollen
geheim sein und Goodyear und die Gesellschaft werden nach besten
Kräften dafür sorgen, solche Jnformationen geheim zu halten und
nur ihren betreffenden notwendigen Angestellten und Personal
zugänglich machen, ausgenommen die Uebermittlung solcher Angaben
welche zum Verkauf von Luftschiffen unvermeidlich ist.

§ VIII.

Sobald ein endgültiger Vertrag für den Bau eines Zeppelin-
Luftschiffes von grösserem Typ als in der Wingfoot-Halle her-
stellbar, vorliegt, dann soll Goodyear die bestmöglichen Anstrengungen machen zur Finanzierung der Gesellschaft, entweder
durch Verkauf von Sicherheiten der Gesellschaft, oder in anderer
Weise, in dem Umfang, wie es notwendig ist zur Errichtung einer
modernen Halle und angemessener Hilfsmittel, alle ausreichend
für den sachgemässen Bau von Luftschiffen bis zur Grösse von

Cubikfuss. Es ist jedoch vereinbart, dass Goodyear,
kraft ihrer Stimmenmehrheit in der Gesellschaft die Bedürfnisse
der Gesellschaft finanzieren darf auf dem Wege des Verkaufs
von Sicherheiten der Gesellschaft in einem Betrag bis zu,
jedoch nicht mehr als 2'000'000.-Dollars. Jegliche Finanzierung über den Betrag von 2'000'000.- Dollars darf nur vor-
genommen werden mit Genehmigung von nicht weniger als 95 % der
ausgegebenen Stammanteile.

Es wird ferner vereinbart, dass alle zum Verkauf gestellten Sicherheiten der Gesellschaft, einschliesslich sowohl
die oben erwähnten 2'000'000 Dollars, als auch jeglichen Betrages,
welcher über die oben erwähnten 2'000'000 Dollars, wie oben gesagt,

./.

finanziert wird, in jedem Fall zuvor an Goodyear und Zeppelin
im Verhältnis ihres Besitzes an Stammanteilen angeboten werden
soll, zu dem Preis, welchen die Gesellschaft dafür auf dem
amerikanischen Markt erhalten kann.   Zu diesem Zweck bestimmt
Goodyear ihren Präsidenten und Zeppelin bestimmt Herrn Vissering als die Personen, an welche die Angebote solcher Sicherheiten gemacht werden sollen und es wird vereinbart, dass die
Gesellschaft frei sein soll, die Sicherheiten bestens auf dem
amerikanischen Markt unterzubringen, wenn solche Angebote nicht
innerhalb 10 Tagen angenommen werden.

In dem Falle dass feste Aufträge erhältlich sind
für den Bau von Luftschiffen grosser Typen, und dass Goodyear
nachdem ihr angemessene Möglichkeit gegeben war, die Finanzierung der Gesellschaft entweder durch Verkauf von deren
Sicherheiten oder in anderer Weise, wie oben gesagt, nicht zustande bringt, oder im Falle, dass solche Finanzierung nicht
erreicht werden kann, ausser durch Verkauf von Stammanteilen,
welche ursprünglich an Goodyear und Zeppelin ausgegeben waren,
dann soll der Fall als eingetreten gelten, dass Goodyear in
seinen Bemühungen um die Finanzierung versagt hat.

Bis zu dem Umfange in welchem Zeppelin Vorrichtungen,
Werkzeuge, Material oder Ausrüstungsteile besitzt, welche die
Gesellschaft für ihren Betrieb benötigt, hat Zeppelin das Recht,
solche Werkzeuge, Vorrichtungen, Material und Ausrüstungsteile
zu übertragen und überschreiben als Zahlung für Sicherheiten
welche ihr wie oben gesagt, angeboten werden sollen, wobei
solches Material, Ausrüstung usw. für diesen Zweck mit den Ge-
stehungskosten für Zeppelin, abzüglich angemessener Abschreibung
oder mit den Wiederbeschaffungskosten in Amerika bewertet werden
soll, und zwar zu dem jeweils geringeren Betrage.

./.

§ IX.

Goodyear verpflichtet sich, zu keiner Zeit sich mit dem
Bau und Betrieb von Starrluftschiffen im Wettbewerb entweder mit
der Gesellschaft, oder mit Zeppelin im Falle der späteren Auflösung der Gesellschaft zu befassen. Andererseits verpflichtet
sich Zeppelin, sich während des Bestehens der Gesellschaft nicht
mit Bau von Starrluftschiffen innerhalb des der Gesellschaft
zugesprochenen Gebietes zu befassen.

§ X.

Jm Falle dass und sobald Goodyear in ihren Bemühungen ,
die Gesellschaft wie oben gesagt zu finanzieren, versagt hat,
soll Zeppelin, wenn gewünscht, eine angemessene Gelegenheit
haben, solche Finanzierung zustande zu bringen. Jm Falle dass
keine Partei Erfolg hat, dann soll auf Antrag irgend einer Partei
die Gesellschaft aufgelöst und liquidiert werden, mit der Ein-
schränkung jedoch, dass Zeppelin an Stelle dessen die Jnteressen
von Goodyear ab besagter Gesellschaft zu einem angemessenen Wert
erwerben kann.   Wenn die Gesellschaft aufgelöst wird, so gilt
als abgemacht, dass von den in ihrem Besitz befindlichen Werten
zunächst an Goodyear alle nach diesem Vertrage als Darlehen gegebenen Gelder zurückbezahlt werden, und dass alle Werte welche
danach verbleiben, an die Anteilbesitzer im Verhältnis ihres betreffenden Besitzes verteilt werden sollen.   Alle Lizenzen, Patent-
rechte etc., welche von Zeppelin an die Gesellschaft erteilt waren
sollen rückgängig gemacht werden und sämtliche Patente, welche
die Gesellschaft erhalten hat, wie auch schwebende Anmeldungen
sollen an Zeppelin übertragen werden.   Es ist jedoch vereinbart,
dass nichts in diesem Abkommen als ein Hindernis für Goodyear
ausgelegt werden soll, sich wiederum auf anderen Luftfahrtgebie-
ten, als Starrluftschiffen im Falle der Auflösung der Gesellschaft
zu befassen.

.⁄.

§ XI.

Jm Falle, dass Meinungsverschiedenheiten zwischen den Vertragsparteien bezüglich der Gestaltung und Deutung irgendwelcher Bestimmungen desselben auftreten, dann sollen solche Fragen 3 Schiedsrichtern vorgelegt werden, einer von Goodyear und einer von Zeppelin ernannt und diese beiden sollen den dritten Schiedsrichter ernennen. Wenn die ersten beiden sich über den dritten Schiedsrichter nicht einigen können, so soll dieser von einem zuständigen Gerichtshof bestimmt werden.

§ XII.

Dieser Vertrag soll für keine der Vertragsparteien bindend sein, ehe er nicht von den betreffenden Aufsichtsräten bestätigt und gutgeheissen ist.

Jn Betreff dieser Bestätigung des Vorstehenden ist dieser Vertrag vollzogen von Zeppelin und Goodyear durch deren zuständige und rechtmässige befugte Vertreter. Alles unter eingangs niedergeschriebenem Tag und Jahr.

Goodyear Tire & Rubber   Luftschiffbau Zeppelin G.m.b.H
Company, Ohio   Friedrichshafen

7.3 Abkommen vom 11. Oktober 1935 über die Nutzung von Einrichtungen der US-Navy durch das Luftschiff LZ 129 „Hindenburg"

Widerrufliche Genehmigung

Da die Luftschiffbau-Zeppelin GmbH Friedrichshafen, Deutschland, die in den USA durch Herrn F. W. von Meister, 354 Fourth Avenue, New York City, vertreten wird und die in diesem Fall durch ihre Tochterfirma, die Deutsche Zeppelin-Reederei GmbH, Berlin, operiert, einen Vorschlag hinsichtlich Luftschiffverkehr in die Vereinigten Staaten unterbreitet hat, demzufolge die kommerzielle Nützlichkeit von Luftschiffen im Außenhandel unter Beweis gestellt werden soll; und

da entsprechender Antrag auf Erlaubnis zur Nutzung der Luftschiff-Landeeinrichtungen der Marineluftstation Lakehurst, New Jersey, und der Marinereserve-Luftbasis in Opa-Locka, Florida, im Zusammenhang mit dieser Beweisstellung gestellt wurde, woraus der US-Regierung keinerlei Unkosten erwachsen; und

da in den Vereinigten Staaten keine geeigneten privaten Landeeinrichtungen zur Verfügung stehen; und

da die Erteilung einer derartigen Genehmigung unter den nachstehend aufgeführten Bedingungen dem öffentlichen Interesse dient;

wird hiermit folglich kraft meines Amtes als Secretary of the Navy von Gesetzes wegen dem vorerwähnten Unternehmen, nachstehend Antragsteller genannt, die Genehmigung erteilt, die nachstehend aufgeführten Luftschiffeinrichtungen im Zusammenhang mit einer Reihe von Fahrten des Luftschiffs LZ 129 in die Vereinigten Staaten zu benutzen, und zwar die Marineluftstation Lakehurst, New Jersey, die Marinereserve-Luftbasis in Opa-Locka, Florida, sowie anderswo wie folgt:

In Lakehurst, N. J.:

Halle; Landemast; Bodeneinrichtungen; Haltemannschaft in Stärke von 90 Mann; Lager für 1 Mio. Kubikfuß Wasserstoffgas; Füll- und Nachfülleinrichtungen; Wetterdienst; Sicherheitsvorkehrungen; und andere solche Einrichtungen und Dienstleistungen, welche üblicherweise für die Landung, das Ankern und Docken und die Wartung eines Luftschiffs erforderlich sind, wobei eine Halle benutzt wird, wie die der Marineluftstation Lakehurst, New Jersey, zur Zeit ausgestattet ist.

In Opa-Locka, Florida:
der Expeditionslandemast und dessen dazugehörige Landeausrüstungen

Anderswo:
die Sicherstellung von bis zu 7 Tankwagen, welche für den Transport von ca. 200 000 Kubikfuß Wasserstoffgas ausgerüstet sind.

Vorkehrungen zur Kontaktaufnahme mit Marinefunkstationen gemäß eines bewilligten Planes zum Zwecke der Einholung von Wetterberichten und anderer nicht kommerzieller Nachrichten, die für den sicheren Verlauf der Fahrt des Luftschiffs auf dem Wege in die Vereinigten Staaten und zurück erforderlich sind.

Diese Genehmigung wird vorbehaltlich der nachstehenden Bestimmungen und Bedingungen erteilt.

1. Diese Genehmigung basiert im allgemeinen auf der Voraussetzung, daß die Benutzung der in dieser Genehmigung benannten Einrichtungen auf Risiko des Antragstellers und ohne finanzielle Belastung für die Vereinigten Staaten erfolgt. Sollten den Vereinigten Staaten doch irgendwelche Unkosten entstehen, so verpflichtet sich der Antragsteller, diese den Vereinigten Staaten zu erstatten.

2. Die in dieser Genehmigung benannte Nutzungsdauer beschränkt sich auf sechs (6) Monate, beginnend dreißig (30) Tage nach der Benachrichtigung seitens des Antragstellers bezüglich der Aufnahme des hierunter benannten Luftschiffverkehrs, sofern diese Genehmigung nicht schriftlich durch den Secretary of the Navy verlängert wird. Es steht im Ermessen des Secretary of the Navy, diese Genehmigung jederzeit zu widerrufen. Es wird erwartet, daß eine Benachrichtigung hinsichtlich der Bereitschaft zur Aufnahme des Verkehrs am bzw. um den 15. 9. 1935 erfolgt, und daß diese Genehmigung dreißig (30) Tage danach in Kraft tritt.

3. Der Antragsteller verpflichtet sich, die ihm zur Verfügung gestellten Einrichtungen lediglich in Verbindung mit einer Reihe von zwölf (12) Hin- und Rückfahrten des Luftschiffs LZ 129 zwischen den

Vereinigten Staaten und Europa bzw. Südamerika zu benutzen, wobei benanntes Luftschiff auf einigen bzw. allen Fahrten Fahrgäste, Post und Fracht befördert.

4. Der Antragsteller verpflichtet sich weiter, dem Navy Department vor dem Inkrafttreten dieser Genehmigung einen Fahrplan mit den voraussichtlichen Terminen der Ankünfte und Abfahrten des Luftschiffs vorzulegen sowie das Navy Department und dessen am Bestimmungsort befindlichen Vertreter unverzüglich über etwaige Änderungen dieses Fahrplans zu unterrichten. Insbesondere verpflichtet sich der Antragsteller, dem Navy Department mindestens vier Tage im voraus endgültige Termine der An- bzw. Abfahrten bekanntzugeben. Absicht dieser Bedingung ist, das Navy Department jederzeit und frühestmöglich im voraus über Datum und Uhrzeit der zu erwartenden Ankünfte und Abfahrten des Luftschiffs auf dem laufenden zu halten.

5. Der Antragsteller hat sich allen Bundes- und Landesgesetzen, -bestimmungen und Anfordnungen sowie speziellen Anweisungen, die durch eine für den Einflug, Betrieb und die Abfertigung zuständige Behörde für das benannte Luftschiff während seiner kommerziellen Nutzung erteilt werden, zu unterwerfen.

6. Dem Antragsteller wird das Recht auf freien Zu- und Abgang zu und von den in diesem Dokument behandelten Fahrtrouten und Räumlichkeiten gewährt. Während des Aufenthalts auf der vorerwähnten Marinestation bzw. Marinebasis haben der Antragsteller, dessen Vertreter und sämtliche Fahrgäste allen bestehenden Marinebestimmungen Folge zu leisten.

7. Der Antragsteller verpflichtet sich, auf der Marineluftstation Lakehurst und der Marinereserve-Luftbasis Opa-Locka, Florida, einen oder mehrere Vertreter für eine angemessene Zeit vor, während und nach der jeweiligen Ankunft eines Luftschiffs LZ 129 zur Verfügung zu stellen, die sowohl qualifiziert als auch berechtigt sind, im Namen des Antragstellers evtl. aufkommende Fragen oder Angelegenheiten genereller bzw. technischer Art zu erledigen.

8. Der Antragsteller hat alle angemessenen Vorkehrungen zu treffen, die einen überlegten Umgang mit der Öffentlichkeit gewährleisten. Insbesondere verpflichtet sich der Antragsteller, keinerlei Informationen zu veröffentlichen, die zu der irrigen Annahme führen

könnten, das Navy Department sei aufgrund der hierunter erteilten Genehmigung in irgendwelcher Weise für die Handlungen des Antragstellers verantwortlich. Ferner muß jeder Eindruck vermieden werden, daß der Antragsteller aufgrund des Tatbestands, daß die benutzten Anlagen und Einrichtungen Regierungsbesitz sind, eine bevorzugte Behandlung irgendwelcher Angelegenheiten in Verbindung mit seinen kommerziellen Ausübungen genießt.

9. Der Antragsteller darf ohne vorherige Genehmigung seitens des Secretary of the Navy bzw. dessen Bevollmächtigten keinerlei Änderungen, Reparaturen oder Verbesserungen an den vorbenannten Luftschiffeinrichtungen vornehmen. Der Antragsteller verpflichtet sich weiterhin, die übernommenen Einrichtungen nach Ablauf dieser Genehmigung in dem gleichen Zustand wie bei der Übernahme zu übergeben bzw. in einer Verfassung, die den Secretary of the Navy zufriedenstellt.

10. Es wird vereinbart, daß für die Landung und das Docken des LZ 129 auf der Marineluftstation Lakehurst eine Landemannschaft von 90 Marineangehörigen bereitgestellt wird, hingegen ist der Antragsteller für die Bereitstellung einer Landemannschaft in Opa-Locka selbst verantwortlich. Sollte aufgrund schlechter Witterungsbedingungen oder anderer besonderer Umstände die Verstärkung der Landemannschaft auf der Marineluftfahrtstation Lakehurst ratsam erscheinen, so hat der Antragsteller dies selbst zu veranlassen und dafür Sorge zu tragen, daß die zusätzliche Mannschaft dem befehlshabenden Offizier in Lakehurst unterstellt wird, und zwar zu Bedingungen, die für selbigen zufriedenstellend sind. Die Befehlsgewalt über Marinepersonal liegt bei Marineoffizieren; falls vom Antragsteller fallweise angefordert, übernimmt ein Marineoffizier die Aufsicht (in Lakehurst) über die Landung und das folgende Anlegen oder Docken der LZ 129, und zwar unter Anwendung der für Marineluftschiffe gebräuchlichen Methoden oder in der vom Antragsteller abgeänderten Art. Das Marinepersonal kann jedoch in keinerlei Weise für irgendwelche evtl. sich ereignenden unglücklichen Zwischenfälle haftbar gemacht werden.

11. Es wird vereinbart, daß die Kompetenzbereiche des Navy Departments, des Antragstellers sowie anderer beteiligter Stellen durch örtliche Vertreter des Departments der Navy und des Antrag-

stellers geregelt und im voraus festgelegt werden, inwieweit das machbar ist, damit die Kompetenzbereiche von den Vertretern aller Vertragspartner anerkannt werden.

12. Der Antragsteller hat für die Bereitstellung von Treibstoff, Wasserstoffgas, Proviant und Unterkünften sowie die Beförderung von Passagieren und Mannschaften auf dem Lande selbst Sorge zu tragen.

13. Nachdem der Antragsteller ausführlich über die Abmessungen und die technische Ausstattung der derzeit auf der Marineluftfahrtstation Lakehurst und der Marinereserve-Luftbasis Opa-Locka vorhandenen Lande-, Abfertigungs-, Dock- und Nachfülleinrichtungen informiert wurde, akzeptiert er selbige als für seine Zwecke geeignet und stimmt hiermit zu, das Luftschiff LZ 129 auf die bestehenden Gegebenheiten auszurüsten. In Fällen, in denen eine Umrüstung des LZ 129 mittels Paßstücken, speziellen Außenzubehörs oder anderer Vorrichtungen auf die vorhandenen Einrichtungen erforderlich ist, hat der Antragsteller alle erforderlichen Paßstücke und Außenzubehör und -vorrichtungen im voraus zu beschaffen.

14. Sicherheitskräfte, die für die Aufsicht der zu erwartenden Besuchermenge ausreichend sind und dem örtlichen Vertreter des Navy Departments als geeignet erscheinen, werden in Übereinkunft zwischen dem Vertreter des Navy Departments und der Gemeindeverwaltung aufgestellt. In Lakehurst stellt der Kommandant für solchen Zweck ein Kontingent zur Verfügung, das üblicherweise für Sicherheitsaufgaben vorhanden ist. Der Kommandant erteilt die Vorschriften und übernimmt die Kontrolle der allgemeinen Sicherheitsvorkehrungen. In Opa-Locka hingegen unterliegt dem Kommandanten die Vorschriftsausübung für die allgemeinen Sicherheitsvorkehrungen, aber er stellt keine Ordnungshüter.

15. Voraussetzung für die hierunter erteilte Genehmigung zur Benutzung von Tankwaggons zum Transport von Wasserstoffgas ist die Zustimmung der zuständigen Aufsichtsbehörde. Dem Antragsteller werden in Lakehurst Tankwaggons zur Verfügung gestellt und danach in Übereinstimmung mit bestehenden Marinevorschriften geleitet und bewegt; und zwar zwischen den vom Antragsteller schriftlich angeforderten Zielpunkten und Zeiten. Das Navy Department wird über Fracht und andere Kosten, die bei der Benutzung dieser

Waggons entstehen, Buch führen. Der Antragsteller zahlt den Betrag in voller Höhe, abzüglich Gutschriften, aus der betrieblichen Nutzung der benannten Waggons. Ferner wird zur Bedingung gemacht, daß der Antragsteller keinen Vorzugsfrachttarif erhält, der daraus resultieren könnte, daß diese Waggons mit Regierungsfrachtbriefen reisen. Es ist mithin die volle Fracht zu zahlen, die bei der Verwendung von privaten Waggons entstünde.

16. Die Vereinigten Staaten lehnen ausdrücklich jegliche Verantwortung für jedwedige Zwischenfälle, die sich evtl. aus der zur Verfügungstellung von Tankwaggons zum Transport von Wasserstoffgas sowie von Lagerräumen auf der Marineluftstation Lakehurst für bis zu 1 Mio. Kubikfuß Wasserstoffgas ergeben könnten, ab. Nach erfolgtem Transport von Wasserstoffgas sind auf Kosten des Antragstellers alle Tankwaggons, Lagertanks und Leitungen zu reinigen und in ihren ursprünglichen Zustand zu versetzen. Zudem übernimmt der Antragsteller volle Haftung für jegliche etwaige Schäden, die sich aus der Benutzung solcher Tankwaggons, einschließlich ihrer Instandsetzung in den ursprünglichen Zustand, ergeben könnten.

17. Der Antragsteller verpflichtet sich, die vorbenannten Einrichtungen der Marineluftstation Lakehurst und die in Opa-Locka während der zugestandenen Nutzungsdauer im Wert von fünfhunderttausend US-Dollar ($ 500 000) bzw. fünfundsiebzigtausend US-Dollar ($ 75 000), und zwar gegen Gefahren durch Feuer, Explosion und Schäden von außen bei einer renommierten Versicherungsgesellschaft bzw. -gesellschaften, nach Genehmigung des Secretary of the Navy, zu versichern. Die Versicherungspolicen dürfen keine Rückversicherungsklauseln beinhalten, sondern sind so zu konzipieren, daß alle Schadensansprüche an den Secretary of the Navy zahlbar sind. Diese Versicherungspolice bzw. -policen sind in Kopie beim Marinegeneralanwalt zu hinterlegen.

18. Der Antragsteller verpflichtet sich zum Abschluß einer Versicherung, ausreichend zur Schadensdeckung von sieben (7) Eisenbahntankwaggons für Wasserstoffgas gegen unmittelbaren Schaden durch äußeren Einfluß; und zwar bei einem Versicherer, gegen den seitens des Secretary of the Navy keine Einwände bestehen. Die Versicherungspolicen dürfen keine Rückversicherungsklauseln beinhalten, sondern sind so zu konzipieren, daß alle Schadensansprüche an den

Secretary of the Navy zahlbar sind. Diese Versicherungspolice bzw. -policen sind in Kopie beim Marinegeneralanwalt zu hinterlegen.

19. Der Antragsteller verpflichtet sich ferner zum Abschluß einer Haftpflichtversicherung gegen Todesfälle, Körperverletzungen und Sachschäden, die im Zusammenhang mit den in dieser Genehmigung benannten Aktivitäten entstehen könnten. Versicherer und Deckungssumme bedürfen der Zustimmung durch den Secretary of the Navy. Die Versicherungspolice bzw. -policen dürfen keine Rückversicherungsklauseln beinhalten, sondern sind so zu konzipieren, daß alle Schadensansprüche an den Secretary of the Navy zahlbar sind. Diese Versicherungspolice bzw. -policen sind in Kopie beim Marinegeneralanwalt zu hinterlegen.

20. Der Antragsteller hat zu jeder Zeit eine Mindesteinlage in Höhe von fünftausend US-Dollar ($ 5 000,00) auf einem Sonderkonto des Navy Departments zu unterhalten, gegen welches Forderungen aus der Nutzung vorbenannter Einrichtungen auf der Marineluftfahrtstation Lakehurst und der Marinereserve-Luftbasis Opa-Locka und deren Instandhaltung in einem Zustand, der die jederzeitige Abfertigung des LZ 129 gewährleistet, gemäß nachstehender Aufstellung verrechnet werden:

Hundert US-Dollar für jeden Zeitraum von 24 Stunden, bzw. anteilmäßig für Bruchteile davon, an denen Luftschiffhalle und Landeeinrichtungen in Lakehurst zur Ankunftsabfertigung des LZ 129 in Bereitschaft stehen. (Anmerkung: Gebühren werden aufgrund der nach § 4 festzusetzenden Termine und Ankunftszeiten berechnet.)

Dreihundert US-Dollar für jeden Zeitraum von 24 Stunden, bzw. anteilmäßig für Bruchteile davon, an denen das Luftschiff in Lakehurst festgemacht bzw. in einer Halle untergebracht ist.

Dreißig US-Dollar für jeden Zeitraum von 24 Stunden, bzw. anteilmäßig für Bruchteile davon, an denen Landeeinrichtungen in Opa-Locka in Bereitschaft stehen.

Hundert US-Dollar für jeden Zeitraum von 24 Stunden, bzw. anteilmäßig für Bruchteile davon, an denen das Luftschiff in Opa-Locka festgemacht ist.

Bei jedem Start und jeder Landung auf der Marineluftstation Lakehurst eine Bearbeitungsgebühr in Höhe von zweihundertfünfzig US-Dollar für die Landemannschaft von 90 Mann.

Zweihundertfünfzig US-Dollar je Waggon, je angefangenen Monat, als monatliche Nutzungsgebühr für Tankwaggons.

Fünfundzwanzig Cent (US-$ 0,25) je 1000 Kubikfuß, je angefangenen Monat, für die Benutzung von Gas-Lagereinrichtungen in Lakehurst.

Überführungskosten der Tankwaggons (abzüglich Meilengelder des Eigners).

Für alle anderen Ausgaben, einschl. Kosten für Strom und Licht, sowie Reparaturen und Änderungen sowohl am Luftschiff als auch am Regierungseigentum, die durch das Luftschiff bedingt sind, werden die von der Marinefinanzstelle tatsächlich errechneten Beträge in Rechnung gestellt, zuzüglich Mehrkosten in Höhe von 20 v.H. der Gesamtausgaben für Löhne, Materialien und unmittelbare Kosten. Diese Mehrkosten stellen die geschätzten Unkosten zur Deckung etwaiger entstehender zusätzlicher Mehrausgaben seitens der Regierung dar.

21. Der Antragsteller verpflichtet sich, die Marineaktivitäten auf der Marineluftstation Lakehurst, New Jersey, und der Marinereserve-Luftbasis in Opa-Locka, Florida, durch seinen in dieser Genehmigung definierten Betrieb nicht über Gebühr zu behindern.

22. Keinerlei Handlung bzw. Handlungen geben dem Antragsteller oder einem in seinem Namen handelnden Dritten unter diesem Vertrag das Recht auf Dauernutzung bzw. Besitz irgendwelchen US-Regierungseigentums.

23. Diese Genehmigung ist beschränkt und nicht ohne die vorherige Zustimmung des Secretary of the Navy übertragbar. Im Falle einer so zugestimmten Übertragung gelten alle vorbenannten Bestimmungen und Bedingungen für die übernehmende Partei.

24. Den Vereinigten Staaten dürfen aus dieser Genehmigung oder aufgrund dieser Genehmigung bzw. Teilen davon keinerlei Ausgaben bzw. Haftansprüche entstehen. Der vorbenannte Antragsteller verpflichtet sich, die Regierung gegenüber sämtlichen Ansprüchen jedweder Art schadlos zu halten, die evtl. aus bzw. im Zusammenhang mit dieser Genehmigung entstehen und die nicht auf ausdrückliches Verschulden der Vereinigten Staaten oder deren Beamten oder Beauftragten zurückzuführen sind.

25. Der Kommandant der Marineluftstation in Lakehurst, New Jersey, bzw. der Kommandant der Marinereserve-Luftbasis in Opa-Locka, Florida, werden hiermit beauftragt und ermächtigt, als örtliche Vertreter innerhalb ihrer Kompetenzbereiche in allen im Zusammenhang mit dieser Genehmigung auftretenden Verwaltungsangelegenheiten zu handeln.

Urkundlich dessen, bescheinige ich durch meine Unterschrift und das Amtssiegel des Navy Departments die Gültigkeit dieser Genehmigung.

11. Oktober 1935

UNITED STATES OF AMERICA
vertreten durch:
(gez. Claude A. Swanson)
Secretary of the Navy

Diese Genehmigung wird ebenfalls im Namen der Luftschiffbau Zeppelin GmbH, Friedrichshafen/Deutschland, und der Deutschen Zeppelin-Reederei GmbH, Berlin/Deutschland, in Anerkennung und Annahme der darin benannten Bedingungen ausgeführt.

LUFTSCHIFFBAU ZEPPELIN GmbH
Friedrichshafen/Deutschland
vertreten durch:
(gez. Dr. Dürr ppa. Lehmann)
Geschäftsführer

gez. F. W. von Meister
Sonder-US-Bevollmächtigter

DEUTSCHE ZEPPELIN REEDEREI GmbH
Berlin/Deutschland
vertreten durch:
(gez. Lehmann ppa. Oesterle)

7.4 Antrag auf Einfluggenehmigung des Luftschiffes „Hindenburg" von Deutschland in die USA für das Jahr 1937

Hiermit beantragt die Deutsche-Zeppelin Reederei GmbH die Erlaubnis, mit ihrem Luftschiff „Hindenburg" eine begrenzte Anzahl von Versuchs- und Vorführfahrten von Deutschland in die Vereinigten Staaten während des Jahres 1937 durchzuführen. Zweck dieser Fahrten ist die weitere Erforschung der Wetterverhältnisse im nordatlantischen Raum während Frühling, Sommer und Herbst. Es soll der Versuch unternommen werden, während der Monate August und September wöchentliche Hin- und Rückfahrten gemäß nachstehendem Fahrplanentwurf durchzuführen. Zweck: um festzustellen, ob der Betrieb eines Luftschiffs vom Typ „Hindenburg" im wöchentlichen Turnus bei der vorhandenen Entfernung durchführbar ist.

In Beantwortung der vom US-Handelsministerium vorgegebenen Fragen werden vom Antragsteller die nachfolgenden Angaben gemacht:

1. Frage: Datum des Antrags:
   Antwort: 8. Februar 1937
2. F.: Genauer Firmenname:
   A.: Deutsche Zeppelin-Reederei GmbH
3. F.: Allgemeine Firmenanschrift:
   A.: Berlin W 8, Unter den Linden 41
4. F.: Name, Titel und Postanschrift des Firmenbevollmächtigten, an den der Schriftverkehr bezüglich der Versuchsfahrten zu adressieren ist:
   A.: F. W. von Meister, Vize-Präsident der American Zeppelin Transport, Inc., 354 Fourth Avenue, New York, New York, USA, US-Generalvertretung des Antragstellers.
5. F.: Firmenorganisation einschließlich Art der Firma, ob Betriebs- oder Dachgesellschaft, oder andere; Name und Staatsangehörigkeit des Vorsitzenden und der Direktoren; Sitz und Ausübungsort der Gesellschaft.

A.: Antragsteller ist eine GmbH, nach deutschem Recht organisiert und betrieben. Zweck dieser Gesellschaft sind Besitz und Einsatz von Zeppelinluftschiffen.

Vorstandsmitglieder:

Dr. Hugo Eckener, Vorsitzender, Friedrichshafen a. B.

Ministerial-Dirigent A. Mühlig-Hofmann, Berlin

Direktor Martin Wronsky, Berlin

Betriebsleitung:

Ernst A. Lehmann, Geschäftsführer, Frankfurt

Carl Christiansen, Geschäftsführer, Magdeburg

Julius Oesterle, Prokurist, Friedrichshafen a. B.

Heinz M. Wronsky, Prokurist, Frankfurt

Alle Mitglieder des Vorstands und der Geschäftsleitung sind deutsche Staatsangehörige.

Die Firma wurde in Berlin gegründet und übt ihre Geschäfte dort aus. Eine Abschrift der Handelsregistereintragung der Deutschen Zeppelin-Reederei wurde dem Handelsministerium am 29. April 1936 eingereicht. (Anlage 1)*

6. F.: Ungefähre Termine für beabsichtigte Fahrten zwischen dem Ausland und den Vereinigten Staaten mit fahrplanmäßigen Daten.

---

* Anlagen sind hier nicht wiedergegeben

Fahrt Nr.	Abfahrt Frankfurt	Ankunft Lakehurst	Abfahrt Lakehurst	Ankunft Frankfurt
1	3. 5. nm.	6. 5. vm.	6. 5. nm.	9. 5. vm.
2	11. 5. nm.	14. 5. vm.	14. 5. nm.	17. 5. vm.
3	22. 5. nm.	25. 5. vm.	25. 5. nm.	28. 5. vm.
4	2. 6. nm.	5. 6. vm.	5. 6. nm.	8. 6. vm.
5	12. 6. nm.	15. 6. vm.	15. 6. nm.	18. 6. vm.
6	22. 6. nm.	25. 6. vm.	25. 6. nm.	28. 6. vm.
7	3. 7. nm.	6. 7. vm.	6. 7. nm.	9. 7. vm.
8	11. 7. nm.	14. 7. vm.	14. 7. nm.	17. 7. vm.
9	13. 8. nm.	16. 8. vm.	16. 8. nm.	19. 8. vm.
10	20. 8. nm.	23. 8. vm	23. 8. nm.	26. 8. vm.
11	27. 8. nm.	30. 8. vm.	30. 8. nm.	2. 9. vm.
12	3. 9. nm.	6. 9. vm.	6. 9. nm.	9. 9. vm.
13	10. 9. nm.	13. 9. vm.	13. 9. nm.	16. 9. vm.
14	17. 9. nm.	20. 9. vm.	20. 9. nm.	23. 9. vm.
15	28. 9. nm.	1. 10. vm.	1. 10. nm.	4. 10. vm.
16	8. 10.nm.	11. 10. vm.	11. 10. nm.	14. 10. vm.
17	19. 10.nm.	22. 10. vm.	22. 10. nm.	25. 10. vm.
18	30. 10.nm.	2. 11. vm.	2. 11. nm.	5. 11. vm.

vm. = vormittags   nm. = nachmittags
Fahrplanänderungen vorbehalten

7. F.: Eine Karte mit eingezeichneter Reiseroute oder -Routen und Endzielen oder Zwischenlandungen bei der Überquerung ist einzureichen. Die Strecke bzw. Strecken, die nachts beflogen werden, sind gesondert zu kennzeichnen.

A.: Eine Karte mit den geplanten Reiserouten wurde vom Antragsteller am 29. April 1936 eingereicht und markiert (Anlage 3). Die tatsächlich eingehaltenen Flugrouten werden jedoch von den zur Zeit des Fluges vorhandenen Wetterverhältnissen abhängen.

8. F.: Stellen Sie Namen des Flugpersonals, das die Testflüge durchführen wird, mit Angabe der Pilotenscheinnummern oder anderer Bezeichnungen zur Verfügung.

A.:Nachfolgend eine Aufstellung der vorgesehenen Mannschaft des Luftschiffs „Hindenburg", vorbehaltlich Änderungen im Fall von Versetzung oder Ausfall durch Krankheit.

Name:	*Position:*
E. A. Lehmann	Schiffskapitän

Offiziere

M. Pruss	Wachoffizier
A. Sammt	Wachoffizier
H. Bauer	Wachoffizier
W. Ziegler	Navigationsoffizier
M. Zabel	Navigationsoffizier
F. Herzog	Navigationsoffizier
K. Schönherr	Obersteuermann
J. Geier	Obersteuermann
H. Gluud	Steuermann
M. Schulz	Steuermann
E. Huchel	Steuermann
G. v. Mensenkampff	Steuermann
L. Felber	Steuermann
H. Lau	Steuermann

Funkingenieure

W. Speck	Oberfunkingenieur
E. Hartwig	Funkingenieur
G. Wieduwild	Funkingenieur
E. Schweikard	Funkingenieur

Segelmacher

L. Knorr	J. Freund	E. Spehl

Maschinisten

R. Sauter	1. Flugingenieur
A. Grözinger	2. Flugingenieur
R. Halder	Maschinist

J. Schreibmüller	A. Deutschle	Maschinist
E. Schäuble	W. Scheef	Maschinist
W. Dimmler	A. Fischer II	Maschinist
G. Zettel	W. Banholzer	Maschinist
R. Schädler	W. Döbler	Maschinist
E. Bentele	H. Fiedler	Maschinist
H. Rothfuß	R. Moser	Maschinist

Elektriker

Ph. Lenz	G. Kunkel	J. Leibrecht

Stewards

H. Kubis		Obersteward
M. Henneberg		Steward
M. Schulze	E. Nunnenmacher	Steward
F. Deeg	W. Balla	Steward
X. Maier		Koch
A. Grözinger		Koch
A. Stöffler		Bäcker
A. Rigger		Page

Die Mannschaftslisten stehen bei jeder Ankunft des Luftschiffs zur Verfügung.

9. F.: Geben Sie die folgenden Informationen über das zum Einsatz kommende Flugzeug:

   (a) Eigner
   (b) Lufttüchtigkeitsbescheinigung oder Lizenznummer mit internationalen Kennzeichnungen
   (c) Fabrikat, Typ und Modell des Flugzeugs
   (d) Anzahl und Art der Motoren
   (e) Mannschaftsstärke sowie Fahrgastkapazität
   (f) Datum der Herstellung und kurze allgemeine Beschreibung

A.: (a) Deutsche Zeppelin-Reederei GmbH
   (b) Lufttüchtigkeitsbescheinigung vom 20. 3. 1936, ausgestellt durch das Reichsluftfahrtministerium, Lizenznummer D-LZ 129

(c) Lenkbares Luftschiff, erbaut von der Luftschiffbau Zeppelin, D-LZ 129

(d) Vier 16-Zylinder-Daimler-Benz-Dieselmotoren von je ca. 1 100 PS

(e) Mannschaftsstärke ca. 50 Mann, Fahrgastkapazität 72 Personen

(f) Erbaut 1932–1935. Für vollständige Angaben s. technische Beschreibung des Luftschiffs, wie am 29. 4. 1936 dem Handelsministerium vorgelegt (Anlage 4).

10. F.: Bitte geben Sie an, ob zuständige Behörde erforderliche Funklizenz bzw. -lizenzen erteilt hat.

(a) Standorte aller Bodenfunkstationen, die in den USA in Anspruch genommen werden.

(b) Ist das für den Einsatz bestimmte Flugzeug mit ein- oder zweiseitigem Funksystem ausgerüstet?

(c) Ist das für den Einsatz bestimmte Flugzeug mit Leitstrahlfunkfeuer ausgerüstet?

A.:(a)s. beiliegende Liste mit Antrag von 29. 4. 1936 (Anlage 5)

(b) zweiseitig

(c) ja

11. F.: Kurzbeschreibung des vorhandenen Wetterdienstes entlang der Fahrtroute bzw. -routen einschl. Quellen und Standorte der berichterstattenden Stationen, Frequenz und Methode der Erfassung und Ausgabe von Wetterberichten.

A.: Das Luftschiff bedient sich regelmäßig der von der Hamburger Seewarte, Hamburg, ausgegebenen europäischen Wetterberichte. Beim Anfliegen und Verlassen des US-Luftraums übernimmt das Schiff auch die allgemeinen Wetterberichte des US-Wirtschaftsministeriums und der Marine.

12. F.: Kurzbeschreibung des Betriebsplans einschließlich des Personals, des Flugzeugs, des Funksystems und Wetterdienstes; der Angabe, ob Instrumenten- oder Over-Top-Flug erwägt ist, sowie solcher zusätzlichen und bezogenen Informationen, die dem „Bureau of Air Commerce" zur Koordination der Regulierung derartiger Flüge mittels inländischer Luftnavigation dienen und es dieser Behörde ermöglichen, die geplanten Ver-

suchsflüge mit allen ihr zur Verfügung stehenden Mitteln zu unterstützen.

A.: Insgesamt sind 18 Versuchsfahrten zwischen Frankfurt/M. und Lakehurst, New Jersey, geplant. Die voraussichtliche Mannschaftsstärke wird 50 Mann betragen, einschließlich 1 Kommandanten, 3 Wachoffizieren, 3 Navigationsoffizieren, 1 Chefingenieur, 1 Hauptfunkoffizier, 1 Arzt, 1 Postassistenten, 1 Oberstewart und 1 Koch.

Lande- und Wartungsvereinbarungen mit der Marineluftfahrtstation wurden beantragt. Dem Antragsteller wurde von der US-Marine inoffiziell mitgeteilt, daß die Erteilung einer Erlaubnis für die Benutzung der Marineluftschiffeinrichtungen nach erfolgter Zustimmung der US-Regierung seitens des Secretary of the Navy erfolgen wird. Die vom Secretary of the Navy erteilte widerrufliche Genehmigung bezieht sich auf technische Fragen sowie Fragen der Haftung und der Gestellung einer Kaution, über welche die Bearbeitungsgebühren verrechnet werden können, usw.

13. F.: Angabe, ob eine Genehmigung für die vorgesehenen Versuchsfahrten seitens der Regierung des Antragstellers vorliegt.

A.: Ja

Es wird hiermit höflichst ersucht, die Bearbeitung dieses Antrags bevorzugt abzufertigen und daß sowohl das Navy Department als auch der Antragsteller über den Verlauf informiert werden, damit technische sowie kommerzielle Vorbereitungen für die sichere und pünktliche Durchführung der vorgesehenen Versuchs- und Vorführfahrten zum frühestmöglichen Termin in Angriff genommen werden können.

New York, N. Y., den 8. 2. 1937

im Auftrag der
DEUTSCHE ZEPPELIN-REEDEREI GmbH
durch
AMERICAN ZEPPELIN TRANSPORT, INC.
General United States Agents

gez. F. W. von Meister
Vice President (Vorstand)

7.5 USA-Fahrten von LZ 127 „Graf Zeppelin"

7.6 USA-Fahrten von LZ 129 „Hindenburg"

s. englischen Teil Seiten 138/139

Receipt for the first mail delivery by Zeppelin airship (LZ 127 "Graf Zeppelin" on October 15, 1928).

Empfangsbestätigung für die erste Postsendung per Zeppelin-Luftschiff (LZ 127 „Graf Zeppelin", 15. Oktober 1928).

8.
LITERATUR- UND QUELLENVERZEICHNIS

Adams, H.: The Education of Henry Adams: An Autobiography (1918). Boston 1961, Houghton Mifflin.

Battles and Leaders of the Civil War, Vol. II. New York 1956, Castle Books.

Botting, D.: The Giant Airships. Alexandria, Virginia, 1980, Time Life Books.

Clausberg, K.: Zeppelin, die Geschichte eines unwahrscheinlichen Erfolges. München 1979, Schirmer/Mosel GmbH.

Cornish, J. J.: The Air Arm of the Confederacy. Richmond, Virginia, 1963, Richmond Civil War Centenial Committee.

Dick, H. G.: The Golden Age of the Great Rigid Airships. In „Inside the Control Car", Issue 27, Feb. 1979.

Eckener, H.: Im Luftschiff über Länder und Meere. München 1979, Wilhelm Heyne Verlag.

Eckener, H.: Zeppelin-Pläne für Nordamerika. In „Werkzeitschrift der Zeppelin-Betriebe" Nr. 4, 12/1936.

Hansen, Z.: The Goodyear Airships. Bloomington, Ill., 1977, Airship International Press.

Hildebrandt, H. (ed.): Zeppelin-Denkmal für das deutsche Volk. Stuttgart 1925, Germania-Verlag.

Holthusen, H. E.: Amerikaner und Deutsche – Dialog zweier Kulturen. München 1977, Verlag Georg D. W. Callwey.

Italiaander, R.: Graf Ferdinand von Zeppelin. Konstanz 1980, Verlag Friedrich Stadler.

Italiaander, R.: Hugo Eckener, ein moderner Columbus. Konstanz 1979, Verlag Friedrich Stadler.

Knäusel, H. G.: The Zeppelin History. Peoria, Ill., 1978, Lakeview Center for the Arts and Sciences.

Knapp, M., Link, W., Schröder, H. J., Schwabe, K.: Die USA und Deutschland 1918–1975. München 1978, Verlag C. H. Beck.

Lehmann, E. A.: Auf Luftpatrouille und Weltfahrt. Berlin 1936, Wegweiser Verlag.

Meyer, H. C., Gallup, S. V.: France Perceives the Zeppelin, 1924–1937. In „South Atlantic Quarterly", Winter 1979.

Meyers großes Personenlexikon. Mannheim/Zürich 1968, Bibliographisches Institut.

Miller, F. T.: The World in the Air, Vol. II. New York/London 1930, G. P. Putnam's Sons.

Moltmann, G.: Die Luftschiff-„Hindenburg"-Katastrophe und das Heliumproblem. In „Wehr-Wissenschaftliche Rundschau", 11. Jahrgg., Nov. 1961, Berlin/Frankfurt, Verlag E. S. Mittler & Sohn.

Piltz, Th. (ed.): Zweihundert Jahre deutsch-amerikanischer Beziehungen. München 1975, Heinz Moos Verlag.

Pochhammer, B.: ZR III, das deutsch-amerikanische Verkehrsluftschiff. Freiburg 1924, Theodor Fisher Verlag.

Samhaber, E.: Weltgeschichtliche Zusammenhänge – Perspektiven für die Zukunft. Gütersloh/Berlin/München/Wien 1976, Verlagsgruppe Bertelsmann GmbH.

Schiller, H. von: Zeppelinbuch. Leipzig 1938, Bibliographisches Institut AG.

Schiller, H. von: Zeppelin – Wegbereiter des Weltluftverkehrs. Bad Godesberg 1966, Kirschbaum Verlag.

Sheperd, J.: The Adams Chronicles, 1750–1900. Boston/Toronto 1975, Little, Brown and Company.

Smith, R. K.: The Airships Akron and Macon. Annapolis, Maryland 1965, Naval Institute Press.

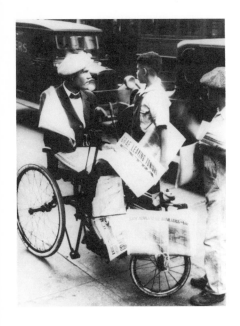

New York, June 3, 1930
New York, 3. Juni 1930

Following the America flights and the world voyage, Dr. Eckener and his crew were always given enthusiastic welcomes in Germany, too.

Nach den Amerikafahrten und nach der Weltfahrt wurden Dr. Eckener und seine Mannschaft auch in Deutschland immer begeistert empfangen.

9.
NAMENS- UND
ORTSREGISTER

Die *kursiv* gesetzten Seitenzahlen beziehen sich auf Abbildungen
im englischen Teil (bis Seite 140).

ZEPPELIN

Ein bedeutendes Kapitel aus dem Geschichtsbuch der Luftfahrt
88 Seiten, ca. 170 teils mehrfarbige Bilder, Fotos,
Zeichnungen und Urkunden.
Kunstdruck. Fester Einband in Ganzleinen, Schutzumschlag.
27×21 cm. Preis DM 19,50 zuzügl. Versandspesen.
5. Auflage 1981

Das Buch schildert den ungewöhnlichen Aufbau des Zeppelin-Konzerns vor und nach dem Ersten Weltkrieg, die Entwicklung und Konstruktion der Luftschiffe von den Anfängen bis LZ 130. In allgemeinverständlicher Form werden die physikalischen Probleme erläutert, Landemanöver, Entwicklung der Fahrgasträume u.a. dargestellt. Eigene Kapitel sind den wichtigsten Zeppelin-Fahrten gewidmet. Mit Bilddokumenten deutscher Städte wird der Band beschlossen. ISBN 3-9800552-3-X

H. G. Knäusel

LZ 1 – Das erste Luftschiff des Grafen Zeppelin
Eine Dokumentation

112 Seiten mit zahlreichen, teils mehrfarbigen Abbildungen auf Kunstdruckpapier. Fester Einband in Leinenimitation, Schutzumschlag 30×21 cm. Preis DM 24,– zzgl. Versandspesen.

Die Dokumentation umfaßt den Zeitraum von 1874 bis 1906 und schildert ausschließlich durch die Wiedergabe einmaliger Zeitdokumente die Entstehung des ersten Zeppelin-Luftschiffs und die Reaktionen der Zeitgenossen auf den ersten Aufstieg, der am 2. Juli 1900 erfolgte. „Ein bemerkenswertes Werk über die Anfänge der Luftschiffahrt...", schrieb die Schwäbische Zeitung, „a beautiful and unique collection" nannte es die Lighter-Than-Air Society, Akron/Ohio, in ihrem Mitteilungsblatt vom April 1976.
ISBN 3-9800552-2-1

Zeppelin-Bildmappe

Eine Serie der schönsten Zeppelinbilder nach Originalaufnahmen. 24 Bilder im Format 30×40 cm auf Chromolux-Hochglanzkarton in Wellpapp-Versandschuber. Preis DM 24,– zzgl. Versandspesen.

Bestellungen an Zeppelin-Druckerei, LZ-Gelände
D-7990 Friedrichshafen 1
oder Ihre Buchhandlung